STYLE IN MODERN BRITISH FICTION

JOHN RUSSELL

STYLE IN MODERN BRITISH FICTION

STUDIES IN JOYCE, LAWRENCE,
FORSTER, LEWIS, AND GREEN

THE JOHNS HOPKINS UNIVERSITY PRESS
BALTIMORE AND LONDON

To Bett

This book has been brought to publication with the generous assistance of the Andrew W. Mellon Foundation.

Manufactured in the United States of America

The Johns Hopkins University Press, Baltimore Maryland 21218
The Johns Hopkins Press Ltd., London

Originally published, 1978
Second printing, 1979

Library of Congress Catalog Card Number 77-22477
ISBN 0-8018-2029-4

Library of Congress Cataloging in Publication Data
Russell, John David.
  Style in modern British fiction.

  Includes bibliographical references and index.
  1 English fiction—20th century—History and criticism. I. Title.
PR881.R8   823.9'1   77-22477
ISBN 0-8018-2029-4

CONTENTS

AUTHOR'S NOTE

The choice of the nine books dealt with in this study calls for a brief explanation. I wanted to examine those British writers who were most responsible for the creative advances made over the first half of this century in the art of the novel. But from their works I wanted to choose specimens that, while mature and decidedly original, were not highly experimental in form. To give an account of their styles and, at the same time, to have some sort of norm to which one could refer—a norm of realistic fiction, in short—was the aim. Their highly individualistic styles, I felt, could be most profitably focused if works comparable to one another were chosen rather than, say, vast "eccentric" books like *Ulysses* and *The Childermass*.

Of the writers of the first generation, Joyce, Lawrence, Forster, and Lewis have the reputation of being great "moderns," masters of idiosyncratic style. Among those who followed them in the postwar generation (including Waugh, Powell, and Isherwood), I judge Henry Green to be the prose stylist most equatable with them, a choice partly warranted by the adaptability of his novels to the "pairing up" technique that is the main critical method of this study.

Following a guideline of studying relatively nonexperimental works, I chose *Dubliners* as a natural starting point, since it allows for comparisons within itself (as Joyce modifies his style within the main "blocs" of stories), and, at the same time, offers a realistic groundplan throughout. The other pairs of novels chosen continue this realistic pattern and share other features as well. For one, they are all presented through third-person narration; for another, there are no sorts of temporal dislocations or shifts of narrative voice in them; for a third (Lawrence the mild exception), all are nearly generically "pure" as novels. I have sheered away from the romance genre (thus, Forster's early fiction), and from Menippean satire (the greater part of Lewis's work). The Lawrence choices, *Kangaroo* and *The Lost Girl,* are less pristine as novels, but that accords with my purpose of presenting him at his most typical, which means working at a sort of "half capacity," writing prose in which artistic care is not, essentially, his first concern.

As these considerations worked themselves out in the book's planning stages, decisions had to be made as to which writers to exclude. Perhaps, under other guidelines, at least twice this number of writers could have been brought in, giving this study of modern British style greater scope, in a much longer work.*

So my critique, which could have been about ten figures or so, settles down to five. There are some statistics in it; they are there to point out rather marked proclivities. They were compiled with care, but I do not vouch for unremitting accuracy. The numerical counts only show trends; it is the percentages that seem of value, for they are accurate to the point that an improved count would produce changes only to the third or fourth decimal place.

While the compilations took effort, I consider them interesting chiefly as satisfiers of curiosity. If a writer uses a device (connective, say, or morpheme, or clause-type) more than his fellows, that can be indicated as a fact, and may give point to some discussion. But how the usages tie in with others, what their multiple effects are on a style—these are what the study tries to indicate. It has two main methods of pursuing its quarry: the amassment of groups of similar utterances from a text, with descriptive comments, and the analysis of passages in their contexts. The statistics are mentioned in passing, and, beginning with the Lawrence chapter, tables are placed at relevant points in the discussion of each novelist. The tables are comparative, averages for the writer in question being rated against those of the other novelists in the study, who thus form a "control" group of sorts.

None of these authors has thus far been subjected to stylistic study of this scope, and while I hope the proof of their individualism be-

---

*For example, Virginia Woolf's major novels do not hew to these straightforward criteria. Ford might have been included, but *Parade's End,* hard to reject, would have caused imbalance judged alongside a single novel; style departures within the tetralogy would have been an issue, too. Isherwood posed a problem by having first-person or mixed narration all through his fiction. Waugh I pondered longest over, but felt the key work to examine would have had to be the war trilogy. Single-issue books of his, if compared to one another, would not be revealingly different (so I felt). As for Powell, his *Music of Time* is a 12-volume work, his early novels all of a piece; his "two distinctive styles" I did examine, however, in the 1970 study I did of his work.

comes apparent by the juxtapositions—each so different from the others—I can foresee that readers may wish to come to a book like this to confront a single writer at a time. This can certainly be done without imbibing the whole product.

Not by design, one curious consistency seemed to fall into place with respect to the books examined. The novels of earlier date—*The Lost Girl, Howards End, Tarr,* and *Back*—tended to deal with youthful protagonists in the midst of formative experience; the later novels of the same authors deal with characters who are beyond the pivotal experiences of their lives. These later books—*Kangaroo, A Passage to India, Self Condemned,* and *Concluding*—become something like twilight works. The authors' styles reflect these differences (though by no means in a uniform or even "mellow" direction). If anything, the late works show ways in which the authors respect a kind of controlling force "out there," which makes each of them adopt a somewhat less jaunty manner in telling the later tale. This also happens to be true of the direction *Dubliners* takes as it makes its way to "The Dead." Perhaps it was natural to have selected pairs of works where such playing-off of style against style would become perceptible. I mention my unconscious decision because these artists would have been responding, as stylists, to something unanalyzed by them, but something that would cause modulation in their writing: the impress of the fictional situation they had placed themselves in.

I owe thanks to the editors of *Style* for allowing me to reuse material that first appeared there in chapter two. I would also like to thank the General Research Board of the University of Maryland for two summer grants that aided in the completion of this study.

A NOTE ON THE TEXTS

In most cases, recent American editions were used for citation in this study. For both Forster novels and for Green's *Concluding*, Penguin editions were chosen because the number of words per page corresponded more closely with pagination for the other authors (citations were checked against hardcover issues). For Lewis's *Tarr* there was no American edition available.

Abbreviations used in the study are as follows:

Dubliners	James Joyce, *Dubliners* (1914; New York: Viking Critical Edition, 1969).
LG	D. H. Lawrence, *The Lost Girl* (1920; New York: Viking, 1968).
K	D. H. Lawrence, *Kangaroo* (1923); New York: Viking, 1960).
HE	E. M. Forster, *Howards End* (1910; Harmondsworth: Penguin, 1960).
PI	E. M. Forster, *A Passage to India* (1924; Harmondsworth: Penguin, 1971).
T	Wyndham Lewis, *Tarr* (1928, rev. ed.; London: Calder and Boyars, 1968).
SC	Wyndham Lewis, *Self Condemned* (1954; Chicago: Henry Regnery, 1965).
B	Henry Green, *Back* (1946; New York: Viking, 1950).
C	Henry Green, *Concluding* (1948; Harmondsworth: Penguin, 1964).

NOTE: With the exception of *Back*, the novels are nearly commensurate as to pagination, containing roughly 375–400 words per page. *Back* has only some 300 words per page, and thus the figure given for its pagination in the tables is 180, to make it correspond with the others. *Dubliners* is not included in the tables, which were derived in order to measure the novel pairs against one another.

Unless otherwise indicated, all italics in quoted material are mine.

1 ADVANCE AIM

More authors learn to think and feel in the laborious process of learning to write than have ever mastered the art of writing under the pressure of urgent thoughts and violent emotions.
    PETER QUENNELL

DECISIONS AND DISCOVERIES

An insurmountable problem faces the would-be analyst of prose style. It comes to this: while he is doing one thing, there are several other things he might have been doing. For this reason, probably the most dangerous posture a critic of style can assume is a militant one. If not directly, then implicitly, as soon as he sets out his wares he comes under the attack of proponents of methodologies he may have scanted or failed to employ at all—perhaps without even paying them lip-service.

While remaining insurmountable, this problem should be recognized as inherent to the practice of criticism. Just as textual scholars avoid the inferences of literary historians or as structuralists approach interpretation from different paths than New Critics, so in the criticism of style does one tend to encounter polarized terms like "subjective" and "objective," "evaluative" and "descriptive," "qualitative" and "quantitative"—terms that are meant to identify proclivities, and that have often been brought to bear by critics of one camp casting animadversions on those of another.

In critiques of style that have been appearing in the 1960s and 1970s, a tendency to advocate "objective-descriptive-quantitative" standards has been noticeable, along with a growing wariness toward impressionistic approaches to style. I would like to think that this study of five stylists who brought modern British fiction to its zenith is based on descriptive (and quantitative) criteria, yet I recognize that impressionism accounts for the germ of the whole thing. This is not something to dwell upon, if only because criticism is itself a quasi-

1

literature. Selectivity must start it into being. One commences with a sense of the value of the authors selected. This granted, the principal reason to analyze their styles is to refocus their themes—that is, to reaccount for their power and singularity: only, not through a study of their work in skeletonized or girdered form (structures, motifs, deployment of symbols), but, rather, through a study essentially of their sentences. Context becomes an indispensable guideline in determining how these authors' sentence habits establish fictional strategy. Naturally enough, occasions for going beyond sentences arise, when paragraphs and even longer tracts are brought in focus; the material also requires emphasis on smaller-than-sentence units (phonemic/morphemic usages, for instance, or even punctuation). And, whereas "absolute 'style' in an isolated text may not be found by analysis," as G. W. Turner has said, an appreciation that "texts differ in relation [a] to each other and [b] to what they might have been"[1] offers a sort of major and minor rationale for discussing *pairs* of novels by the writers herein (or, in Joyce's case, for launching the enterprise by looking at the discrete substyles of *Dubliners*).

The major rationale is simply that different works of an author, examined near one another, will yield elements of his "ground style" along with departures from it that the individual works tend to induce, and, moreover, that there are ready-made comparisons available as the works of other authors are likewise compared and then cross-compared. The minor rationale supposes that conjectures as to "what might have been" occasionally offer a resort for speculation about what is making existing sentences work, as Turner implies.

Paramount in this approach is a regard for command. It hardly matters whether one writer meticulously revised his work (as Lewis did with the 1928 *Tarr*) and another disavowed all but haphazard connection with it (Lawrence's situation with the unrevised *Kangaroo*). How any of them put their words and sentences together is not recoverable; *what* they produced remains tractable to analysis. Arguing their command over their material simply cautions the critic not to assume exhaustibility of his own subject. As Forster said in a Harvard lecture in 1947, contrasting the critical and creative states, "The critical state . . . is grotesquely remote from the state responsible for the works it affects to expound." Not only is the creative state a different order of prehension (it learns "what it has said *after* it has said it,"[2] says Forster), but, just as importantly, artists of very high caliber, one must suspect, have reserves of power which those who are normally proficient in language may set false limits to. As personal as a genuine work of art must be, it will never encompass the personality or creativity of its begetter. The gift for parody alone—conspicuous in Joyce and

Lewis (but one need think only of the rantings of a few of their characters to see that Lawrence, Green, and Forster share that gift)[3]—should remind the reader that novelists like these suggest an almost illimitable range of verbal constructs. My point is that working with a couple of the products of each, and even uncovering some solid indices to their styles, is not tantamount to delimiting their linguistic resources. It would be wiser, when dealing with writers of the first order, to assume protean abilities, namely, their mastery of forms upon forms of language—indeed, if they lacked a fascination with forms upon forms, they would not, I think, be great writers at all.

All this is by way of a disclaimer. For, even though statistical justifications are offered all along in these chapters, they do no more than offer proof, on the strength of incidence, that a given writer happens to be resorting to this or that special form of utterance in his text. Evaluative comments are in order after each such illustration, for statistics can never be considered determinant. That is, they do not bind an author or affix a style to him that one finally calls *his*. Considerations of context, especially in affective works like novels, can often yield nonce usages or other radical departures from normally consistent patterns, which may be indicative of urgencies—even of slacknesses—in theme as revealed through style. "Command," while it need not be conscious, will certainly be as well characterized by departure as by continuation. One might go as far as to say that a high quantitative count illustrates an author's yielding to an instinctive syntactic or verbal pattern—and that a departure could indicate resistance to that instinct—but his style will be a compound of that yielding and resisting; the resistance will not be *foreign* to it.

For example, E. M. Forster, as shown in chapter four, is an inordinately heavy user of antithesis—not only in the two novels discussed, but in all six novels he wrote (he once commented that the conjunction "but" was a word that bedeviled his prose). All the same, in Forster's tales one encounters next to no antithesis. In one sense this is a phenomenal fact; in another, an indication that there must be a felt control in Forster's writing, probably owing to his sense of decorum, what he feels his tales should read like. Does it, then, become right to say that Forster's real style has nothing to do with the style of Forster's tales? If we put precedence in quantitative yield we would have to make the error of saying that, or at least of calling the tales atypical. But why be maneuvered into a false dilemma like this? The alternative would be to make note of such quantitative evidence, without presuming to derive inherent as opposed to exiguous qualities from the two different performances: in other words, not let a quantitative approach presume to dictate appetencies and circumscribe abilities. It would be far more interesting to speculate on what may have been the narrative aspects of Forster's tales that caused him to curtail antitheses. Pondering that question would be a task of criticism and yet, of course, it would be "evaluative-subjective-qualitative."

One of the more quarrelsome books that batten on a statistical method is Louis Milic's *A Quantitative Approach to the Style of Jonathan Swift* (1967), to which we owe a great deal, but sometimes for reasons other than those Milic puts forward. (For example, concerning the sentence I just wrote: I had forecast a different phraseology at first, then checked at Milic's title and interpolated the "to which" clause. I had meant to begin a new sentence with the idea of our owing Milic's book a good deal. But it fit my scheme better, on nearing that idea, to cast it as a subordinate construction. There was no question of revision, only of adjustment along the way. As a relative clause the idea—while conceding merit—remains minimal in impact on the main clause, where Milic is deemed quarrelsome.)

I permitted myself that parenthesis because Milic states categorically that writers do not tamper with their syntax—rather, he avers that this comes to them unconsciously. He maintains they reserve their emendations for their vocabulary. In effect, his opinion is that Jonathan Swift was incapable of doing what I just did.

"During his period of apprenticeship," according to Milic, "a writer develops a certain variety of [syntactic] structures, strictly his own, which he continues to use and re-use with scarcely any change during the period of his mature writing. It is like his handwriting, unmistakably his but *almost beyond his power to modify to any significant extent.*"[4]

A statement like this is so reductive that it borders on the irresponsible. It is matched later by this rigorously held preconception: "The search for Swift's syntactical consistency is based on the belief— indeed the necessity—that such consistency is characteristic of all his work, regardless of subject matter."[5] Such a doctrine forces all unconscious choices made by a writer into the realm of syntax (Milic's idea of where one's real "style" is to be found), and all conscious choices into the lexical realm: " . . . the individual choice of word is far more readily tampered with than the grammatical mold," he supposes. Likewise, "It takes more effort to modify the syntactical structure of thought than the lexical component. . . . Thus it seems probable that vocabulary is intimately connected with Style (1), the rhetorical level, but that [the critic's or computer's] emphasis on syntax will reach Style (2), the expressive level."[6] The latter level Milic prefers to appropriate as the just-about-unalterable wellspring of the writer.

This is to fail to take account of the mystery of writing. It most certainly begs the mystery of genius. Just to give one alternative position: J. Middleton Murry, in one of the six lectures that formed *The Problem of Style* (1922), took on himself the enactment of a creative perception when he tried to inform his audience of his lecturer's emotion of depression and thought of a peach tree stripped by wind. "I have," he explained, "if you like, 'selected' that from the host of attendant circumstances, though I assure you I did nothing of the kind. The peach-tree seemed to fit my case pretty well; it simply rose up before my mind when I determined to make the attempt to convey the particular quality of my feeling."[7] Here it is diction (or image)—a peach tree—that rises to the mind's eye and needs (conscious) syntactic embodiment. My point is merely this: that what may move the writer initially can as well be a word or words, or can alternatively be a syntactic method of combining words; what he decides deliberately to impose on his text—again—may be a word or image, or may be a structure over which he is master. One can imagine Murry's peach tree materializing from nowhere and the writer devising a dozen ways for it to be brought particularly to his page, maybe finessing half of those tries in a spirit that would not warrant the verb "devising." In fact such decisions and discoveries operate para-consciously. Factors of momentum, experience, fortuity, all enter into play, and it is impossible to split apart lexical and syntactic components as though one underpinned the other and the critic could rest his case on isolating that one.

For purposes of critical distinction, one might define the imposed quality of a writer's message as his tone and the unconscious or personal quality of his message as his voice. But it would always be true to say that syntax *and* diction are capable of yielding tone, as both are capable of rendering voice.*

In identifying the syntactic hallmarks of Swift, Milic singles out his heavy use of verbals, his variety of connectives, and his pressured, often asymmetrical series-making. These are features of the great

---

*The quality of "voice" might be said to mark the way unsummoned words and phrases well up, whereas "tone" could mean the way a writer tapped that well. But one should not be simplistic as to the presence of some Style (1), comprising rhetoric, as opposed to some other deep-syntactic Style (2), where the real writer lies, hidden even from himself. He might be gratified to feel the surge of his own true accents, yet he will hardly feel cheated over something he has applied to advantage tonally. Art is not pure, it is tampered with, after all. But the tamperings cannot *all* find their line back to one command center. For, "It can be stated as a general psychological law that any creative search involves holding before the inner eye a multitude of possible choices that totally defeat conscious comprehension." (Anton Ehrenzweig, *The Hidden Order of Art* [Berkeley: University of California Press, 1971], p. 35.) For the critic, it would be fine to feel one had separated tone from voice, but the assignment of those labels entails educated guesswork.

satires like *Gulliver* and *A Tale of a Tub*. But had Milic done the same analysis of Swift's sermons, he would have found all three hallmarks wanting. Of course Swift composed those sermons gravely, permitting himself no flourishes, so all this may seem needless carping—except that Milic expressly dismisses those critics, like Paul Fussell and William Ewald, who acknowledge Swift's great range of impersonation and—without quantitative backup—assert his adoption of differing styles. On the analogy of Forster's tales and novels, it needs admitting that the unhortatory, enumerative style of the sermons is as truly Swiftian as the restless style of the satires.

The main objection to Milic is simply that he is such a zealot. He sweeps the board clean of "impressionistic" critics, presumes to derive from his tables the *unmonitored* voice of an artist who—as the "Polite Conversation" alone tells us—was absolutely infested with the swarms of vernacular phrases our native speakers have developed, being as addicted to variety as Joyce. Still, Milic's discoveries about Swift's syntax are rewarding, and the emphases he places on word order and nonconnotative lexical items like conjunctions and prepositions do bring to the fore possibilities for stylistic investigation that all too often have been overlooked.

A critic also employing a quantitative method, but, happily, without the quarrelsomeness of Milic, produced the first stylistic study of a twentieth-century British writer. This was Richard Ohmann, whose *Shaw: The Style and the Man* appeared in 1962. Both in his book and in his landmark essay "Prolegomena to the Analysis of Prose Style," Ohmann contends for a definition of style as "epistemic choice." That is, admitting the stylist is limited by the "methods of knowing" preorganized by the mother tongue, Ohmann holds that great varieties of nuance remain open, and that certain linguistic choices repeatedly seized on indicate a writer's "persistent way of sorting out the phenomena of experience."[8] Ohmann offers some examples of what he means: "A heavy dependence on abstraction, a peculiar use of the present tense, a habitual evocation of similarities through parallel structure, a tendency to place feelings in syntactical positions of agency, a trick of underplaying causal words: any of these patterns of expression, when repeated with unusual frequency, is the sign of a habit of meaning...."[9]

In *Shaw: The Style and the Man*, Ohmann isolates from the essays of Shaw some appetencies of this sort—in fact, 21 different ones—and by measuring frequency counts from Shaw against those from a control group (of contemporaries like Chesterton and Russell) illustrates the components of Shaw's narrative style. One of the categories that emerges (related to Shaw's predilection for "all-or-nothing determiners" like "everybody," "any healthy person") comprises "degree words," essentially adverbs of intensification like "extraordinarily," "thoroughly," "revoltingly." An insight to Ohmann's good sense all through his study is afforded when his count shows Bertrand Russell surpassing Shaw in numbers of degree words per thousand from the samples (some 16 for Russell to 12 for Shaw). But, says Ohmann, "A glance at [Russell's] degree words shows that they are not generally intensifiers . . . but the very opposite. His prose is full of thoughtful, qualifying, hesitating degree words such as 'fundamentally,' 'essentially,' and 'more or less'. . . . That a high score in such a count can mean extravagance for Shaw and caution for Russell is unfortunate but true, and goes to show once again that statistics cannot at present be the final refuge of stylistic criticism."[10]

Admissions like the last are invaluable. They enable one to take the results of intelligently applied statistics at face value and, moreover, to confide in a critic who does not simply mill out his findings. Ohmann, like Milic, worked from samples of continuous prose: in Ohmann's case, 2600-word aggregates, in Milic's, aggregates of varying lengths (10,000 words, 1000 sentences, etc.). Beginning with different hypotheses, though, the authors' conclusions reflect their original partiality to those hypotheses. Ending his book on the attribution to Swift of "A Letter of Advice to a Young Poet," Milic goes as far as to say that "Swift's nearly unadulterated style is present in the middle section . . . [whereas] something went wrong at the two ends" (he includes the possibility of an alien hand to account for this), and this because the two ends of the letter do not conform statistically with the "proved" Swiftian pattern.[11] Ohmann is characteristically less dogmatic. He concludes, since all his "controls" resemble one another in contrast with Shaw's deviance (on the 21 counts), that "the generalization very tentatively indicated is that a writer's characteristic style is largely the product of relatively few idiosyncratic variations from the norm, out of the vast number possible. This hypothesis makes sense if style does reflect epistemic choice, for no writer, surely, differs from the rest in his entire epistemic alignment. Even a great eccentric is likely to share in large part the conceptual scheme, and hence the style, of his fellows."[12]

The scientific drive for proof affects Milic more drastically than it does Ohmann, who is willing to remain much more speculative. Their strategy—determining the style and the man and allowing for little self-modulation (or none at all)—makes valid enough the choosing of more or less random samples of writing to be investigated quantitatively. My own quantitative efforts differ entirely. My purpose is not to extrapolate style but, rather, styles, and along with that, to concentrate on how some novels have been made and "how" they mean. No random sampling is offered at all. On certain major issues I recur to statistical counts for each writer to reinforce qualitative emphases. But usually I offer conclusions about style that, in context, seem self-evident enough not to require statistical verification.

Since I deal with five writers, all of whom might be admitted among the "great eccentrics" alluded to by Ohmann, there is, as I said, a set of "controls" available for the making of comparisons. Thus when a statistical check seems to reveal a lot about, say, Wyndham Lewis's proclivity for the conjunction "as," or D. H. Lawrence's for the anterior positioning of appositives, four-fold comparisons are pressed into service. But such a supply of data will be sporadic, not automatically part of the program. More crucially at issue will be the comparisons arising within the author's canon. Therefore, the chapters that follow produce nothing like point-by-point resemblances to one another. The immanence of theme tends to dictate the working plan of a chapter. In the end, the sentences culled from the novels and from *Dubliners* try to perform a double service: while they represent the style of the author, they aim to discover meanings in the fiction.

BELLETRISTS, LINGUISTS, AND THE FORM-CONTENT ISSUE

Most works on prose style feel an obligation to define style and, in doing so, to come to grips with the form-content controversy. I shall be willing, in a moment, to give a short though binary definition of what I feel style is. However, I do not believe a definition *need* be wrestled with, nor do I think the form and content issue a salient one over which to become embroiled.

In books and articles over the last quarter-century, say, that have dealt with style—a time coinciding with the rise of the New Criticism, on the one hand, and of the study of stylistics as a branch of linguistics on the other—there has been a tendency for the linguistically oriented critic to argue a separation of form and content, and for the critic who is aesthetically oriented to deny this separation. Inevitably, the position taken by either exponent comes back to what he or she considers to be the presence (or *ur*-presence) of "situation." Ordinarily the linguist assumes a situation that can be manifoldly treated; he suggests that there are many ways of saying virtually the same thing, and that the small differentiations observable—while roughly the same thing gets reported—constitute "style." However, the belletrist counters by saying that every utterance is unique to itself, and *becomes* situation; each whole utterance can be regarded as uniquely "styled."

Not only is the position of either party defensible; it actually becomes incontrovertible, once perspective is brought into play. The problem is one of temporal orientation. And, in the context of the time perspective of each arguer, each is right. The nearest analogy is to the quandary of predestination (which is why the issue is unfruitful to pursue, though it does seem to need to be rehearsed). At any one point in the linguist's time perspective—which is that of the future and a situation yet to be verbalized—a stylistic choice can be made, and a notion refined, added to, or modified, so that the one expression chosen, on the point of its production, will differ slightly from what might have been. Some linguists in fact devote their whole energies to the recovery, through transformational grammar, of the processes by which a sentence's "deep structure" did emerge into the deviant, special surface structure figured in its final form.[13] (When stylistic analyses are then made, they are in the direction of indicating what the "transforms" have been, the modes of levering the simply-extant material—in the deep structure—into forms favored at that time by the sentence-maker: such practices as the construction of an appositive by the deletion of a predicate: "They achieved their victory: [they won] a great reprieve.")

The aesthetic critic argues, feeling his position unassailable where artifacts are concerned, that only the thing done is pertinent. His viewpoint is implicitly that of the past: it resembles the predestinarian's, which says, "it has come to this," and in saying so denies or deems irrelevant the erstwhile element of choice. He may know of a preexistent version of the utterance in question (e.g., a rough draft), but will maintain that the words on the page and what they do are all the critic has the right to deal with.

This latter, "monistic" argument need not lead to a dead end. What it will do, always, is downplay any recourse to "deep structure" as an advantage in identifying style. Stanley Fish may be cited as an outspoken opponent of the transformational method whose own countermethod involves a temporal approach to sentences as they unfold before a reader. For the question "what does this sentence mean?" he would substitute "what does this sentence do?" and he would investigate expectancies word-by-word along the sentence line, as productive of an "experience" or an "event" rather than of a statement.[14] Fish precludes delving for linguistic *ur*-structures, and is in favor of the building linear effect of writing, on the principle of the reader's responding to an author's strategies. For example (passages from Browne and Pater well illustrate his point), surface structures would have to be seen, at least to some degree, as *misleading* by linguists, who would solve them for their original-statement matrices. "In my account of reading, however," says Fish, "the [reader's] temporary adoption of these inappropriate strategies is itself a response to the strategy of an author; and the resulting mistakes are part of the experience provided by that author's language and therefore part of its meaning."[15]

Fish's reemphasis on surface structure does seem a valid corrective. It gives primacy to a response that remains "on edge," so to speak, while deferring to a writer's often complex motives for letting what has arrived on the page stand. Fish's approach would dislodge another linguistic system as well: the "deviation" theory of Michael Riffaterre, which argues that an author, "at the points he deems important along the written chain," will veer from expected pattern, forcing on his reader's attention *"inescapable elements,"* which, to engage the reader's active imagination, *"will have to be unpredictable."*[16] Though gravitating toward the linguists' view of a "situation" being managed ("the points he deems important"), Riffaterre does not oversimplify matters: he has a complex view of the unforeseeable contexts within which all manner of stylistic devices may develop. And he is talking about a widely held concept, that of "defamiliarization"[17] as a necessary concomitant of verbal art. The contention here is that strangeness, out-of-placeness, is what prevents elliptic, facile "decoding" (Riffaterre's word) on the part of readers.

Fish's reason for quarreling with Riffaterre seems theoretically sound (he would avoid the latter's "atomism"), yet may be practically dangerous. Riffaterre seems ready to apprehend only the "treated" and "inescapable" stretches of a text. But transparency itself, for Fish, is worth noting when it is evident in a writer's style; to state this another way, he is wary of "deviation theories [narrowing] the range of meaningful response [with the result that reader experience] will become binary in structure, a succession of highlighted moments alternating with . . . intervals of contextual norm . . . [during] a large part of [which], nothing will be happening."[18] While this sounds athletically right as a warning, may it not also be possible to be too finely on one's guard? Are there not welcome dross-spots in the experiencing of the greatest art? Isn't there a rhythm, an unguarding of perception and attention as the eye follows words, that even in lyric poems invites to relaxation (when "nothing will be happening") before concentration? One might be wary of Fish's over-regard for a continually arresting context, for he may cause the reading to be more wrought than the writing, and not allow for rhythm that is the essence of art.

10

Take his criticism to its ultimate application, that is, to the experiencing of *syllables* while one reads, and it will be seen to be overstated. The very attentiveness the mind gives to words will be to *portions* of words chiefly, their unstressed portions being assimilated during intervals where "nothing will be happening."

I only make this scruple because criticism itself can hardly continue without the element of purism discarded. It *will* be atomistic in the end; criticism of prose has got to deal with highlights. "We find an uncertainty principle at the very foundation of stylistics," says G. W. Turner, "which ensures that however nearly its goal, if this is the particularity of language, is approached, it will never be reached. We might make narrower and narrower generalizations but we generalize to the last, until there is nothing left to do but quote. . . . Stylistics must therefore deal with a particularity it can never reach, ever indicating and lighting up what it cannot capture."[19] His phrase, "lighting up," really comes straight back to "highlighting." Of course there may be transparencies to be accounted for in prose styles, as well as opacities. But even the act of describing the transparent must involve singling it out as special. And, in the end, the doing of some justice to even the most idiosyncratic prose will include the acknowledgment that there are pedestrian elements which will go unaccounted for but for which no reader will be ungrateful.*

Critics who take into account the facts of the matter—who uphold the uniqueness of art but who hesitate to idealize its forms—can announce fairly rigorous theories about nonparaphrasability while at the same time accommodating the relativist views of linguists. Susan Sontag and David Lodge are two such critics. Controversial as Miss Sontag often is, she offers, in her essay "On Style," the sort of reminder that must disarm any "purist" interpreter. "The role of the arbitrary and unjustifiable in art has never been sufficiently acknowledged," she points out; she goes on to say, "Usually critics who want to praise a work of art feel compelled to demonstrate that each part is justified, that it could not be other than it is. And every artist, when it comes to his own work, remembering the role of chance, fatigue, external distractions, knows what the critic says to be a lie. . . ."[20] The

---

*A caveat of Middleton Murry's might also illustrate the likelihood of stretches of duller decoding coming up in long works of prose. "It seems to me," says Murry, "that the truth is not so much that an author must himself possess a great power of visualization . . . as that he must possess the power of making his readers see things on occasion." (*The Problem of Style*, p. 92.) Of the writers in this study, Wyndham Lewis pretty well violates Murry's stricture, but in doing so, may seem to bear it out. Murry could have had Lewis in mind when he continued, "If anything, I should say that a writer would be embarrassed by an exceedingly exact visual memory."

11

whole view of art as process, even in some respects as the result of luck, is manifest here, along with the useful coda that a writer is not specially concerned minute-by-minute with what the critic will later be pinning down as his ineluctable style. David Lodge comes close to the same reminder about the process of art when he likens the envisioned structure of a novel not to a "framework of pillars and arches" but to something that is more akin to "scaffolding, without which the building cannot be started, but which is altered and dismantled in the process of construction."[21] Even though this accounts for the provisional element that must accompany the writing of novels (and note how the critical perspective is thrown toward the future, the thing as yet undone, admitting of choice, the linguists' view), Lodge, in his earlier and major work on style, *Language of Fiction* (1966), remains a stickler for the thing done, with its provisional entailments "cut."

In this work Lodge contends for the inseparability of matter and form by debarring contingent situation from the realm of art. He takes his lead from the demonstration of the philosopher J. M. Cameron that "the entailments . . . are cut in fictional discourse,"[22] meaning that the text allows for no alternative conjecture as to what is transpiring, there being no real prior state of affairs to which one can make an appeal.

Yet, in one sense, to react at all to style will force some alternative conjectures into play. The warnings of "belletrist" critics against our taking novels as "statements," against our apprehending quasi-verifiable data in them, must be regarded as valuable cautions against thinking of novelists as overlaying their material with style. The novelist does create only what is there in black print on the page. But to respond to the life that is in that page, the reader in practice has to be doing two things: he has to be adjusting his own linguistic experience, and he has to be appealing to life experience as well. The former act of attention is possibly less conscious than the latter.

A brief illustration from a parody in *Punch* may indicate what sort of mental purchase on words a reader is likely to be making at every step. The title, "The Artificial Respiration Controversy," is somewhat of a giveaway because of the last word, which suggests contending factions. The opening sentence tells us that a delegate to a conference started the controversy when he "remarked in an interview that he thought that Artificial Respiration." (No [sic] is involved, either here or in the rest of the extract.)

> . . . Little more was heard, apart from an official denial, and most people thought that a natural death; however, a week later, an official announcement was made, on behalf, that they considered that Artificial

Respiration, but in much stronger terms than. The original delegate responsible resigned from, saying that misquotation.

A question was asked in the House, replying to which the Parliamentary Under said that he had given the matter due.

"Bearing in mind," he continued, "and despite, the government is obliged to refrain from on this matter. We prefer to keep an open."[23]

The writer of this parody can dare delete words from every sentence to create this ménage of nonsentences because he knows the reader is linguistically maneuvered into supplying the gaps for himself. In fact, what would have been lifeless, in full form, is given life by the omissions. Yet what exactly does one mean by life? By it, I suppose, one means the conscious strand of imagination that must be ignited so as to impel the reader from a passive attitude of intake to an apprehension that something different could or even ought to have been there. In this specific instance, sentence-by-nonsentence, he is reminded that he is hearing the voice of a report, a committee-spawned one, no less. It would seem to achieve its own special vitality from its having dared to stand out from other reports through its omissions of the weighty committee words themselves. But in thinking of those other reports the reader (here more consciously) has to be projecting into *life* situations, just as he has to be doing this in his experiencing of novels. Thus, even "belletristic" critics like Lodge and Sontag—or, say, the structuralist Roland Barthes, who would go them one better and insist exclusively that *beyond* the discourse "begins the world"—even such advocates of the artifact have to edge back to some middle ground before what they tell us about the artifact can make sense—unless they quote it. And a good critic from the linguist camp, Seymour Chatman, has made this clear, it seems to me. Applying the principles of Barthes to an examination of Joyce's "Eveline," Chatman, while assured that "the analyst should limit himself to what is immanent in the work of art," is forced to the empirical conclusion that, after all, "our chief pleasure in reading modern fiction ... depends radically, it seems to me, on outside knowledge." For "art seems to need life-information. ... The very inferences that are necessary to the establishment of [structural] indices can only be formed by references to the real world."[24]

To follow Chatman's lead is to credit a reader with an alternate instinct that takes him from text to world (for appreciation of the text, of course). As the *Punch* parody shows, what the writer does *not* supply is something a responsive reader takes in. I would expand this to a general principle; such tacit comparisons are indispensable for stylistic appreciation.

Paying tribute to a writer's style need not begin with finality—"he could not have said it another way." Rather, a closer approximation of the creative process would sense what syntactic or lexical options the author was *preventing* himself from taking. But the key word remains "tacit." By no means must there be a constant and active posing of alternates to the mind for a critic to say things about style.

Simply, for example, to mention a term like "inversion" and count on its being understood indicates that a "normal order" of sequence is (roughly) shared among readers of a language. Critic need not remind reader of this normal order. He can virtually say "here are a set of inversions" and rely on a stylistic disinterment being made. Or let us, by extension, take expletives ("It was Alexander who conquered the greatest territory"). Of this special pattern in the syntax of the copular, Louis Milic has said accurately, *"There* and *it* as expletives signal that a grammatical inversion has taken place."[25] That is, the utterance is really saying, "Alexander was [the one] who conquered the greatest territory." When "it" replaces "the one," the proper noun is then thrown behind the verb ("It was Alexander"). Not much apparently seems changed as the statement accepts further compression to "Alexander conquered the greatest territory."

The important thing, though, should a critic be talking about expletives (and here the notion of inversion signifies), would be to say that in the first and second (but not the third) sentences about Alexander an implicit question has been lodged. Whenever a reader encounters a lengthening out by way of expletive, he is also being set up to suppose he himself has asked a question. That is what happens in this sentence from *A Passage to India:*

> Still, the men tolerated him for the sake of his good heart and strong body; it was their wives who decided that he was not a sahib really. (PI 62)

Reading the second clause (and, incidentally, here would be an application of Stanley Fish's method: seeing what happens word-by-word through time delay), we feel as though we are collusive with Forster on the point of the women's culpability—as though our question, "Who was it, then?", had been answered.

An analyst can provide commentary like this, pointing to the resultant emphases, while rarely needing to refer to the alternative ways the thing might have been done. He simply relies on a moot agreement between himself and the reader: as between artist and audience, so between critic and audience, this interplay is part of communication anyway, an implicit test being undergone all the time. (Some linguistic analysts, I think, are unnecessarily chary of this sort of

14

getting-on-with-it; perhaps they should be more willing to be wrong, less prone to want to make graph paper out of ruled paper.)

Especially in the study of achieved style this sense of alternatives needs to be assumed between critic and audience. Even when it conveys the qualities of "seamlessness, inevitability,"[26] art will be informed by an element of torsion. Peter Quennell, whose aphorism about artists heads this chapter, reminds us in another passage from his autobiography that the best writing combines "a natural facility and an acquired difficulty."[27] It would seem the two halves of this formula satisfy the two needs a creative writer has to meet. The more effluent of the two, one might suppose, is the capacity to impress readers; the more exacting, perhaps, the satisfactory expression of self.[28] From this idea the binary definition of style promised earlier develops.

Of all the definitions of style with which I am acquainted, the swiftest valid one, to me, is Kenneth Burke's. "In its simplest manifestation, style is ingratiation."[29] From the rhetorician's point of view held by this critic, I see no reason to take exception to the definition. Admittedly, though, it has a transitive, writer-to-audience ring to it, whereas the "acquired difficulty" spoken for by Quennell would seem to mark the writer's writing for himself. Think of Joyce resisting the well-meant suggestions for changes that came to him from Grant Richards. Richards wanted to publish *Dubliners,* but was badgered by, among others, the very printers who had been consigned the accepted manuscript! "Ingratiation" would serve as no word for Joyce's firm attitude; yet, unquestionably, he ingratiates readers of all subsequent generations who have been helped to their own scrupulosity by such a writer championing exactitude in his way. He may have had an *ultimate* corps of readers projected, but he himself was his own first one.

To the degree, then, that a writer must keep his readers in mind, it is fair to say that style is ingratiation; but to the degree that he must not, it is emergency. I would define its existence in terms of no more than the suggestibility of those two nouns. This does not make for a very probing definition, only for a kind of ranging one. It would forestall but still endorse idiosyncrasy, at one and the same time.

Idiosyncrasy, crucial to art, imperils an artist when indulged. One knows the sensation of being let down by craftsmen who slip to self-parody: the best American novelists of this century—James, Faulkner, Hemingway—have been peculiarly charged with this failing. The writers encountered in the present study also, one time or another, have been so criticized. In the chapters to come, no effort is made to assess such possible shortcomings. (For one thing, in the choice of

15

books like *The Lost Girl* and *Self Condemned,* where the writers seem less self-monitored than usual, or *Concluding* and *A Passage to India,* which are the authors' masterpieces, there is an element of implicit reprieve from charges of self-repetition.) The styles to be met are idiosyncratic, by all means, but there is measure or resistance at work in them— there is not a great deal that is spectacular.

The emergency of great writing cannot help but require idiosyncrasy. As John Crowe Ransom said in 1950, style is a necessitous force freeing an author "from the restrictions of logical prose," and operating thus urgently because a kind of side-of-the-eye seeing must be at work. The job at hand is to retranscribe, into pages of fiction, objects that demand to be quickened with life rather than mastered or possessed or exhausted.[30] For "the great effort of stylization means to expand them [perceived things] into the concrete objects which they were all the time if we could have had reason for stopping to see them fully. The effort goes against the grain of our linguistic conditioning; the labor it requires is paradoxical since it must concentrate upon a certain dissipation of the normal act of attention."[31]

What Ransom seems to mean in his last clause is that the key effects of good fiction will work through off-focus schemes; writers have to engineer their own readiness to let slip into their narration things that surprise themselves.

Yet for a writer to commence with the conviction that he must be deliberately idiosyncratic, stem to stern, would probably be ruinous. As personal as most novelists admit to being, it is not surprising to find that few (Joyce is an exception here) are willing to say that what they are evolving is idiosyncratic style. It is probably missing the main point to say that the idiosyncrasy of a good novelist is deliberate; his secret, if he is really good, is more likely to have been this: that his deliberation has been idiosyncratic.

2 JAMES JOYCE: *DUBLINERS*

Don't talk to me about politics. I'm only interested in style.
        JAMES JOYCE TO STANISLAUS JOYCE, WHILE WRITING *DUBLINERS*

FORMAL COMPOUNDING: JOYCE'S NORMS AND SOME DEPARTURES

A stylistic analysis, like any other critique of Joyce's *Dubliners*, should be able to contribute to an understanding of the whole work. Where the focus of any sound traditional study would be forced, to some degree, onto the collection's organizing principles, the aim of a style study might be described differently, as that of disclosing a principle of utterance.

As readers we pore over words and words and words—and the best result of traditional criticism has been to teach us to detect the structural placings of the key words (or images, or scenes) that reveal the artist's shaping. It is the *deployment* that counts. Here is part of a sentence from "Clay": "and though Fleming had said that for so many Hallow Eves, Maria had to laugh . . . and the tip of her nose nearly met the tip of her chin." The kind of critic I am talking about will emphasize deployment by noting that just as Hallow Eve is mentioned we are given the witchlike description of Maria. A critic of style (in this case, myself) might be led to emphasize a different facet of the sentence entirely: here, the choice of the incomplete intensive construction "for so many Hallow Eves"—an idea that will be returned to later. It is not so much the deployment as the *rendition* of the image that interests the critic of style. By pointing out something about the timing, that other critic would be paying heed to architectonics. But as Evelyn Waugh once said about his writing, "You see, there are always words going round in my head. . . . I think entirely in words. By the time I come to stick my pen in my inkpot these words have reached a

17

stage of order which is fairly presentable."[1] Ideally a critic of style should be able to illustrate something about the words and their fairly presentable order that will supply meanings through intensive patterns. The characters and events revealed to us through the medium of sentences may thus be brought across with more of their author's authority, if our apprehensions of the sentence patterns are sharpened by accurate descriptions of them.

But these descriptions will have to be somehow reincorporated into the wider scheme of the whole work. When Joyce or any other artist creates his sentences, he is doing so against the pressure of his own memory. He has to retain what has gone before and then, too, project forward a "memory" that grasps the shape and sound of the work's final form while it is yet inchoate. Far from being produced in any actual vacuum of "words going round," the sentences pressed out under a pen nib will have past and future dictates to guide them to the form they reach. Thus matters of structure and theme have to be kept by the critic in the middle distance at least. A concern with them cannot be put aside; decisions about which stylistic matters to pursue will, it seems to me, have to be made in accordance with what value they have as conditioned by consideration of the entire work (as much as by piecemeal detection of things done within sentences).

To illustrate: an ordinarily minor matter like punctuation might get extra consideration from an analyst of style, whose antennae may be out for tinier-than-usual signals bearing on an author's practice. Suppose he finds a disposition toward a certain form of punctuation; suppose then, from outside the text, he hits on a certain fact that seems related to his first discovery. Is it possible that through the combination the minor discovery may turn major? One must keep one's eye out for just that sort of possibility. Broadly speaking, this only means keeping alert for structural clues to enhance textural findings. In other words, what is discovered stylistically may have doubled import when reinforced by placement.

I shall be trying to show in a moment that the key emotive mark of punctuation in *Dubliners* is the colon. This requires some evidence and, also, a qualitative sense of Joyce's employment of this mark. Now, from outside the text (Joyce's letters after his submission of the manuscript), we know these two things: he was bent on describing Dublin as the center of Irish paralysis, and before he wrote "The Dead," his story "Grace" was to have ended the collection, which had been begun by "The Sisters." Here is the first sentence of "The Sisters": "There was no hope for him this time: it was the third stroke." And similarly for "Grace": "Two gentlemen who were in the lavatory at the time tried to lift him up: but he was quite helpless."

18

Two examples cannot show a predilection for anything. Yet it is a fact that Joyce starts out these framing stories by registering helplessness, and that he resorts to the colon to set up relationships across the clauses. The first is a continuing relationship (no hope: third stroke), the second a contravening one (tried to lift: but he was helpless), but the effects are radically similar. Since Joyce's use of the colon is found to operate consistently with such precision, it is germane to assume that he was drawn to the usage to start off his framing stories. My interest just now, though, is in the fact that support can be gained, from knowledge not having anything directly to do with style, for a stylistic point that can be come by via the more normal (quantitative) approach. A knowledge of structure (the placing of "The Sisters" and "Grace") and of theme (Joyce's intention to record his country's paralysis) become factors in arriving at a stylistic perception that can not only be corroborated by a quantitative check, but can also be seen as *worth* citing and pondering further as a Joycean hallmark.

Since Joyce's early fictional style has received little critical attention,[2] a focus on how he makes his sentences should be interesting in itself. As far as method is concerned, Nils Enkvist's breakdown of approaches to stylistic analysis proves convenient. Enkvist indicates how phonemic and morphemic attention to particles offers one line of approach, and larger considerations of lexis and syntax another. A fifth category added by Enkvist involves the mechanics of punctuation and capitalization.[3]

In the present study of *Dubliners*, lexical and syntactic analysis takes central position (some important morphemic variants figuring here). As for phonemic yield, I have felt that a demonstration of Joyce's cadences makes for a suitable conclusion, in that results purely referable to sound qualities may remind us that the writer's ear and his pulse could be the ultimate dictating forces behind his choice of words and word order.* Initially, however, I would like to illustrate something about mechanics—the rather formal punctuation that helps impress the ground style of *Dubliners* on the reader. It points to some partiality in Joyce for compound constructions, a trait underlined by his pronounced use of connectives. These in turn can be discarded when logical, formulaic linking is no longer desired and linkings of greater immediacy are required.

In going over the proof sheets of the first edition of *Dubliners*

---

*In the final chapter of this study, where Henry Green is the subject, I return to the matter of cadences and present comparative findings for all the authors treated. While avoiding any ironclad suppositions, one might venture to say that a writer's "voice" takes over from tone when rhythms tend to become dominant.

(1914), Joyce, as Scholes and Litz point out, "made over a thousand corrections—mainly removing commas that had been introduced by the printer."[4] For all the quickening of narration this fact implies, the pace of the stories is usually kept in some measure retarded. One of the ways Joyce maintains a judicial air is through a rather liberal use of colons and semicolons.

In the 216 pages of *Dubliners* (exclusive of their appearance in dialogue or introducing dialogue), there are 155 semicolons and 115 colons: 270 occurrences, or well more than one per page, when the two marks are taken in combination.[5] Their general import is to convey a sense of rectitude on Joyce's part: a consideration for the congruence of ideas or feelings in many sentences. But the fact that he departs from basic usages (in the four adolescent stories plus "A Painful Case" and the dramatic story "Ivy Day") is most interesting of all.

After employing a uniform style in "The Sisters," "An Encounter," and "Araby," Joyce occasioned his manner to change. The three stories of childhood gave way to four of adolescence, followed by four dealing with maturity and three on public life. Placed as a capstone, "The Dead" reechoes but mellows the predicaments experienced in the shorter stories. Dropping first-person narration after "Araby," Joyce also "developed a system," Scholes and Litz say, "whereby the events and characters . . . determined the diction and syntax of the narrative prose."[6] This is most strikingly felt in the stories of adolescence—"Eveline," "After the Race," "Two Gallants," and "The Boarding House." For, as the stories of maturity are launched, there is some tendency to return to the more elegant prose with which the collection had begun, this being most evident in the first of the new bloc, "A Little Cloud."

So, along with the resiliency of variation, there is the resiliency of return. By adverting to Joyce's "formal" punctuation we can begin to point out some standard Joycean constructions and then some variations that accord with these thematic changes.

If first it is remarked that of the 155 semicolons in *Dubliners*, 88 are followed by clauses introduced by coordinate conjunctions, one becomes aware of a recurrent sentence type amounting to a Joycean predilection. In the 20 pages comprising "The Sisters" and "An Encounter" there are 16 semicolon usages, and every one involves a compound sentence ligature including the conjunction. For example:

> It murmured; and I understood that it desired to confess something. I felt my soul receding into some pleasant and vicious region; and there again I found it waiting for me. ("The Sisters")

> He would love that, he said, better than anything in this world; and his voice, as he led me monotonously through the mystery, grew almost affectionate. . . . ("An Encounter")

These examples capture moments of mental excitation, in fact, of collusion. Insights of a more painful sort are caught in the final sentences of "Araby" and "A Little Cloud"; the "and" after both semicolons transfers cause to effect:

> Gazing up into the darkness I saw myself as a creature driven and derided by vanity; and my eyes burned with anguish and anger. ("Araby")

> He listened while the paroxysm of the child's sobbing grew less and less; and tears of remorse started to his eyes. ("A Little Cloud")

With "A Little Cloud" reverting to the more "curried" style (Hugh Kenner's phrase), where "Araby" had left off, it is revealing that Joyce should return to his formal compounding. For that is what he has done. In the intervening four stories something different had been going on. Of the 155 semicolons mentioned before (roughly 11 per story), 49 appeared in that adolescent bloc (about the same average). However, only 12 (one-fourth) of those work in the compound connective way. In the stories outside the adolescent bloc, three-fourths of the usages are compound connective (76 of 106). The situations in the adolescent stories have the characters more in a welter than elsewhere—lunging, trapped, or waiting. The stresses seem to account for structures like these:

> He knew Corley would fail; he knew it was no go. ("Two Gallants")

> He had money enough to settle down on; it was not that. ("The Boarding House")

> That was a long time ago; she and her brothers and sisters were all grown up; her mother was dead. ("Eveline")

Deprived of conjunctions, these compound sentences are staccato. More pronouncedly than anywhere else in *Dubliners,* the adolescent stories have this tautened effect. Most breathless of all is "After the Race," which has 18 semicolons—the highest number in the collection—but of these, 15 are employed atypically:

> Rapid motion through space elates one; so does notoriety; so does the possession of money.

> Besides Villona's humming would confuse anybody; the noise of the car, too.

> . . . it had been his father who had first suggested the investment; money to be made in the motor business, pots of money.

> What excitement! Jimmy was excited too; he would lose, of course.

In the first example, "so does" tries to keep pace with factors that make for excitement. In the last, the final clause is a *non sequitur* (almost dismissed because of excitement). In the two inside examples, fragments to the right of the semicolon appear for only time in *Dub-*

21

liners. Neither the sentences nor the main character have had time to stabilize themselves, and these constructions mirror the confusion to which Jimmy is prey all along.

From the "maturity" stories that follow we can abstract what may be regarded as the most typical Joycean compounds. ("A Painful Case" is not represented.)

> He had slightly emphasised his tone and he was aware that he had betrayed himself; but, though the colour had heightened in his cheek, he did not flinch from his friend's gaze. ("A Little Cloud")

> The man glanced from the lady's face to the little egg-shaped head and back again; and, almost before he was aware of it, his tongue had found a felicitous moment. ("Counterparts")

> But no one tried to show her her mistake; and when she had ended her song Joe was very much moved. ("Clay")

In this pattern there is an interruption after the connective, at which point an adverbial clause of time is inserted, creating some periodicity to help along the ironic connotation of the close ("did not flinch," "found a felicitous moment," "was very much moved"). This is a pattern indigenous to Joyce. It serves well to bear out Kenner's assertion that the prose is "scrupulously overwritten . . . a faded patent-leather prose that never quite recedes from the reader's attention. . . ."[7]

That the pattern is foreign to "A Painful Case" is owing to the character of Mr. Duffy. Every rhetorical emphasis in this story is based on his categorical nature, and so, instead of development, we get dogmatism. In the compound sentences this is managed when the second clause serves to reinforce a prior conviction rather than carry an idea along associatively.

> Not merely had she degraded herself; she had degraded him.

> He went often to her little cottage outside Dublin; often they spent their evenings alone.

> He could not have carried on a comedy of deception with her; he could not have lived with her openly.

> He gnawed the rectitude of his life; he felt that he had been outcast from life's feast.

There are many such redundancies in "A Painful Case," so it is noteworthy that the "public life" story that follows, "Ivy Day in the Committee Room," is kept clean of them—with one notable exception. It has to do with the character Crofton, Duffy-like in his aloof superiority. To put him into the unsympathetic camp of Duffy, Joyce breaks his easy sentence patterns through the nonce use, in this story, of a semicolon. Crofton, we are told, "was silent for two reasons. The first reason, sufficient in itself, was that he had nothing to say; the second reason was that he considered his companions beneath him." I am convinced Joyce contrived this occasion by which to deal stodginess a blow through a pompous construction. There are no others remotely like it, and the story's otherwise dramatic purity could have some bearing on why Joyce named it his favorite.[8]

Rather than illustrate the semicolon at further length (since its employment in "A Mother" and "Grace" is a return, basically, to Joyce's norm), I shall turn to "The Dead" to show how semicolon and colon crowd in once the climactic region of the story is reached.*

"The Dead" is 50 pages long. Through the first 38 pages there are only 19 colons and semicolons; through the last 12 there are 14 of them. More important is that both types cluster, over different three-page spans, near the end. Heavy formal compounding begins right after Gabriel has been stirred by the figure of his listening wife and they have ventured into the night air. Here are three of five examples:

> A dull yellow light brooded over the houses and the river; and the sky seemed to be descending.

> The blood went bounding along his veins; and the thoughts went rioting through his brain, proud, joyful, tender, valorous.

> Under cover of her silence he pressed her arm closely to his side; and, as they stood at the hotel door, he felt that they had escaped from their lives and duties, escaped from home and friends and run away together with wild and radiant hearts to a new adventure.

The first sets atmosphere. The others end with a sense of overspill (each last clause amplified by a series voicing Gabriel's hopes). But Gabriel is not to have his cravings come to fruition. As the story moves to its climax, Joyce presses into service not the semicolon but the colon. It clusters six times in the last five paragraphs, beginning with "So she had had that romance in her life: a man had died for her sake." As with the opening sentence of Dubliners ("... it was the third stroke"), a statement like this is a simple truth-teller. What counts is what lies to the right of the colon: "a man had died for her sake." Unlike the semicolon continuator, the colon sets up an end statement and the lead-in to the left exists only for that. Two others of the six at the end of "The Dead" illustrate this factor remarkably well. The first

*It is well to interject Joyce's conviction about the difference between the two marks. James Stephens reported, on meeting Joyce, "He ... confided the secret to me ... that, grammatically, I did not know the difference between a semi-colon and a colon ... and that I should give up writing...." (Richard Ellmann, James Joyce [New York: Oxford University Press, 1959], p. 345.)

involves Gabriel's premonition that Aunt Julia will shortly be dead. "Yes, yes: that would happen very soon." Neither scrupulous over-writing nor scrupulous meanness (Joyce's label for his style) applies here. It is not scrupulous anything. It is unself-regarding emotion, Joyce's plainest prose, appropriate here for Gabriel who is now also unself-regarding. So Joyce repeats the intonation a little further down the page: "Yes, the newspapers were right: snow was general all over Ireland."

In each story Joyce can be counted on to provide structures like this, for they represent his finest method of retardation, letting him underscore pressing situations for his characters. Since "The Sisters" and "Grace" have already afforded examples along with "The Dead," I here list the best respective examples from the stories between them. I deliberately hold back examples from "The Boarding House" and "Ivy Day."

1. But real adventures, I reflected, do not happen to people who re-main at home: they must be sought abroad. ("An Encounter")
2. These noises converged in a single sensation of life for me: I imag-ined that I bore my chalice safely through a throng of foes. ("Araby")
3. Jimmy, under generous influences, felt the buried zeal of his father wake to life within him: he aroused the torpid Routh at last. ("After the Race")
4. He was drawing her into them [the seas of the world]: he would drown her. ("Eveline")
5. His eyes searched the street [for Corley and the girl]: there was no sign of them. ("Two Gallants")
6. He turned from the page and tried to hush it: but it would not be hushed. ("A Little Cloud")
7. The evening was falling and in a few minutes they would be lighting the gas: then he could write. ("Counterparts")
8. Somebody said something about the garden, and at last Mrs Don-nelly said something very cross to one of the next-door girls and told her to throw it out at once: that was no play. ("Clay")
9. We cannot give ourselves, it said: we are our own. ("A Painful Case")
10. But she would see that her daughter got her rights: she wouldn't be fooled. ("A Mother")

The fact that Joyce registers a full thought after the colon is normative; and though (as with [6] and [7]) he will occasionally intro-duce his thought with a connective, much more often he puts the thought down unsupported. In this list I have inverted the order of "Eveline" and "After the Race," and should like to examine a further feature of the sentences by looking at them starting with the second half of the list. Observe that there is a good deal of oppression in the circumstances of sentences (6) through (10) and that after the colon in each case the rhythm is spondaic:

: bút ĭt woúld nót bĕ húshed.
: thén hĕ coúld wríte.
: thát wăs nó pláy.
: wĕ aŕe oúr ówn.
: shé wouĺdn't bĕ fooĺed.

The prose gets most abrasive as the characters become most frustrated. All monosyllables as well after these colons—a way of getting the spondees into play. Something not entirely different operates in (4) and (5), but here there is a dying fall achieved after a strong diphthong accent:

: hē woūld drówn hēr.
: thēre wās nó sĭgn ōf thēm.

Forlornness, perhaps we could say, is superadded by way of this variant. I have no wish, however, to press farther on the dangerous venture of ticketing rhythms with emotions; I only wish to indicate that some of Joyce's most serious moments are rendered in the syntactic form being described and that they are rhythmic. Turning to examples (1) through (3), we see that under more high-hearted circumstances the rhythms correspondingly change: solid affirmative iambs march in. In number (1) we have a trimeter line: "they must be sought abroad." In (2) and (3) (a "sixteener" and a tetrameter), the first foot requires anapestic notation but from there on again we have pure iambs:

: Ī ĭmaǵinēd thát Ī bo(r)e m̄y cháli(c)e sáfel̄y thróugh ā thróng ōf foés.
: h̄e āro(u)séd t(h)e tórpīd Roúth a(t) lást.

While the first of these ends one of the famous sentences of *Dubliners*, one could as easily vote for the second as a phonal accomplishment hardly surpassed by Joyce. Jimmy, in "After the Race," has felt the "buried zeal" of his Irishness take fire against the Englishman Routh. Part of the buoyancy of the moment is felt in the perfect assonance running across from first to third "foot": "aroused the torpid Routh at last." But Routh is not torpid in the card game that ensues, where Jimmy meets disaster. Thus the climactic sentence in "After the Race" is two words long and has no interest in eloquence: "Routh won."

I did not consider "The Boarding House" because of the idiosyncrasies to be found there. Aside from "The Dead," "The Boarding House" contains the most colon constructions—14. A sentence characterizing Mrs. Mooney shows why more are to be found, for the colon is the cleavage mark of punctuation: "She dealt with moral problems as a cleaver deals with meat: and in this case she had made up her mind." Through the determinate middle paragraphs of the story—a group of 16 sentences—there are seven usages worked in by Joyce. They include:

> Things were as she had suspected: she had been frank in her questions and Polly had been frank in her answers.

> To begin with she had all the weight of social opinion on her side: she was an outraged mother.

> He had simply taken advantage of Polly's youth and inexperience: that was evident.

What is different is that there is no sense of discovery in these sentences. The portion to the *left* of the colon is what counts; the other side merely gives reinforcement. (This resembles the semicolon arrangements in "A Painful Case.") In effect, the colon serves as an argumentative device in "The Boarding House." Mrs. Mooney clinches arguments before they are started. Thus we find another variant, coming up twice in the story, and only resorted to two other times by Joyce—the colon construction with a single truncated appositive to the right of it.[9] The result is again idiosyncratic, illustrating conviction rather than revealing a full thought. So the story opens:

> Mrs Mooney was a butcher's daughter. She was a woman who was quite able to keep things to herself: a determined woman.

("Determined" can mean not only wilful but also "set for a predestined end"; the colon constructions abet this meaning.) And so, at the end of the decisive 16-sentence span, Joyce says, "For her only one reparation could make up for the loss of her daughter's honour: marriage."

But I have reserved the single incident of colon construction in "Ivy Day" for a different purpose, which appears at the end of this chapter.

LEXIS AND SYNTAX: SOME SPECIAL VARIANTS

The generalization made earlier, that Joyce's style changes at the break between the third and fourth stories and then returns to a somewhat more formal mode with "A Little Cloud," gives occasion for demonstration over the last part of this chapter of what some of the differences amount to. Within any of the story blocs there are still shades of extra variation attainable because of the fusion Joyce keeps

26

making between style and character. The reason "A Little Cloud" tends to readmit the earlier stylization is that, with "maturity" on tap, a more precise sensitivity begins to be registered. Meanwhile the opening stories had recounted the doings of a precocious boy, as sensitive as anyone in all of Joyce.

My purpose thus is to make four examinations: first, of the opening bloc in its entirety, then of single stories out of the adolescent, maturity, and public life sequences. These examinations deal with style within story rather than exhibiting favored devices used across the stories, as heretofore. As for the stories after the first three, I mean to deal with those taking the most pronounced departures from the mainstream style. These are "Eveline," "Clay," and "Ivy Day in the Committee Room."

Of the adolescent group, "Eveline" carries farthest a use of vernacular idiom that is symptomatic of this foursome. Even more than in the others, Joyce keeps the register depressed as he follows the thoughts of the unsophisticated girl. He does something similar with "Clay," only here he elevates the register. What Kenner calls "feminine modes" of narration come into play most designedly in these two, which are treatments of two virgins. Conversely, with "Ivy Day," Joyce achieves pure neutrality, conforming to Stephen Dedalus's strictures about the dramatic mode, which calls for the artist to refine himself out of the picture.

"The Sisters," "An Encounter," "Araby"

The special stylistic yield of the first stories pertains to the self-monitoring capacity of the boy who narrates them. His attraction to odd words, his collusion with the simoniac priest, his careful notations of his dreams, all register his precocity in "The Sisters." In that "pleasant and vicious region" of his dreams where he meets the smiling priest, he finds himself in that man's role: "I felt that I too was smiling feebly as if to absolve the simoniac of his sin."

Joyce's point in the early stories is that to have a capacity for enormities, one must have an acute intelligence. It takes that kind of mind for the boy to be led into refined indulgence (witness the Eastern imagery in the three stories). His prescience in "The Sisters" concerning sacrilege becomes foreknowledge of the sexual in "An Encounter" and "Araby." Against it all some moral resistance is exerted by the boy. These are the schemes of tension in the first stories.

The style must bear such conditions out, otherwise ordinary childhood confusion might be assumed to be involved. This boy is aware of where his confusions are taking him. As a result, words like "puzzled" and "uneasy" are not as simple to gloss as might be expected—they refer to moral rather that mental bewilderment. The best example comes from "An Encounter," where the boy proves clairvoyant about the green eyes of a sailor that disturb him. He senses some affinity for abandonment, borne out at the climax when he listens to a pervert make a case for flagellation, and says, "I met the gaze of a pair of bottle-green eyes peering at me from under a twitching forehead." In fact, the mounting poignancy in the early stories results from the fact that the child is not confused. As he confides at one point in "An Encounter," "The sun went in behind some clouds and left us to our jaded thoughts" (the adjective is glorious); as he says at another in "Araby," "I had hardly any patience with the serious work of life which, now that it stood between me and my desire, seemed to me child's play, ugly monotonous child's play."

The counterparts in the style that vouch for precocity go beyond the category of diction. They include certain predominant morphemes, certain recursions to reflexive constructions, and a tendency (pointed out once by Ohmann[10]) to formulate abstract words and engineer them into positions of agency. These three hallmarks may appear unrelated when baldly listed like this, but are actually linked together intrinsically to produce, independently or in combination, one repeated effect. This is nothing less than to show *what it is like* to have a prehensile mind—a mind that instantaneously assimilates experiences and also monitors its own ongoing reactions to those experiences.

Even in the examples I just gave (though humorous from one point of view), the tendency to perceive abstract things in positions of agency is observable. It was the disappearing sun that "left us to our jaded thoughts"; the "serious work of life" that "stood between me and my desire." The boy conceives these operations taking place through finite verbs. He constructs presences out of forces felt in the air, as it were—just as, in the sentence with which Ohmann was concerned, the boy says he felt himself being "driven and derided by vanity." Ohmann showed the processes of transformational grammar from which the sentence derived, whereby "vanity" in one of the substructures would have been subject of the verbs "drive" and "deride."

Such abstract forces are not limited to grammatical substructures. Here are some other sentences produced by the boy's conceptual tendency:

A silence took possession of the little room and, under cover of it, I approached the table and tasted my sherry and then returned quietly to my chair in the corner. ("The Sisters")

A spirit of unruliness diffused itself among us and, under its influence, differences of culture and constitution were waived. ("An Encounter")

The career of our play brought us through the dark muddy lanes . . . to the dark odorous stables. . . . ("Araby")

The first two are similar in that "silence" and "spirit" take command, and then, under their "cover" and "influence," more things get accomplished. In the third, the boy perceives an abstraction *of* an abstraction as the agent. "Our play" would ordinarily have served, but the scope of this narrator leads him to chart the "career of our play."

His sense of apportionment even causes him to refine persons, sometimes, to their attributes. If in "An Encounter" he says, "I saw Mahony's grey suit approaching," in "Araby" he will say, "I kept her brown figure always in my eye." That kind of epitomizing aids his imagination, and, in the next paragraph, subject and object are reversed: "Her image accompanied me even in places the most hostile to romance." This soon modulates to "her image came between me and the page I strove to read."

The fact that the boy gets put into the position of grammatical object is important, and a second stylistic resource helps make this happen rather often: the narrator's affinity for reflexive constructions. These cause the subject to reappear and be acted on by the verb. In the last sentence in "Araby" the operative main clause was "I saw myself as a creature." Even when nothing abstract is involved, the reflexives mark an ability to visualize an action as summed up and complete, as in these sentence-openers from "An Encounter": "We banded ourselves together"; "We revenged ourselves on Leo Dillon"—the reflexive pronoun is superfluous in the first and avoidable in the second. The style is really earmarked when the reflexives operate together with abstract phrases of agency, as in "The Sisters":

The reading of the card persuaded me that he was dead and I was disturbed to find myself at check.

. . . I felt annoyed at discovering in myself a sensation of freedom as if I had been freed from something by his death.

The priest's death and the reading of the card are the agents in these sentences. They pull the boy up, but with the secondary effect of having him pull *himself* up—"disturbed to find myself," "felt annoyed at discovering in myself." Any element of surprise becomes muted because of the monitoring that habitually comes in. A final example from "An Encounter" presents "the spectacle of Dublin's commerce" on the Liffey, but the reflexive opening tempers the experience. At the same time, this passage affords a view of a last stylistic feature of the early stories, which integrates with the other two.

29

> We pleased ourselves with the spectacle of Dublin's commerce—the barges signalled from far away by their curls of woolly smoke, the brown fishing fleet beyond Ringsend, the big white sailing vessel which was being discharged on the opposite quay. Mahony said it would be right skit to run away on one of those big ships and even I, looking at the high masts, saw, or imagined, the geography which had been scantily dosed to me at school gradually taking substance under my eyes.

In the first element of the series after the dash, the word "signalled" looks like a verb. However, for it to be one, "by" would have to become "with," and the integrity of the series would be lost. Joyce has worked up a more sophisticated construction than that of the predicate "the barges signalled." Here the meaning is "the barges [which were] signalled." Passive voice is implied, the clause being elliptical; hence the operation of some agency again becomes involved. A transformational grammarian would take us back to the active form ("the curls of woolly smoke signalled the barges"). This indicates how awkward "to signal" can be as an active verb. (It sounds something like the modern ad, "travels the smoke.") But in participial form (e.g., a signaled intention, a well-traveled man) there is more harmoniousness, because of a certain resource our language offers. Since the past participle of a verb can be transformed into an adjective, English is afforded many -*ed* adjectives: not only that but, by extension, many nouns can attract affixes and turn into adjectives (e.g., a wooded lot—and note that "signal" is a noun as well as a verb; the -*ed* suffix could as well be a morphemic change turning noun to participle as it could be one that changed verb to participle). Because of this flexibility in our language, many good writers who would avoid the direct transcription of noun to active verb ("hosted the show" and similar barbarisms) make sharp use of nouns transformed to past participles. I think it is one of the great small secrets of good writing.[11] This is a morphemic change Joyce makes use of in the early stories; in the passage just quoted, a fine example can be seen in the boy's recognition of "the geography which had been scantily dosed to me at school." The precocity we sense here can be attributed to the simple ability to handle such transforms. The nouns "coffin" and "house" are treated in the same way in "The Sisters" and "Araby":

> He had been coffined. ("The Sisters")
>
> If my uncle was seen turning the corner we hid in the shadow until we had seen him safely housed. ("Araby")

There is a leap of mind involved in seeing the priest coffined, the uncle housed. It is a way of envisioning encirclement as if this were *done to* the men, and is thus allied to the boy's reflexive habit and his ascription of agency to abstract concepts. All point to the greatest characteristic in the boy's makeup: his capacity for seeing things under their completed aspect. Thus in "Araby," when he is in the "flaring streets," we recognize his sense of the enclosed, complete thing he cherishes—his adoration of Mangan's sister, conveyed in the protected image of the chalice. All this is further connected with his dreaming, with that swooning complex he has and how it is enhanced by smacking of the secret and illicit. Thus the style brings us full circle, emphasizing the boy's powers to see inchoate things as already completed, the very index of what precocity is all about.

"Eveline," "Clay," "Ivy Day in the Committee Room"

To move from the dialogue (not the narration) of the early stories is to arrive at the prose style of "Eveline." One of the sisters in the first story uses the idiom "latterly" and the phrase "only for Father O'Rourke." In "Eveline" these have become embedded in the narrative: "latterly he had begun to threaten her and say what he would do to her only for her dead mother's sake." Scholes and Litz point out that in the first version, printed in the *Irish Homestead,* Joyce had written that sentence differently—"saying what he would do if it were not for her dead mother's sake"—replacing the formal phrase with "only for" in the *Dubliners* version.[12] Joyce by no means continues sentence-by-sentence with such Irish locutions, but even when the language is formal, it will not evoke what the earlier language evoked. Instead, along with the idioms, it works toward limiting the heroine imaginatively (though not reducing her emotionally).

Joyce delimits Eveline's imagination by placing odd repetitions where substitutes might have been expected. He does this with both diction and syntax. The second paragraph begins: "Few people passed. The man out of the last house passed on his way home. . . ." It is odd that the same verb is repeated, a strange depletion of vocabulary for *Dubliners.* A heavy leaning on the verb "used to" begins in this paragraph—and for that verb to be reinforced by "usually" is indeed unresourceful: "Her father used often to hunt them out of the field with his blackthorn stick; but usually little Keogh used to keep *nix* and call out when he saw her father coming." The third paragraph describes some furnishings in her house that threaten to detain Eveline because of nostalgic association: the paragraph is flanked by sentences that repeat themselves not only lexically but syntactically: "Now she was going to go away like the others, to leave her home. . . . She had consented to go away, to leave her home." The style shows something defeating about the way the girl's mind runs in tracks. In trying to drive herself on, she can come up with only one sort of rangeless

31

emphasis, that which can only *double* a thing. "Then she would be married—she, Eveline." And again, "Frank would take her in his arms, fold her in his arms." The feeling may be intense but its intended force is lost in inarticulateness.

The worst of her problem is that the counter ideas, the ones that command her to stay, also surge up in doublet forms. She is reminded of "the promise to her mother, her promise to keep the home together"; then, again in an appositional way, of "her mother's life . . . —that life of commonplace sacrifices closing in final craziness." One sees that Eveline always tries once to redefine an issue, pro or con, but can do no more, get no farther to one side or the other of it. The crucial passage in this regard has to do with her father:

> Her father was becoming old lately, she noticed; he would miss her. Sometimes he could be very nice. Not long before, when she had been laid up for a day, he had read her out a ghost story and made toast for her at the fire. Another time, when their mother was alive, they had all gone for a picnic to the Hill of Howth. She remembered her father putting on her mother's bonnet to make the children laugh.

Here the syntactic repetition operates across sentences instead of within them: "Not long before. . . . Another time. . . ." It is a good example of style serving theme and yielding meaning. Eveline is foiled of an insight because counting to two is as far as she can go, and this suffices for her. What the reader can recognize she cannot: the colossal emotional blight of her father. For she can recall only the two bare occasions of generosity, and for one of them she has to cast all the way back to a time her mother was alive. Yet the memories are enough to seal her in a monstrous situation.

Joyce cuts all lines of hope in a stylistic departure he takes in the story's last sentence. It obliges us to mark that the last word is his, purely objective, no longer chiming with Eveline's point of view. Her fiancé has called to her from the ship; she has remained transfixed: "Her eyes gave him no sign of love or farewell or recognition." It is a polysyndetic series, enforcing the differentness of the three things she denies him, in worsening order. "Recognition" does not even belong in a series in which familiarity is denoted by "love" and "farewell." With Eveline's denials extending beyond the usual paired matrices, Joyce describes how her whole being is closed to the man who might have saved her.

There is undeniable pathos in Eveline's predicament, but the feminine mode of narration used for "Clay" produces something different. Here Joyce falsifies emotion by bringing in debased qualifiers that purport to lend meaning and value to the rounds Maria makes.

Far from being a peacemaker, Maria is a time-usurper, makes everyone cheerless, and has to be suffered and humored ad nauseam. Though two camps of criticism have sprung up about this story, one attesting Joyce's sympathy for Maria and the other his antipathy, only the second camp deserves a hearing once the debased style is comprehended.

Maria, we read, spoke "always soothingly," "was always sent for... always succeeded in making peace." When Richard Ohmann wrote on Shaw, he coined the phrase "all-or-nothing intensifiers" to handle adverbs like this. Shaw's style was replete with them, but they are foreign to Joyce's, except in "Clay." Here, too, the adverb "very" occurs 16 times in 112 sentences; the bland adjective "nice," 12 times. Quantity is telltale in this story. Eleven sentences begin with coordinate conjunctions—10 percent of the total, while the average for the other stories is under 3 percent. As for paragraphs, outside of "Clay," Joyce begins only eight with coordinate conjunctions; but of the 19 paragraphs in "Clay," six begin with "but," "and," or "so." Throwing out the first paragraph (which could not have begun this way), we find the extraordinary average of one out of three commencing in this odd manner.

Why does Joyce do it? To get a sense of false bounce, when there's really nothing springy there at all. None of the four "but's," for instance, announce an adversative transition (e.g., "But wasn't Maria glad when the women had finished their tea...."). And everything always grades the same. "Everybody said: *O, here's Maria!*"; "Everybody had a solution for the mystery"; "Everyone was so fond of Maria." These devices are all working as ameliorations, in the direction of proving that Maria is living a life engaged with everyone else's and is liked by everyone. The party she attends is the crabbiest on record and yet we are given the false report that "soon everything was merry again," and "they were all quite merry again...." This is not mere wishfulness, it is more a species of wilfulness. It marks Maria's tendency, since no joy does accompany her anywhere, to call what is where she is by the name of joy. That way there is no need to measure the abrasiveness of her presence. Joyce has a way of making the disruptive power break through anyway. Meanwhile he reserves another device to record her habit of blanketing things in the all-or-nothing way.

Anyone who has ever been warned, in his own writing, to "avoid intensive 'so,'" should not fail to detect the major stylistic device reserved for "Clay." The split conjunctions "so... that" and "such... that" are standard for introducing clauses of comparison. When "so" and "such" alone are used, and the comparisons not filled out, we are victims of what grammarians call "feminine intensives." The implication is that this or that person/event was *so* interesting/thrilling/remarkable—and the *that* is left up in the air: the freed adverb contains *such* a tone of sincerity that to hunt down a comparison becomes otiose.

The feminine intensive is a natural sentence aborter, employed to guarantee the feel of intensity when none may happen to be there. On 14 occasions in "Clay," an average of twice per page, we are subjected to this crutch language. (In only three other sentences in *Dubliners* does the feminine intensive appear.)

> Everyone was so fond of Maria.
>
> He was so different when he took any drink.
>
> She used to have such a bad opinion of Protestants . . . but the matron was such a nice person to deal with, so genteel.
>
> . . . she looked with quaint affection at the diminutive body which she had so often adorned. In spite of its years she found it a nice tidy little body.

Semantically the device has self-cancellation built into it. It pretends to quick sensibility but automatically closes the door to any application of that sensibility. The four statements above not only use the device but end paragraphs with it. It is Maria's trademark.

Joyce's way of breaking through her blind involves a certain inadvertence, a *non-sequitur* quality in "Clay," which underscores the fact that the characters recognize they are oppresssed by this insensate creature. That they put the clay before her is one symbolic mark of their oppression. It is an irritation to have to create substance in the humored life of someone bringing along none of her own (another meaning of "clay"). Thus some giveaways steal into the style. Three times we hear how different people are "nice with her." The idiom ought to be "nice to her," but the "with" substitution suggests the furniturelike nuisance of the woman. Similarly, in the last part of the story, rude verbs of command take charge in *non-sequitur* situations that hint of continued provocation. The children are "made" to say thanks to her; Maria is "made" to take a glass of wine—"Joe insisted"; "They insisted then on blindfolding Maria and leading her up to the table. . . ."

Thus the air is impregnated with bad temper (rightfully), though Hallowe'en is supposed to be festive. The story ends with another *non sequitur*, as Joe, the irascible head of the family, becomes sentimental over Maria's song.

> . . . his eyes filled up so much with tears that he could not find what he was looking for and in the end he had to ask his wife to tell him where the corkscrew was.

34

Bathetic this may be, but to do Joe credit we might observe the construction "so much . . . that." Intensive "so" did not get in its vile innings, despite this decrepit finale.

In moving from "Clay" to "Ivy Day," we move from Joyce's least austere to his most austere sentence arrangements.

In trying to achieve neutrality, Joyce to all appearances took special pains with predication. "Ivy Day" is quite a long story, and has proportionately the greatest amount of dialogue. In every case when a narrative sentence is embedded in the dialogue, a single verb, unmodified, will indicate the act of speech. Outside of the dialogue packets, there are 100 sentences in the story, and a good deal of uniformity is to be marked in them. To me, the few departures then become of intense interest. Anticipating for the moment, we may say that of the 100 sentences, five are significant in having three or more finite verbs in the main clause. The five become important because of prevailing patterns in the other sentences.[13]

Almost half of the total (49) are either simple sentences with a single verb or complex sentences with one verb in the main clause. All these are short and unobtrusive. The longer sentences, on the other hand, conspire to set up a rather regular beat. With the exception of the special few just mentioned, all of "Ivy Day's" longer sentences have either a double predicate or two independent clauses with single predicates. Two main-clause verbs are thus produced in all these sentences (44 of them); and since they have some length and resonance, the reader gets used to their double predication setting the pulse of the story—they allow for scarcely any modulation.

A sizable number of examples may demonstrate the impact of this double predication. Regardless of increases in complexity, Joyce keeps a rein on all the items here by allowing them no more than two governing verbs.

1. Old Jack raked the cinders together with a piece of cardboard and spread them judiciously over the whitening dome of coals.

   He opened his very long mouth suddenly to express disappointment and at the same time opened wide his very bright blue eyes to express pleasure and surprise.

2. Imminent little drops of rain hung at the brim of his hat and the collar of his jacket-coat was turned up.

   A denuded room came into view and the fire lost all its cheerful colour.

3. Mr O'Connor tore a strip off the card and, lighting it, lit his cigarette.

   Mr Hynes laughed and, shoving himself away from the mantlepiece with the aid of his shoulders, made ready to leave.

4. Mr O'Connor shook his head in sympathy, and the old man fell silent, gazing into the fire.

He retreated from the doorway and Mr Henchy, seizing one of the candlesticks, went to the door to light him downstairs.

5. Mr O'Connor, a grey-haired young man, whose face was disfigured by many blotches and pimples, had just brought the tobacco for a ciga-rette into a shapely cylinder but when spoken to he undid his hand-iwork meditatively.

Mr O'Connor had been engaged by Mr Tierney's agent to canvass one part of the ward but, as the weather was inclement and his boots let in the wet, he spent a great part of the day sitting by the fire in the Committee Room in Wicklow Street with Jack, the old caretaker.

It almost comes to seem dependable, a regular pattern of "this and that" predication. And it may well be that readers subconsciously get to expect it. These five sentence types do differ a little from one another. In the examples from the first two groups, simple and com-pound sentences respectively, two verbs handle the action, with no punctuation. When a third action is involved, as in groups (3) and (4), Joyce pauses and demotes one of the sequential actions to participial status. In the compound-complex samples in group (5), he continues to rely on two main-clause predicates. Note too that, regardless of other segmentation, he moves swiftly from one main clause to the other by neglecting to punctuate before the connective (in these cases, "but"). This runs counter to what was demonstrated earlier about standard Joycean punctuation, where clauses were poised against each other via the semicolon. Joyce eschews all such occasions in "Ivy Day," not seeming to want to create pauses and links that have any-thing momentous about them.

For the reader, an effect of this neutralizing style is to find the ward heelers of "Ivy Day" not highly differentiated. They wear ivy in their lapels to celebrate the anniversary of Parnell, but they are lukewarm Nationalists who have put up a compromise candidate—a man who will not be obnoxious to the Clericals or the Conservatives (represented by the latecomers to the committee room, Lyons and Crofton). The exception is Hynes, who, on coming in, has the "immi-nent" raindrops clinging to his hat. He has gone over to the Labour-ites, but it is he who will read the elegiac lines on Parnell at the end. Still he does not appear much different, initially, from the others.

But if the dead Parnell cannot make a real bond, something else can—the "dozen of stout" that the candidate has ordered for his can-vassers makes all well. The fact that the corkscrew has been carried off by the delivery boy makes it necessary for the latecomers' bottles to be opened by heat at the fire. It is in connection with this that Joyce makes the story's stylistic coup.

For he breaks his verb patterns three different times where the stout is concerned, the first in connection with the delivery boy (a budding Dubliner), the other two with Lyons.

> As the old man said nothing further the boy took the bottle, said: *Here's my best respects, sir* to Mr Henchy, drank the contents, put the bottle back on the table and wiped his mouth with his sleeve.

> [Mr Henchy] took two bottles from the table and, carrying them to the fire, put them on the hob. Then he sat down again by the fire and took another drink from his bottle. Mr Lyons sat on the edge of the table, pushed his hat towards the nape of his neck and began to swing his legs.

> In a few minutes an apologetic *Pok!* was heard as the cork flew out of Mr Lyons' bottle. Mr Lyons jumped off the table, went to the fire, took his bottle and carried it back to the table.

Alongside the verbal patterns I have been identifying occur now these multiplied-verb variants: took, said, drank, put, wiped; sat, pushed, began to swing; jumped, went, took, carried. Joyce's intention, once the variant is detected, seems to me obvious: he is grouping finite verbs for those actions that are truly important. One gets the illusion a sort of authorial nonchalance has dominated, and then all of a sudden a challenge comes up from the material. The drink matters (the only thing that can stimulate factitious loyalty). So the economy achieved by the other sentences becomes forfeited. This would be easy to overstate, yet the actions pertaining to the bottles on the hob are not offhandedly subordinated or transposed to verbals, because they have some exigency to them. Likewise for Crofton. With him, Joyce doesn't multiply his verbs, but he does resort to incriminating diction: "Mr Crofton sat down on a box and looked fixedly at the other bottle on the hob." "Fixedly" gives him away. And, after a time,

> *Pok!* The tardy cork flew out of Mr Crofton's bottle. Mr Crofton got up from his box and went to the fire. As he returned with his capture he said in a deep voice:
> —Our side of the house respects him [Parnell] because he was a gentleman.

His would-be compliment is annulled by the noun "capture": ponderous and guarded though he is, the *Pok!* has made him show his true colors. They do not burn for Parnell.

Hynes, on the other hand, is made to shine as a result of Joyce's meddling with established sentence patterns. Triplicate predicates assigned to Hynes should not be regarded as innocuous. In his case, verbs given in finite, weighted form imply importance to simple manual motions—repeated, since he happens to make two entries to the room.

> Mr Hynes took off his hat, shook it and then turned down the collar of his coat, displaying, as he did so, an ivy leaf in the lapel.

> Mr Hynes hesitated a little longer. Then amid the silence he took off his hat, laid it on the table and stood up.

Both passages are hieratic, as Hynes "uncovers." In the first, honor due Parnell is accorded by the naming of the ivy; the second precedes the reciting of the poem to him. Hynes's deliberate manner is unassuming but touching. After he speaks the poem, Joyce follows through with another little tribute, employing, for once only, a colon.

> When he had finished his recitation there was a silence and then a burst of clapping: even Mr Lyons clapped.

The climax of the story is not the reading of the poem but the single sound of a cork popping that now follows.

> *Pok!* The cork flew out of Mr Hynes' bottle, but Mr Hynes remained sitting, flushed and bareheaded on the table. He did not seem to have heard the invitation.

It is brilliant that a third ritualistic *Pok!* is heard, especially because Hynes does not reach for his bottle. He is separated from the fellow travelers, his sentiment for Parnell not dictated by the stout. He is a world away from Crofton, who is asked to comment on Hynes's poem, closing off the story: "Mr Crofton said that it was a very fine piece of writing." The dampened enthusiasm of this answer is caught through Joyce's recording it as the only specimen of indirect dialogue in the story.

CADENCES

A critique of Joyce once demonstrated his aversion for pat endings: "'Ivy Day in the Committee Room' ends on an anti-climactic, inconsequential remark. 'Grace' closes in the middle of a sermon. The ending of 'Clay' skirts the irrelevant. . . ."[14] These were the best examples that could have been offered—they are the three stories Joyce ended bathetically. Taking an erroneous step further, James Atherton once ranged the conclusion of "The Boarding House" against that of "Ivy Day." The final sentence there refers to Polly, called away from her reverie by her mother: "Then she remembered what she had been waiting for." This, wrote Atherton, "is a flat, undistinguished prose sentence, completely without emotion, without rhythm."[15]

But this is a mistake. The sentence is rhythmical. There is a bell-clear accentuation in that last noun clause, for the girl hears in her mother's voice nothing less than a marriage summons. Only the three stories "Ivy Day," "Clay," and "Grace" end with impaired rhythms, and only these three are anticlimactic in intention. An attempt to supply accent marks proves the point about the rhythm:

Mr Crófton sáid that ī̄t wās ā véry fíne pieče of writing.

. . . and īn the end hē hád tō ašk hīs wífe tō tell hīm where the corkscrew wás.

. . . Ī will réctify thís and thís. Ī will set ríght my accoúnts.

Nothing can be made of this scansion. The endings are all flawed: "a very fine piece of writing" checks the momentum of two iambs by suddenly crossing them with two trochees; "tell him where the corkscrew was" produces a running unaccentuated pattern against which are jammed up two accents in the three finishing syllables. (If the sentence ran "tell him where the corkscrew had been put," a repetitive rhythm, antipathetic to Joyce's purposes, would have resulted: he wanted to eclipse resonance instead.) The last sentence in "Grace" catches Father Purdon's exhortation in midparagraph. Six words long, its fitful start, pyrric to spondee ($\frown^{-}\textit{//}$), is suddenly halted by an anapest where more was expected. (Even "I will set right my account book" would have made the sentence more euphonious by repeating the pyrric-spondee rhythm.)

I offered those alternatives because it is harder to show why a sentence is unrhythmical than why it is rhythmical—my point is that in those three Joyce refused to let a sound effect heighten the finish; he simply dropped things, which is bathos.

Only in "Counterparts," where the ending is hysterical, does something similar happen. The pace is roughened by ellipses as the small boy begs not to be beaten: "—O, pa! he cried. Don't beat me, pa! And I'll . . . I'll say a *Hail Mary* for you. . . . I'll say a *Hail Mary* for you, pa, if you don't beat me. . . . I'll say a *Hail Mary*. . . ."

This emergency language can't have cadence or scan (though of course there is no question of bathos here).

But for the other eleven stories, Joyce supplies well-modulated rhythmic closes; he never jams accents at their conclusions. For four of them he supplies one basic sort of accentual ending, and for the other seven, a different one.

Joyce, no more than any other prose writer, could have overused rhythmic technique and remained any good. As Morris Croll has pointed out, where the rhythms of verse keep the writer's energy expenditure "higher than that of the ordinary human occupations and movements," prose does not "move uniformly on this high level. Its foundation is laid on the basis of common and matter-of-fact speech: instead of forcing the physiological processes to adapt themselves to it, it yields and adapts itself to them."[16] Yet at conclusions of discourses, and at certain other moments where the prose will bend toward the accommodations of verse, it virtually asks that its direction by recognized.

I should like to indicate how the rhythmic ending of "The Dead" (discerned by many critics) falls in with the cadential endings of three other stories:

> His soul swooned slowly as he heard the snow . . . falling, like the descent of their last end, upon all the living and the dead. ("The Dead")
>
> He felt that he was alone. ("A Painful Case")
>
> He listened while the paroxysm of the child's sobbing grew less and less; and tears of remorse started to his eyes. ("A Little Cloud")
>
> A small gold coin shone in the palm. ("Two Gallants")

A consistent feature about these closes is that, while they are composed in rising rhythm and end on the masculine syllable, they also prevent that final syllable from being an iamb. They do not permit another accent near it, and, therefore, though the reader's voice has been moving rhythmically toward the final word, it encounters a small pattern of unstressed syllables before it gathers to that final word. In the last phrase group of "The Dead," the accents are separated by one extra syllable in each instance: ¯ ′|¯ ¯′|¯ ¯ ¯′ In "A Painful Case," what resonance there is has been achieved by anapestic substitution at the end of another three-beat rising line: ¯ ′|¯ ′|¯ ¯′ The ending of "A Little Cloud" is essentially a tetrameter; each half-line employs trochaic inversion so that one half echoes the other; yet observe once again the admission of one extra unaccented syllable in the last unit: ¯ |¯ ′|¯ ′|¯ ¯′ And so for the conclusion of "Two Gallants." This is the only "surprise" ending in *Dubliners*, its career arrested with spondees; but again, the final half-line supplies trochaic substitution and thus an incursion of suppressed syllables: ¯ ′| ′′| ′¯|¯ ′

In *The Other Harmony of Prose* Paull F. Baum made a study of cadential endings most natural to English, and found the varieties just discussed to be the most dominant where sentence endings were scannable. He was looking in particular for the incidence of the medieval *cursus* (that is, its English equivalent). This cadential ending, also discussed by Morris Croll, derives from Latin oratory. It is a climactic device involving two accents, the first of which is stronger, occurring over the last seven, six, or five syllables of a period. The rhythm is always falling, the second accent being placed one or two syllables from the end. Croll describes the onset of the cursus (at the seventh, sixth, or fifth syllable) as marking "the point at which the tendency to rhythmical form ... restrained earlier in the phrase by the necessities of logical statement, is finally allowed to appear without check. It marks the moment of release of the rhythmical impulse which is half the secret of our delight in oratorical performance."[17] His own sentence, interestingly, ends here on a cursus. "Oratorical performance" is a 6-2 cursus (first accent on the sixth-from-last syllable, second accent on the second-from-last). In Baum's findings, all of the varieties of cursus combined (5-2, 6-2, 6-3, 7-2, 7-3 are the most common) accounted for only 25 percent of the scannable endings of the English sentences he examined.[18] In other words, the medieval cursus is an infrequent cadence in English. But Joyce ended half his stories with it.

The finality of the cursus seems governed by the relationship between the two accents, the first always stronger, along with the falling rhythm—as seen in the 5-2 cursus that ends many Latin prayers: "per omnia saeculá saéculórum." The seven examples in *Dubliners* follow below, their varieties indicated in parentheses. Not one is bathetic—they always indicate a serious disclosure, a shift of attitude, or a new and final outlook on things.

> —... So then, of course, when they saw that, that made them think that there was sómethíng góne wróng wíth hím.... (6-3) ("The Sisters")

> And I was penitent; for in my heart I had always despísed hím a líttle. (5-2) ("An Encounter")

> Gazing up into the darkness I saw myself as a creature driven and derided by vanity; and my eyes burned with ánguísh and ánger. (5-2) ("Araby")

> Her eyes gave him no sign of love or farewéll ór récogníton. (6-2) ("Eveline")

> —Dáybréak, géntlemén! (6-3) ("After the Race")

> Then she remembered whát shé hád béen wáitíng for. (7-3) ("The Boarding House")

> —You did the próper thing, Holohan, said Mr O'Madden Burke, poised upon his umbrélla ín appróval. (6-2) ("A Mother")

The felt sense of a caesura in "—Daybreak, gentlemen!" seems to warrant its inclusion with these other six pure forms of the cursus. Just as interesting as Joyce's reliance on these oratorical cadences is, of course, the fact that on four occasions he aborted his closing rhythms. If he had supplied carefully tuned-out endings to all the stories it would have been a shame. Then however we would have had a lesser artist on our hands.

41

To ask whether an artist like him had it in mind to make use of rhetorical formulae would be to pose an irrelevant question. A writer like this is trying to hear and feel and lay hold of something for himself, not for the reader. Labels are otiose in such instances. He hears the words in his mind's ear; turns them against his palate; senses the encroaching rhythms as they combine; deliberates the pauses; and weighs the end result against his concept of character and mood and what he has said already. One hopes the process will never be described with accuracy. It is not with the process but with the result that the critic works. In moral terms, as Eliseo Vivas has said, "What the writer does is to accept or to reject what is offered to his consciousness from the depths of his mind. His responsibility as artist is to decide whether what is offered to him now belongs with what he has already accepted or has a greater right to survive than what he had already put on paper."[19] His integrity, then, while writing, should be thought of as always being tested out by concrete things for which there are no names. In technical terms, the various substrata of order that can later be sought out under the appearances of plain narration will attest to that integrity, if it is there.

3 D. H. LAWRENCE: *THE LOST GIRL, KANGAROO*

... a narrator who lets the shape of his paragraphs be decided by the immediacy and urgency of the details as they come to him.
RICHARD HOGGART

LAWRENCE'S UNDERCUT PARAGRAPHS

In his career D. H. Lawrence produced ten novels, and if one were to judge them with an eye to differences, *The Lost Girl* (written in two stages across a period of eight years) would be at the farthest remove from *Kangaroo* (completed in four months' time in 1922). As he does in all his books, Lawrence editorializes in these, but *The Lost Girl* is perhaps the story of his most marked by straight narration, the one in which Lawrence is least authorially involved with the protagonist, and *Kangaroo* is probably the novel with which he was most self-embroiled. These books produce two sorts of discursive narration, and were aptly labeled "pseudo-novels" by R. P. Draper in his study of Lawrence.[1] Because of their discursiveness they provide an advantageous starting point for examining Lawrence's style. This is because factors salient in his "purer" novels, largely making for intensification, are found in these two as well, but they also have a store of more random linguistic devices by which the voice of the author, easygoing, ironic, or hectoring, is allowed to be heard with great frequency. While in terms of formal achievement it is often argued that Lawrence's masterpieces are *The Rainbow* and *Women in Love,* his very antiformality, which affects his whole career, makes it seem that his gifts as a stylist might be best disclosed through works in which he wrote sometimes at full pressure and other times almost in disdain of his very art. These comments are offered in explanation of my choice of a pair of well-known but not mainstream Lawrence novels, by means of which I hope to elucidate the leading characteristics of Lawrence's prose.

It happens that *The Lost Girl* and *Kangaroo* are almost identical in length, so a one-to-one ratio is in force for the judging of quantitative data.[2] While the findings reported here may well prove consonant with Lawrence's other work, any quantitative evidence will naturally be subject to revaluation should differences arise when other novels are brought into consideration.

One of the most marked similarities between *The Lost Girl* and *Kangaroo* has to do with the way Lawrence ends paragraphs in them. It is a striking enough feature to begin with in characterizing his style. Fifty percent of his paragraphs end on sentences of 10 words or under—sentences or fragments of them that in length comprise less than a line of print. Critics traditionally denominate Lawrence a rhythmic writer; furthermore, his paragraphs and their sentences are as a rule quite long, developed under impulsion that does not conduce to restriction of word flow. Repetitive as he is, he resorts to two standard practices to connect sentences without breaking down paragraph rhythm: one is to start new sentences with coordinate conjunctions (paratactic connection), and the other, to employ sentence fragments. The fragments mostly originate from repetitions of key words—they involve portions of sentences that have gone before and some grammatical elision. However, as the following typical sequence demonstrates, these two main transitional techniques do not necessarily produce short sentences in turn.

> And so he craved for marriage: to possess her entirely, and to have her always there with him, so that he was never alone. Alone and apart from all the world: but by her side, always by her side. (LG 301)

The first sentence here provides the coordinate-conjunction transition, the second gives a fragment. Oddly, Lawrence can echo the word "alone" and build anew from it, even though the sense shifts from not being alone to the opposite idea. I chose this illustration as typical because, though the two techniques might be thought of as available for curtailing sentence length, the point is that they just as easily permit sentences to roll onward. In the first, "coordinating," sentence, after the colon what amounts to a long sentence fragment is developed ("to possess . . . and to have . . . so that"); in the next, "fragmented," sentence, after the colon the coordinate "but" comes in to introduce the phrase "by her side" which is then itself repeated.

Readers familiar with Lawrence will, I think, recognize his accents here, and perhaps will grant recollectively that Lawrentian music often moves like this. It depends on amplitude. Lawrence is not essentially a short-sentence writer. Yet the curious fact remains that in the two long novels examined here—one showing him at his most detached and "societal," the other on the verge of being apocalyptic—50 percent of the paragraphs that he writes end on sentences of 10 words or less.

It appears to me that we have here one of the most powerful indices to Lawrence's style. The remarkable thing is to find an incidence even approaching 50 percent. The figures for *The Lost Girl* and *Kangaroo* differ a bit. The ratio of short to longer concluding sentences in *The Lost Girl* is 54 percent; in *Kangaroo* it is 47 percent (see table 3.1). That real disparity is hardly indicated can be confirmed if we check the figures for half a book: the first half of *The Lost Girl* (8 of 16 chapters, 184 of 372 pages) contains 399 short endings to 801 paragraphs—almost exactly 50 percent; the second half of *Kangaroo* (9 of 18 chapters, 189 of 367 pages) works out the same—867 paragraphs, 433 short sentences to end them.

Needless to say, these figures do not create the arresting phenomenon. What might be called arresting is to read page after page of Lawrence, getting a sense of his momentum (whether in the longish discursive passages or in the swifter dramatic interchanges), and dis-

Table 3.1 Paragraph Endings, Ten Words or Less

	Number of Paragraphs[a]	Final Sentences, Ten Words or Less	Percentage
The Lost Girl	1,780	963	54
Kangaroo	1,444	679	47
Lawrence aggregate	3,224	1,642	51
Howards End	702	280	40
A Passage to India	468	130	28
Forster aggregate	1,170	410	35
Tarr	1,292	404	31
Self Condemned	1,004	230	23
Lewis aggregate	2,296	634	28
Back	725	403	55
Concluding	845	385	45
Green aggregate	1,570	788	50

NOTE: Forster and Lewis, Lawrence's contemporaries, are clearly unlike him in terminal brevity. Only Henry Green approaches him in this regard. Green, writing later in the century, might be thought to have imbibed his generation's fondness for clipped narrative. However, this proves a false supposition. It is really because of the tongue-tied hero in *Back* that the dialogue scenes there produce so many short paragraphs of the "He said nothing" type (B 81, 215). *Back*'s lapses in communication cause the 55 percent incidence of truncated paragraphs. In neither *Back* nor *Concluding* (45 percent) is the technique at all related to Lawrence's crisp offhandedness.

[a]The paragraph count excludes passages ending in dialogue or dialogue guides.

covering a sort of metronome at work in his system that dictates to him a necessity for curtailing endings. (As table 3.1 shows, the writers in this study contemporary with him do not approach this half-and-half ratio.)

The question is, what causes him to send his paragraphs along well-worn tracks like these?

> Odd, eccentric people they were, these entertainers. Most of them had a streak of imagination, and most of them drank. Most of them were middle-aged. Most of them had an abstracted manner; in ordinary life, they seemed left aside, somehow. Odd, extraneous creatures, often a little depressed, feeling life slip away from them. The cinema was killing them. (LG 136)

> But alas, it was just too late. In some strange way Somers felt he had come to the end of transports: they had no more mystery for him; at least this kind: or perhaps no more charm. Some bubble or other had burst in his heart. All his body and fibers wanted to go over and touch the other great being into a storm of response. But his soul wouldn't. The coloured bubble had burst. (K 132)

In a rough and superficial way, it might be claimed that sentence lengths alternate here between short and long: only the next-to-last sentences make an exception to that pattern. Other paragraphs would render such a claim challengeable, however. What is more typical is a repetitive drift through the paragraph's main body that is halted by a blunt declarative standing as an unqualified summary. In the sentences running before, one picks up qualifiers: "somehow," "a little"; "in some strange way," "at least." Not so as Lawrence ends the paragraphs. One of the main reasons, in short, for his curtailment of final sentences is to reverse his tendency to dwell overmuch on things. It is as though he is counteracting a shortcoming.

The following paragraphs amplify this strategy; they illustrate Lawrence veering, each time, in one certain direction. This might be called his "proverbial" habit, which often comes pat to him as he finishes a line of thought or a narrative segment.

> No sooner said than done. In came the architect, with whom he had played many a game of chess. Best, said the architect, take off one good-sized shop, rather than halve the premises. James would be left a little cramped, a little tight, with only one-third of his present space. But as we age we dwindle. (LG 22)

> Alvina was indeed speaking at random. She had never thought of being a nurse—the idea had never entered her head. If it had she would certainly never have entertained it. But she had heard Alexander speak of Nurse This and Sister That. And so she had rapped out her declaration. And having rapped it out, she prepared herself to stick to it. Nothing like leaping before you look. (LG 37)

> Poor Richard Lovat wearied himself to death struggling with the problem of himself, and calling it Australia. There was no actual need for him to struggle with Australia: he must have done it in the hedonistic sense, to please himself. But it wore him to rags. (K 22)

> Any more love is a hopeless thing, till we have found again, each of us for himself, the great dark God who alone will sustain us in our loving one another. Till then, best not play with more fire. (K 202)

The paragraphs from *The Lost Girl* begin with brief statements, those from *Kangaroo* starting out a bit more lengthily. The curt finales find Lawrence shifting to indefinite general pronoun usages ("we," "you"), something very common with him; or, without their help, he may evoke proverbial situations, as he does with the idiom "worn to rags" (commensurate with "playing with fire" and "looking before leaping"). Other typical paragraph-enders include "You live and learn and lose" (LG 211) and "We're between the devil and the deep sea" (K 309). The Lawrentian hallmark is that the switches to the proverbial almost invariably take place in patterns like these; those quoted here happen to run six to eight words in length.

In the paragraphs thus far examined, the closings seemed designed to put an end to maundering, but Lawrence depends on his undercutting technique to gain more profound effects as well. Brevity, for him, can serve to intensify what has just been rendered as well as do the opposite—digest it. Situations of intense sexuality often culminate by way of a sharply telescoped sentence. To get profound moments to resonate, Lawrence will frequently employ a fragment, often an infinitive, to create a hovering effect for an experience. In *The Lost Girl* the impact on the heroine of a visit to a coal mine is described early in the novel. It is a symbolic foreshadowing of her compulsion (the perennial saving theme in Lawrence) to lose herself, let herself be extinguished, under the impulse of dark sexual force.

> As it always comes to its children, the nostalgia of the repulsive, heavy-footed Midlands came over her again, even whilst she was there in the midst. The curious, dark, inexplicable and yet insatiable craving—as if for an earthquake. To feel the earth heave and shudder and shatter the world from beneath. To go down in the débâcle. (LG 58–59)

The opening sentence, 26 words long, is supplanted by fragments here. The middle two are each half its length (13 words). In this pair a sense of control (maintained by the serial adjectives "curious, dark, inexplicable") gives way under the push of polysyndetic infinitives (the objective complements "heave and shudder and shatter"). Then the last element again halves the sentence length. This six-word fragment points out a final compulsive direction, and all the actions implied in the earlier infinitives are gathered up in the noun "débâcle."

The idea of going down into it is left lingering, incipient. Again we have foreshortening, this time not to lead us away from the experience but to engulf Lawrence's heroine (and, presumably, his readers) in it.

In *Kangaroo* a kind of reengulfment of author or reader is more the practice, in that Australia evokes "The previous world!—the world of the coal age"(K 179). That world and its claims receive only passing attention in *The Lost Girl.* But, starting with *Kangaroo,* as Leo Gurko has said, Lawrence's fiction went into a phase in which it sought "to meld with the spirits and gods of place." Gurko concludes: "As [Lawrence] moved over the physical face of the earth, he sought to penetrate it psychically. *Kangaroo* has as its hero . . . nothing less than the shape of a continent."[3]

Though Lawrence's hero Somers first reacts in fear to the Australian bush, by stages he is induced to drift to the farthest pole of indifference by the prehuman, almost sexless world. (Lawrence's theme will always involve a legitimate drift to that lulled condition— "Only the great pause between carings" [K 341]—and then a counterflow to a pole of full consciousness and responsibility, what he calls "thought-adventure" [K 226].) It should be stressed that the lethargies induced by Australia are deeper confirmations of the sexual submission endorsed in *The Lost Girl* and *Lady Chatterley's Lover.* They make sex only secondary and instrumental; the yielding to the sex drive itself becomes a kind of legitimate decomposition in which personality and its intentions are subverted while something else (that something is Lawrence's God) is served. Giving in to the somnolent land is a still more primitive shedding of the potential self.

Lawrence's first description of the land accords with the one just examined from *The Lost Girl,* including the shift from full sentence to suspended fragment and the foreshortened close:

> And then one night at the time of the full moon he walked alone into the bush. A huge electric moon, huge, and the tree-trunks like naked pale aborigines among the dark-soaked foliage, in the moonlight. And not a sign of life—not a vestige. (K 8)

"Yet something," the next paragraph begins. An irrational fear now takes hold of Somers, "his hair began to stir with terror, on his head. There was a presence." Fighting this fear brings a different kind of conclusion to this paragraph. Where we had just been given fragments, we get instead definition: "But then to experience terror is not the same thing as to admit fear into the conscious soul. Therefore he refused to be afraid" (K 9). The three infinitives here all work differently than before, completing Lawrence's *finite* structures. "Therefore" finishes the chore of addressing the mind to the problem, the whole evolution caught appropriately in the style. And now the six-word ending is dismissive.

As I have said, only Somers's first reaction to the wilderness is terrified. Later on, regularly through the novel, the land makes resistless appeals. Not always in the many paragraphs forming the motif do the hypnotic fragments take charge. But there remains the tendency to end fragmentarily, as in this instructive instance:

> Somers felt the torpor coming over him. He hung there on the parapet looking down, and he didn't care. How profoundly, darkly he didn't care. There are no problems for the soul in its darkened, wide-eyed torpor. Neither Harriet nor Kangaroo nor Jaz, nor even the world. Worlds come, and worlds go: even worlds. And when the old, old influence of the fern-world comes over a man, how can he care? He breathes the fern seed and drifts back, becomes darkly half vegetable, devoid of pre-occupations. Even the never-slumbering urge of sex sinks down into something darker, more monotonous, incapable of caring: like sex in trees. The dark world before conscious responsibility was born. (K180)

Aside from the last of these ten sentences, only the fifth is a fragment. But the punctuation of all the interior entries goes some way toward retaining an anaesthetized effect. Their last units are responsible. Commas in six of the sentences, colons in the other two,* separate small phrase groups of two, three, and four words, as though the breath gathered anew for those final short expirations: "even worlds," "how can he care," "like sex in trees." In content the passage affords as good an epitome of the fern-world motif as any in the novel. And, once again, Lawrence concludes with a short verbless summary of what it is the paragraph has been evoking.

To summarize: I have really been claiming two opposite achievements for Lawrence in this survey of a major paragraphing practice of his. On the one hand, he often seems fretted by his material. Impatient, even angry with it (or with himself), he throws down his like-it-or-lump it, dismissive conclusions. Conversely, when caught up with rhythmic, ineffable experience, he will favor short but resonating (often repetitive and fragmentary) methods of ending. While the material itself may irritate or overwhelm—while Lawrence may be exhilarated or despondent—there seems to be a curiously recurrent effect, regardless of which circumstance prevails. This I would describe as an impatience not so much toward the material per se (though sometimes it begins there) as toward writing—recording—in general.

---

*These particular colons work very much like the colons supplied by Joyce at the end of "The Dead," discussed in chapter two.

One might label this quality of Lawrence's style as inadvertent sincerity. Now "sincerity" is something critics responsive to Lawrence have always traded heavily on (the Leavis school, for example). But a negative view might hold that sincerity can become far too cloying in Lawrence, especially in some of his natural descriptions. Even an admirer like Anaïs Nin will hesitate in the midst of praise and say of *Kangaroo* that "the descriptions are rather enumerative."[4] Her general reservation about Lawrentian prose also touches on its indulgence: "Very often, in fact, it is the undercurrent of rhythm which makes the careless writing. The words almost cease to have a meaning; they have a cadence, a flow, and Lawrence gives in to the cadence. That is why there are so many 'ands' and *enchainements,* repetitions like choruses, words that are made to suggest more than their own determinate, formal significance."[5] I would submit that many passages prove her right, though not passages having the modulation displayed in the type of paragraphs we have been reviewing.

In his most convincing passages, sexual or of an even profounder laxity, Lawrence avoids "enumeration" by having the will of the participants abrogated. Static, heavy forces actuate them—their experiences are anything but kinetic (no matter what gyrations they may go through). But, like them, Lawrence is apt to fall into and out of mesmerization. When he is out of it, he sometimes fails to monitor himself, secure about his own eloquence because of his almost Biblical earnestness. This is when someone like Anaïs Nin finds a reason to score him. But what if the rough-and-ready feature of his prose then comes in evidence? I grant that it may not come up often enough, yet I feel that Lawrence can reveal his own potential for detecting the very weaknesses that an un-bowled-over critic might detect—the "enumerative" weakness, for example.

It is almost as though one can get to like Lawrence best when he is between stretches of laid-on eloquence, so to speak, times when he does not bother to eliminate or conceal the drossiness along the route. That is why it is worthwhile studying his "dismissive" paragraph-enders. How conscious his strategies may have been is difficult to say. They certainly provide him with occasion after occasion for exhibiting a nonreverential attitude toward writing itself, though that is his craft, his medium for coming at the primitive rhythms and responses in men by which he sets such store. He might be said to regard his art as a sort of seismograph. But when it sputters, as it does a good deal of the time, he is under no compulsion to tidy up the record. It is as good as saying, "What an undignified instrument this is after all. What a lot of trivia it records." Thus when Alvina in *The Lost Girl* is led into a benighted engagement with a medical man, we hear that at his house

Alvina admired the Jacobean sideboard and the Jacobean arm-chairs and the Heppelwhite wall-chairs and the Sheraton settee and the Chippendale stands and the Axminster carpet and the bronze clock with Shakespeare and Ariosto reclining on it—yes, she even admired Shakespeare on the clock—and the ormolu cabinet and the bead-work foot-stools and the dreadful Sèvres dish with a cherub in it and—but why enumerate. (LG 290)

Not even a question mark is reserved for the three-word retraction that ends the catalogue. It is not exasperated, only tired at the pointlessness. That is what I meant about "inadvertent" being a viable word to characterize Lawrence's sincerity. In that passage we have just a stopping off, by means of a formula that is not presumed to have any force as it is used.

In *Kangaroo,* having had his hero argue first that ideas are relative and then that the individual is absolute, Lawrence produces this short paragraph:

So that even relativity is only relative. Relative to the absolute. (K 286)

In one sense, nothing could be more otiose than writing such sentences. They are the kind that anti-Lawrentians find galling. Yet, taken another way, they could represent Lawrence at his best. They record rank sententiousness and allow it to stand. Lawrence not only is depressed but lets it be clear that he is, so much so that he ends the next paragraph: "He preached, and the record was taken down for this gramophone of a novel" (K 286). Gramophone or seismograph, the tendency not to supervise is evident.

Oddly enough, in *The Lost Girl,* the asking of a question without a question mark is a stylistic device repeated many times; similarly, in *Kangaroo,* the odd genitive construction ("this gramophone of a novel") is encountered often, and each in its own way helps characterize the narrative voice of the novel in question. That is a point to be taken up later, when differences between them are inspected. Both indicate inadvertency, but in *The Lost Girl* the style is perhaps kept more sardonic by devices such as the one just named, while in *Kangaroo* there is a greater confessional tendency because of the identification between Lawrence and Richard Lovat Somers.

FRAGMENTATION, TRANSITION, INVERSION

The Lost Girl is a social novel describing Alvina Houghton's estrangement from the town of Woodhouse and, especially, those in her household (her father and two arch women, aptly named Frost and

Pinnegar). *Kangaroo,* on the other hand, is a political novel describing Richard Somers's brush with fascism and socialism (the two alternatives to democracy) and his rejection of all three Western ideologies on the ground that they are based on abstraction and raise up the same bannerword—"love"—as a cover for their real operative byword, "wilfulness." The figures of Kangaroo himself, as chief of the Diggers, and his supporters and opponents from right and left make up the roster of characters with whom Somers comes in contact, Australian politics being imaginatively extended to embody the whole postwar Western dilemma.[6]

The differing social and political contexts produce a different moral scale, and this is reflected stylistically by the narrators. The moral problem in *The Lost Girl* is less weighty, more conventional. Alvina as protagonist is special, granted, and for this reason she goes through the Lawrentian initiation: she becomes "lost," and then is saved from the fates of her mother, of Miss Frost and Miss Pinnegar, from "the terrible crying of a woman with a loving heart, whose heart has never been able to relax" (LG 33). The fact that in Lawrence's eyes she is special and at the same time a tyro accounts for the narrator's tone. "Now so far, the story of Alvina is commonplace enough," he says at one point (LG 97), only to begin his next paragraph with a contradiction:

> But we protest that Alvina is not ordinary. Ordinary people, ordinary fates. But extraordinary people, extraordinary fates. The all-to-one-pattern modern system is too much for most extraordinary individuals. It just kills them off or throws them disused aside. (LG 98)

Talking off-handedly about his story, Lawrence suddenly delivers his "protest" that his heroine is extraordinary. Yet her novice state makes it appropriate for him to remain chatty about her, using the editorial "we" and concluding with statements about people who "just" might be found dispensable because they are different. Essentially, this knowingness of the narrator (even though Alvina escapes being merely tossed aside) is justified, since most of the time narrator and reader know what Alvina knows only incipiently: that she is special and will balk and resist until the right fatal ingredients arrive to allow her to fulfill herself.

As for Somers, by the time *Kangaroo*'s action takes place, his character has already been long formed, he himself long since been through these personal trials and discoveries. If Alvina finds and submits to her sexuality and to Ciccio, Somers has long before, in his marriage to Harriet, learned these lessons of passional life. (The couple are more autobiographical than any of Lawrence's other portraits of Frieda and himself.) Thus the moral scale of *Kangaroo* is more elevated, because the book deals with an initiate, not a tyro.* The psychical trials peculiar to a Lawrence character continue, and one of the polarities that always offers—that of *independence*—is now made to measure itself against political imperatives and the will to improve man's lot—a different thing from improving one man's (or one woman's) lot. The pressure on the narrative voice becomes much greater when the alternatives of reclusion or outward commitment are offered to a mature and tested man, a man who has solved emotional problems and long since risen from "lost" status to positions of conviction, as exemplified by this statement:

> Man is a thought-adventurer. Man is more, he is a life-adventurer. Which means he is a thought-adventurer, an emotion adventurer, and a discoverer of himself and of the outer universe. A discoverer. (K 284–85)

This paragraph contrasts well with that just given from *The Lost Girl,* not only because of the dropping of the editorial "we," but also because of the recursion to the generic noun "man." Where Alvina, when she "went right back on high-mindedness" (LG 43), was rebelling from the attitude of others, Somers has gotten so clear of others' influence that, in effect, he must reexamine the possibility that he may have to get back to movement with men. Men—man, that is, as a cosmic adventurer—is thought of in higher-than-individual terms in such a paragraph from *Kangaroo,* and "high-mindedness" makes new claims now on the Lawrence hero.

I wanted to name this tonal difference now, but not pursue it. Stylistic differences that arise out of it ought to wait on the establishment of more similarities, first at the unit level of the sentence, then lexically. Once this is done, a last section can return to the question of differences.

Having discussed Lawrence's sentence fragments as they often work in paragraphs, I should like to move from examples in the last two extracts toward a glimpse of what generates a Lawrence fragment. Richard Ohmann once proposed that an option favored by Lawrence worked off the principle of deletion.[7] In part the passages just quoted bear Ohmann out. Noun-phrase fragments are common in Lawrence ("Ordinary people, ordinary fates"; "A discoverer"). Predicates are deleted from sentences that might originally have read

---

*Something on this order comes to light with the other pairs of novels we study. Most apparently, the protagonists of *Tarr* and *Self Condemned* recall the beginner-versus-veteran distinction in Lawrence. The young wounded hero of *Back* similarly contrasts with the old scientist Rock of *Concluding.* And from the narrator's point of view, at least, *Howards End* and *A Passage to India* have some affinities here, also.

"Ordinary people [require] ordinary fates" or "[Man is] a discoverer." In another typical form, though, the principle of substitution rather than deletion takes hold. The relative-clause fragment ("Which means he is a thought-adventurer...") derives, of course, from a noun again, but becomes fragmentary because of the substitution of the relative pronoun "which" for the demonstrative "this."

These are the two most commonly encountered sentence-fragment types in Lawrence.

One might go further and say that, setting aside exclamations and related short utterances, there are really four ways to produce fragments. Two would rely on nouns—noun phrases or their adjectival derivatives—and two on verbs, verbal phrases and adverbial clauses. The first are predominant in Lawrence and are discussed here, with equivalency between the two novels. As for verb-derived fragments, not only are they less common, but they produce some statistical discrepencies that are shown, in the last section, to have bearing on the stylistic distinctions the two books offer.

In the cases of noun-derived fragments (deletional and substitutive), one would expect to find the affirmation of a presence or a quality without emphasis on an action. This holds true, though one early distinction might also be made: Lawrence uses the relative-clause fragment most often for derogatory purposes. His narrative can turn easily flippant through this device, and it will often be his means of catching his characters in petulant or fatuous attitudes, as in this extract from *The Lost Girl*, which exposes Alvina's suitor, Dr. Mitchell:

> [The attendant] rushed out of the room, and burst into tears on the landing. After which Dr. Mitchell, mollified, largely told the patient how she was to behave. . . .
> "Oh doctor—"
> "Don't say *oh doctor* to me. Do as I tell you. That's *your* business." After which he marched out, and the rattle of his motor car was shortly heard. (LG 283)

Many similar examples of the "which" substitution can be tabulated. The contexts in all the following cases are foolish or pejorative:

> In which he was disappointed, for he got only eight hundred. (LG 9)
>
> Which it was. And which, in her curious perverseness, Alvina must have intended it to be. (LG 38)
>
> Which is the *reductio ad absurdum* of idealism. (LG 53)
>
> With which cryptic remark he left it. (K 53)
>
> Which state of affairs did not go at all well with *our* friend's sense of self-importance. (K 62)

Which is the bitter pill which Buddhists and all advocates of pure *Spirit* must swallow. (K 308)

Which being so, he proceeded, as ever, to try to disentangle himself from the white octopus of love. (K 335)

All the examples here from *Kangaroo* either begin or end paragraphs, giving them added stridency. Incidentally, the fact that "which" substitutes for "this" so often in fractious circumstances seems related to a curious retention of "this" at other times. For on nine occasions (seven of them pejorative) Lawrence creates fragments by deleting his predicate, to sum up the force of a nasty or swaggering remark.

All this in French. (LG 170)

This as he gazed down on the wan mother in the bed. (LG 282)

"You know I mean what I say, Mrs. Larrick"—this to the wife. (LG 284)

And threaded on this ironical stoicism. (K 55)

This to the Chink. (K 106)

This in a tone of sneering scepticism. (K 259)

All this in a high shrill voice above the waves. (K 337)

But these two sets of examples aside, Lawrence's fragments generally seek to relay matters of serious rather that trifling import. One clear deletion pattern involves the elimination of expletives ("it is," "there are," etc.), causing him to begin right off with the noun or adjective that completes this construction. The effect is that of radical identification between author and situation. I think this quality is absent in most of the "which" substituting, where the relative pronoun is a deliberate logical connective that has to be brought in. The elimination of expletives runs counter to logic as space is cut away in the effort to get to value words.

A paragraph from *Kangaroo* offers a splendid example of a sequence of sentences eliminating expletives (I reprint it with the expletives bracketed):

Awful years—'16, '17, '18, '19—the years when the damage was done. The years when the world lost its real manhood. Not for lack of courage to face death. Plenty of superb courage to face death. But no courage in any man to face his own isolated soul, and abide by its decision. Easier to sacrifice oneself. So much easier! (K 217)

[They were] awful years—'16, '17, '18, '19—the years when the damage was done. [They were] the years when the world lost its real manhood. [It was] not for lack of courage to face death. [There was] plenty of superb courage to face death. But [there was] no courage in any man to face his own isolated soul, and abide by its decision. [It would be] easier to sacrifice oneself. [That would be] so much easier!

Setting the omitted elements in, at least in this example, marks something fairly unusual about Lawrence's writing habits. Notice that the expletives change. Only in the first two sentences could it be argued that exact repetition of the front element occurs, so that the deletion in the second sentence is a simple ruling out of a controlling phrase already felt. While Lawrence's habits of repetition do sometimes cause such patterns in his sentences (as Ohmann has pointed out), this paragraph demonstrates changes in head phrases that will not provide for continuity across the sentences; yet the fragment forms persist. It then becomes less a question of rhetoric for Lawrence and more a sense of author identification with situations, followed along through their suppressed syntactic changes—which says something more for Lawrence than that he operates mainly by incantation.

The next examples illustrate similar direct commencement with the complement, the last set showing a transitional element in use in advance. Out of all two dozen examples, only one, "Time for Miss Frost to die," saw the ellipsis generated from an earlier full-fledged sentence ("It was time now for Miss Frost to die").

   a. Noun complements as headwords

     Time now for a new flight. (LG 22)

     Time for Miss Frost to die. (LG 45)

     No denying it, she was an artist. (LG 182)

     No doubt about it, the Natcha-Kee-Tawaras were under suspicion. (LG 273)

     Pure foolishness, of course, but there's no telling where a foolishness may nip you. (K 9–10)

     Never another sail in sight, never another ship in hail. (K 173–74)

     Bugle at six, and a scramble to wash themselves at a zinc trough in the wash-house. (K 223)

     No strain in any way, once you could accept it. (K 282)

   b. Adjective complements as headwords

     Sufficient that the girl herself worshipped Miss Frost: or believed she did. (LG 27)

     Useless to talk of the distracted anguish of Alvina during the next two days. (LG 61)

     Curious how *dark* they seemed, with only a yellow ring of pupil. (LG 159)

     Ridiculous to be so happy. (LG 261)

Sufficient that Somers went indoors into his little bungalow, and found his wife setting the table for supper, with cold meat and salad. (K10)

No good pretending otherwise. No good playing tricks of being nice. (K 165)

Strange that the torpor had come on him so completely of late. (K 181)

Bitter, in Oxfordshire, to unpack the things he had loved so dearly in Cornwall. (K 256)

c. Transitional elements as headwords

Here the *ne plus ultra.* (LG 7)

In the breasts of the crowd, wonder, admiration, *fear,* and ridicule. (LG 11)

Hence the extreme peril of her case. Hence the bitter fear and humiliation she felt.... (LG 98)

But there—a clocking, shouting, splashing sound. (LG 344)

But near at hand nothing but bungalows—street after street. (K 7)

At her very feet, the huge rhythmic Pacific. (K 77)

Hence the fly in the ointment: embalmed in balm. And our repugnance. (K 285)

But surely a place that will some day wake terribly from this sleep. (K 314)

The last group put adverbial stress on locations or sources of things—very Lawrentian in their compression. Such spatial transitions reduce the need for predication. "At her very feet, the huge rhythmic Pacific"—no need to work a verb in to realize this tableau. Lawrence takes a more surprising turn when he introduces some of his noun fragments temporally. Consider this series from *The Lost Girl,* twice helped along by temporal conjunctions:

> Curtain! A few bars of Toreador—and then Miss Poppy's sheets of music. Soft music.... And so the accumulating dilation, on to the whirling climax of the perfect arum lily. (LG 126)

The peculiar thing here is that the transitions ("then," "so") give a sense of consequence and motion, yet head up noun groups lacking verbs to enforce that sense. It seems it would be hard to write this way (almost going against the grain of such transitions), yet Lawrence does it consistently.

And then, most irritating, a complete *volte face* in her feelings. (LG 32)

Yet all the time, his lustrous dark beauty, unbearable. (LG 227)

And then—the unknown vengeance of the authorities. (LG 275)

And so, through Folkestone to the sea. (LG 327)

Yet the strange exposed smile she gave him in the dusk. (K 27)

Now this little kingfisher by the sea. (K 84)

So then man. . . . The mob, then. (K 301)

But still, that sense of sardonic tolerance, endurance. (K 314)

In context, the next-to-last example is the most striking. The two "sentences" head up a pair of long paragraphs in tandem, in which Lawrence starts a diatribe on "the God-urge" within man that is the unrecognized source of mob violence. "So then man" and "The mob, then" represent Lawrence at his most idiosyncratic—the tremendously big concept (of man, of mob) caught in a three-word burst, and himself caught on it, too, twice brought to a stop at the head of a paragraph, gathered, as it were, on the verge of a subject he is about to eviscerate.

Other times this happens in *Kangaroo*, this cessation and gathering. "Yet something," we had read as the terror of the bush gained on Somers (K 8); "And now the war," we read when London is about to be described in the "Nightmare" chapter (K 253). The transitions seem to say "go on," but the nouns stop off.*

It has been common for critics to remark on Lawrence's paratactic connection (here illustrated with fragments). No purpose would be served by an extended tabulation of his use of conjunctions as headwords; nevertheless, one redundancy does become impressive, I think, when attended by statistics. This is his predilection for *doubled* conjunctions as headwords, a style-marker I should now like to consider.

There are two combinations of note: the coupling of "and" and "but" with the conjunctive adverbs "then," "now," and "still"; and the heavy use of "and so" and "and yet" ("yet" and "so" are able to be preceded by "and" where other coordinates are not). In *Kangaroo*, 135 sentences begin with doubled conjunctions of these types; in *The Lost Girl*, 152 sentences do so. Their average occurrence is more than one time for every three pages—a 37 percent incidence in *Kangaroo*, 40 percent in *The Lost Girl* (see table 3.2).

The important thing about these transitions is that in spite of their variety they are all, as Lawrence employs them, semantically

---

*In *The Lost Girl*, a cognate phenomenon happens in the case of Ciccio, portentous to Alvina as the general nouns "man" and "mob" and "war" are to Lawrence-Somers. This helps measure the difference between the two novels: one a girl's story, the other a "thought adventurer's." "Geoffrey followed, heavily," we read. "Then Ciccio" (LG 257). Or, "Useless to deny it. Even to Ciccio" (LG 267). Again, "He was heard talking to some one in the moonlight outside. To Ciccio" (LG 315).

Table 3.2   Doubled Conjunctions as Headwords

	Number of Doubled Conjunctions	Number of Pages	Incidence per Page
The Lost Girl	152	372	.409
Kangaroo	135	367	.368
Lawrence aggregate	287	739	.388
Howards End	6	315	.019
A Passage to India	9	300	.030
Forster aggregate	15	615	.024
Tarr	7	291	.024
Self Condemned	28	386	.073
Lewis aggregate	35	677	.052
Back	9	180	.050
Concluding	10	200	.050
Green aggregate	19	380	.050

NOTE: Obviously no grounds for comparison exist here. The paucity of occurrences— a grand total of 69 in six novels—only underscores Lawrence's appetency for doubled conjunctions.

close. On the face of it, only "and so" would seem to announce direct consequence. The others—"yet," "now," "then," "still"—would seem each to imply an intimation of change, in varying degrees. But in Lawrence this is not the case. Rather, the conjunctive adverbs tend to suggest flow without retaining their logical properties of charting new direction. This is a very hard concept to state, but it is consonant with Lawrence's criterion of the "unstable ego."[8] An *impulse* of directional flow is something he is interested in recording, but as for counterflow, he seems uninterested in any true checking power it may have. Thus he will use this group of transitions interchangeably, sapping their force and clarity. Unstable fluctuation is the result gained, especially suiting his psychic portrayals. Fortunately, though hard to state, the concept is easy to illustrate.

> *But now* Mr. May had laid his detaining hand on James's arm. *And now* he was shaking his employer by the hand. *And now* James, in his cheap little cap, was smiling a formal farewell. (LG 111)
>
> *And then* at last he lifted his head and looked at Somers. *And now* Somers openly hated him. His face was arrogant, insolent, righteous. (K 214)

In its context, the first transition, "but now," has no antithetical force. It simply breaks away from material dealing with Alvina and Miss Pinnegar, who are spying on the two men. The "but now" transition is really indistinguishable from the "and now's" that follow it. Likewise in the second instance—no distinction is felt between "then" and "now," although they pretend to a root dissimilarity. Suppose the third sentence, describing Kangaroo's face, had intervened between the other two (and that would have been quite logical); there would have been more reason to notice the sharp transitional effect of "now." But that doesn't happen, and, instead, the "then" and "now" are run up against one another in virtual repetition of a single mode for recording time shifts.

Similar interchangeability occurs in the following portion of a *Kangaroo* paragraph:

> He half wanted to commit himself to this whole affection with a friend, a comrade, a mate. And then, in the last issue, he didn't want it at all.... All his life he had cherished a beloved ideal of friendship. And now, when true and good friends offered, he found he simply could not commit himself, even to simple friendship. (K 104)

The more interesting fact here is that, had Lawrence truly felt the cleavage between an old desire and a sudden reversion from it, he might more properly have written "*but* then" and "*but* now" at the points of transition. This only serves to show that "anything goes" with such locutions. In the three-sentence sequences from *The Lost Girl* that follow, where Lawrence does conclude with a double conjunction headed by "but," he succeeds, oddly enough, in getting a sense of continuation rather than reversal:

> They all laughed, and sat down to tea.... Fortunately for them, Madame had seen to their table-manners. But still they were far too free and easy to suit Miss Pinnegar. (LG 248)

> And so, from the matron, she learned to crochet. It was work she had never taken to. But now she had her ball of cotton and her hook, and she worked away as she chatted. (LG 281)

> ... But wondering about the Natchas would not help her. She felt, if she knew where they were, she would fly to them. But then she knew she wouldn't. (LG 296)

The curious thing is that the antithetical element in these passages comes in the next-to-last sentence each time, a sentence *not* helped along by a "converse" transition. Meanwhile, the last sentence is helped in this way, but it only reconfirms the initial idea. In short— and of all things that might be said about Lawrence's style, this might in the end prove most fundamental—it must be recognized that Lawrence is not a dialectical writer. Writers as far apart in theme as Forster and Lewis owe their pointedness very much to their dependence on antithetical constructions and a drive toward definition.

Lawrence does not. What his negative transitions represent is something else altogether; he is a writer of *double* antitheses. He mostly creates dialectic in order to cancel it, seeking diffuse effects. In this regard the key Lawrentian transition turns out to be "and yet." It heads 25 sentences in *The Lost Girl,* 23 in *Kangaroo.* (In the more conventional *Sons and Lovers,* this transition occurs only three times.)

"And yet it was still the kangaroo face" (K 111). Thus ends a paragraph describing Ben Cooley's eloquence and the "extraordinary beauty" it kindles in his face. "And yet" next asks us to reserve judgment. Australia, too, seen in a bleak panorama "so unimpressive . . . out of our ken," waits on the transition: "And yet, when you don't have the feeling of ugliness or monotony . . . you get a sense of subtle, remote, *formless* beauty more poignant than anything ever experienced before" (K 73–74). In the first instance beauty is affirmed and then taken away, in the next beauty is taken away and then affirmed. One can imagine Lawrence's readers always on the verge of crying, "But you just said . . ." At the climax of *The Lost Girl* two paragraphs occur, one to affirm Alvina's passion for Ciccio and the other to state her self-sufficient strength. They cancel each other mutually. The first finds her sensing her own pregnancy: "She hardly noticed him. It seemed to her she was with child. And yet in the whole market-place she was aware of nothing but him" (LG 357). That last sentence imposes her lover's power on her, setting up the next major paragraph, which in its turn ends: "His yellow, luminous eyes watched her and enveloped her. There was nothing for her but to yield, yield, yield. And yet she could not sink to earth" (LG 358). Earlier we had been given, "And yet she shrank . . . . And yet she went forward . . ." (LG 236). Or, to turn to Somers's wife, here is a paragraph having no basis for its initial transition. Harriet has not been involved in the foregoing material, Lawrence is only feigning an antithesis:

> But Harriet was waiting for him rather wistful, and loving him rather quiveringly. And yet even in the quiver of her passion was some of this indifference, this twilight indifference of the fern world. (K 180–81)

Each book happens to isolate a protagonist to reveal such vacillation at length, so, rather than spot check the "and yet's" further, I will let these paragraphs serve for summation:

> The food was objectionable—yet Alvina got fat on it. The air was filthy—and yet never had her colour been so warm and fresh, her skin so soft. Her companions were almost without exception vulgar and coarse—yet never had she got on so well with women of her own age—or older than herself. She was ready with a laugh and a word, and though she was unable to venture on indecencies herself, yet she had an amazing

faculty for *looking* knowing and indecent beyond words, rolling her eyes and pitching her eyebrows in a certain way—oh, it was quite sufficient for her companions. And yet, if they had ever actually demanded a dirty story or a really open indecency from her, she would have been floored. (LG 40)

When [Somers] saw a motor-car parked in the waste lot next to Cooee, and saw two women in twelve-guinea black coats and skirts hobbling across the grass to the bungalow farther down, perhaps wanting to hire it: then the devil came and sat black and naked in his eyes. They hobbled along the uneven place so commonly, they looked so crassly common in spite of their tailors' bills, so *low*, in spite of their motor-car, that the devil in him fairly lashed its tail like a cat. And yet, he knew, they were probably just two nice, kindly women, as the world goes. And truly, even the devil in him did not want to do them any *personal* harm. If they had fallen, or got into difficulty, he would have gone out at once to help them all he could. And yet, at the sight of their backs in their tailored "costumes" hobbling past the bushes, the devil in him lashed its tail till he writhed. (K 165–66)

The *Lost Girl* paragraph supplies an interior "yet" antithesis with every sentence, showing Alvina adapting to gross circumstances. Innuendo has built up, especially toward the end. The concluding "and yet" then vitiates the whole catalogue, by revealing that an open indecency would have "floored" Alvina. In their momentum the sentences became looser and looser (right-branching), until the finale, "would have been floored," which is left-branching.

The movement in the *Kangaroo* paragraph is only slightly different. The first two (left-branching) sentences focus on the devil aroused in Somers by the mincing women. Pitted against these are the next three sentences, headed by the first "and yet" transition, which cool off his fury—the women are deemed "nice" and "kindly." (Thus the paragraph's antitheses work across sentence groups rather than within sentences as in the *Lost Girl* sample.) However, this movement is then cancelled by another "and yet." The continual shifting refuses to let an emphasis harden. But that is precisely the effect Lawrence craves. There seem to be echoes in all this of the skilled inadvertency that may be his best-guarded secret. One force overtakes and then is itself overtaken. The result, from one point of view, is a weakening of rhetorical power, but the gain may be the setting up of unstoppable to-and-fro action through antirhetoric.

Can anything more be said? Oddly enough, it can, for there happens to be a short conjunction that is able to imply a retraction, to contradict "yet" and "but" without repeating them. It is the conjunction "only." It is one of Lawrence's favorites, commencing 18 sentences in *Kangaroo* and 14 in *The Lost Girl*.

James was now nearly seventy years old. Yet he nipped about like a leaf in the wind. Only, it was a frail leaf. (LG 110)

... And the boldest [magpie] would even come and take pieces of bread from his hands. Yet they were quite wild. Only they seemed to have strange power of understanding the human psyche. (K 84)

The first example is a paragraph in its own right. The second concludes a long paragraph. The double-antithetical pattern is the same in each. And there are many comparable examples, enough to make one wonder whether any other writer has made the word "only" his property, in this special vernacular sense, to the degree Lawrence has done (see table 3.3 for comparisons).

In the discussions of Lawrence's paragraphs, fragments, and redundant connectives, I emphasized a certain dilution that is characteristic of his prose. Sometimes, however, Lawrence's purposes drive him or his principals onto fixed positions; a last noteworthy feature of his syntax, common to both *The Lost Girl* and *Kangaroo*, has to do with infringements he makes on sentence patterns for the sake of fixed emphasis. They often produce sentences that are inverted, and the inversions, less casual in structure than the fragmented or coordinated elements, almost never appear in conjunction with these others. Thus they purport to bring us at times to stable ground more assuredly that any other of Lawrence's devices.

Table 3.3   Incidence of "Only" as Headword

	Number of Occurrences	Number of Pages	Incidence per Page
The Lost Girl	14	372	.038
Kangaroo	18	367	.049
Lawrence aggregate	32	739	.043
Howards End	0	315	.000
A Passage to India	0	300	.000
Forster aggregate	0	615	.000
Tarr	4	291	.014
Self Condemned	1	386	.003
Lewis aggregate	5	677	.007
Back	1	180	.006
Concluding	2	200	.010
Green aggregate	3	380	.008

NOTE: The figures represent the use of "only" as a negative conjunction. It is, of course, a common transition as an adjective ("Only a real fear of offending Madame drove her down" [LG 230]) or an adverb ("Only then did she notice" [K 194]). The Lawrence figures of 14 and 18 represent conjunctive uses of "only," which occur more frequently in his works than both other types combined.

Lawrence seems drawn to inverted patterns for two main reasons: to record novelty and wonder, or to register a conclusive action or unambivalent state of mind. It is hardly that he becomes more formal at such times. Rather, in the act of writing, he seems to require filled-out statements in lieu of haphazardly joined or abridged ones; under strain this filling-out often takes tortuous form. One of the formal varieties of inversion is chiasmus, and we do find Lawrence ending his "Nightmare" chapter with this figure: "He was broken apart, apart he would remain" (K 265). But there is only one other example in *Kangaroo* of chiasmus: "The Fates lead on the willing man, the unwilling man they drag" (K 268)—and with this sentence Lawrence was translating a Latin motto he had quoted earlier. Similarly, *The Lost Girl* has only one example of chiasmus: "It screamed all the night—all the way from Paris to Chambéry it screamed" (LG 331). Balance of this type, as has already been implied, is foreign to Lawrence. More characteristic are occasions when echoes from forerunning sentences cause him to follow up with inversions, as in this sequence from *The Lost Girl:*

> She laughed in spite of herself. In spite of herself she was shaken into a convulsion of laughter. Louis was masterful—he mastered her psyche. She laughed till her head lay helpless on the chair, she could not move. Helpless, inert she lay, in her orgasm of laughter. (LG 167)

Moving from sentence one to two, the prepositional phrase is inverted; from sentence four to five, the predicate adjective "helpless." The middle sentence controlling this hilarity also involves a partial chiasmus (in the morphemic change from "masterful" to "mastered"). This becomes interesting when it is noted that the flanking sentence pairs also show morphemic changes (from the head phrase "She laughed" to the final phrase "of laughter" in each case). Such are the irregular but quite provocative chiastic structures likely to be found in Lawrence.

As this sample shows, some situations can be conducive to a clustering of inversions. Novelty, surprise, all-or-nothing resolution may lead to more that one uncommon twist. Broadly speaking, the next clusters illustrate the major methods of reorienting syntax: early positioning of adverbial elements and inversion of complements or objects. (Later I illustrate some clusters from *Kangaroo* that work differently, and show a special Lawrence idiosyncrasy.)

> *So easily* she might miss him altogether! *Within a hair's-breadth* she had let him disappear. (LG 235—adverbial elements inverted)

> *So clean,* she felt, so thankful! Her skin seemed caressed and live with cleanliness and whiteness, *luminous* she felt. (LG 280—predicate complements inverted)

Jack's iron bar, for instance, nobody mentioned. It was called a stick. *Who fired the revolvers,* nobody chose to know. (K 327—direct objects inverted)

The second passage here records a moment of elation for Alvina, after she has been temporarily freed from the influence of the Natcha-Kee-Tawaras. (The shifting forward of adjectives can name her condition immediately.) The first and third passages are more alarming, Alvina realizing how near she has come to losing Ciccio, Somers reacting to the suppression of news about murder and mob violence in Sydney. With the help of the following lists, I try to suggest why a *kind* of inversion might crop up for one and then the other sort of context.

a. Adverbial elements inverted

To the women he said not a word. (LG 102)

Of that she was sure, and of nothing else. (LG 214)

Right at the top of the rocks they stood, like pilots. (K 86)

Clear as the air about him this truth possessed him. (K 339)

b. Direct objects inverted

This last degradation the women refused. (LG 54)

But Ciccio it put into unholy, ungovernable temper. (LG 170)

What this pledge consisted in he did not try to define. (K 28)

This Richard Lovat Somers had steadily refused to do. (K 216)

c. Predicate complements inverted

Curiously flat and fish-like he was, one might have imagined his backbone to be spread like the backbone of a sole or a plaice. (LG 75)

Queer, dainty woman, was Madame, even to her wonderful threaded black-and-gold gaiters. (LG 144)

A new sort of bird to her was this little man with a beard. (K 14)

A detestable little brat he felt. (K 288)

In terms of resultant meaning, there seems a closer relationship between lists (a) and (b) than between either of them and list (c), and this seems due to the fact that, whether an adverbial element or a direct object is transposed forward, the result is an intensification of the predicate. While a periodic effect is also created in the third list, the copular verb there cannot sustain emphasis the way the verb can be made to do in the other two classes of inversion.

Thus the predications in the first two lists share a fixity of purpose demonstrable in several ways: through unequivocal negatives ("said not a word," "was sure of nothing else," "did not try to define"); through inexorable connotations in the other predicates ("possessed," "refused," "refused to do"); or through heightened modifiers in the remaining sentences (the reinforced "right at the top" plus the "ungovernable" that completes the predicate about Ciccio).

In the third list, where the verbs cannot be heightened, the inverted complements retain the emphasis themselves. Instead of determination, they tend to give off an aura of surprise. As a general rule—and in all of the sentences in this list—this is the inversion pattern that Lawrence uses when he is struck by novelty. *Kangaroo* offers a sharp exception that proves the rule, a sentence ending with "was" that does not produce an inversion of novelty. However, the reason is that the anterior element is not a complement at all, but the main predicate itself, "was" being in this case not copular but auxiliary. The sentence is psychologically devastating: "But watched and followed he knew he was" (K 254).

The clusters from *Kangaroo* referred to earlier illustrate a last technique. (Certain pronouns are italicized for convenience.)

> In the individual man he was ... they believed with all the intensity of undivided love. But in the impersonal man, the man that would go beyond them ... in *this* man they did not find it so easy to believe. (K 95)

> These moments bred in the head and born in the eye: he had enough of *them*. ... To the visual travesty he would lend himself no more. (K 143)

> To meet another dark worshipper, *that* would be the best of human meetings. But strain himself into a feeling of absolute human love, he just couldn't do *it*. (K 335)

Of these inversions, the two that are familiar are those beginning "In the individual man he was" and "To the visual travesty," a pair of transposed adverbials, both quite forceful. But the lead phrase in each of the other four sentences is operating as an appositive. Its counterpart, a pronoun that anchors the thought to save the syntax, comes along later. This is most impressive when the pronoun comes last: "These moments ... he had enough of them"; "But strain ... he just couldn't do it." Note that the sentences all propound one of Lawrence's strongest themes: his need for "impersonal" emotion, his hatred of specious excitement ("the visual travesty"), his valuation of privacy ("human meetings" that won't violate the innate self).

The construction Lawrence likes to choose here can be called the anterior appositive. A noun cluster is sprung down. The sentence developing out of it, a kind of offshoot, is connected by a late referent pointing back to that cluster. Spontaneity, the necessity of getting the assumptive words down, may seem at the heart of this, but that could have been said of Lawrence's fragment-writing too, whereas here he seems motivated to complete thoughts that have become momentous.

One of the most natural anterior-appositive structures arises when a question is thrust on a character:

> All those other peasant women, did they feel as she did?—the same sort of acquiescent passion, the same remoteness from the world's actuality? (LG 357)

> But all those filthy little stay-at-home officers and coast-watchers and dirty-minded doctors who tortured men during the *first* stages of the torture, did these men *in their souls* believe in what they were doing? (K 269; Lawrences's italics)

Wonder can naturally be provoked this way, or it may turn to violent incredulity, as in the *Kangaroo* example, when the noun phrase swells and swells until a pause finally occurs and a question can be framed to deal with it. Without the question format, however, a real decisiveness attends the structure. In the specimens of the anterior appositive that follow the first and third indicate a character from each novel taking an immovable position:

> That Woodhouse, as a very condition of its own being, hated any approach to originality or real taste, this James Houghton could never learn. (LG 11–12)

> The fierce, savage gods who dipped their lips in blood, these were the true gods. (LG 351)

> The whole trend of this affection, this mingling, this intimacy, this truly beautiful love, [Somers] found his soul just set against it. (K 104)

> But the first, dark, ithyphallic God whom men had once known so tremendous—Struthers had no use for Him. (K 205)

A different kind of emphasis—actually a reverent one—is reserved for the other pair of examples. It is instructive to find that Lawrence there records his convictions about the dark gods and that, in two different fictional worlds, his sentiments take parallel inverted expression. This even though Alvina accepts the gods' reality, while in *Kangaroo* the opposite happens: the socialist leader Struthers "had no use for Him."

In these two novels the anterior positioning of appositives is resorted to more than 70 times (see table 3.4). It becomes one of the striking hallmarks of Lawrence's style. Since the late referent can take various syntactical positions, there is no heavy-handedness in these usages. Once in a while even a negative pronoun can be substituted late for a pre-positioned noun.

> Roads there were none: only deep tracks, like profound ruts with rocks in them.... (LG 354)

> Soul of his own he has none: and never will have. (K 287)

Table 3.4   Anterior Appositives

	Number of Occurrences	Number of Pages	Incidence per Page
The Lost Girl	28	372	.075
Kangaroo	45	367	.123
Lawrence aggregate	73	739	.099
Howards End	21	315	.067
A Passage to India	24	300	.080
Forster aggregate	45	615	.073
Tarr	18	291	.062
Self Condemned	18	386	.046
Lewis aggregate	36	677	.053
Back	0	180	.000
Concluding	0	200	.000
Green aggregate	0	380	.000

NOTE: The somewhat high incidence in Forster seems related to his habit of beginning sentences occasionally with proper nouns in apposition: "Leonard—he would figure at length in a newspaper report" (HE 290); "And Adela—she would have to depart too" (PI 250). Green's abstension from the use of the anterior appositive is noteworthy, and is perhaps attributable to the lack of authorial investment in his prose.

These have an almost Biblical ring to them. As for a really odd example, tortured into being when Somers is raging over those who caused and profited from World War I, we have this: "But the living dead, these he could not reckon with: they with poisonous teeth like hyenas" (K 266). Here "the living dead," in apposition with "these," is in the objective case (since "these" is the object of "with"). Yet immediately a new appositive is created: "they with poisonous teeth like hyenas"— made possible because "living dead" appears to be a subject and in the nominative case. Such is the pressure against grammar when a man's thoughts are really seething. This occurs in the chapter " 'Revenge!' Timotheus Cries," and after this tortuous sentence, the next three words in the text are "Rage! Rage! Rage!"

The Lost Girl does not offer occasions of such vehemence. Thus to conclude the account of Lawrence's syntax I would like to single out a lightener, which he affects, again by way of the appositive, only now in a spirit of sheer redundancy—a technique limited, not only to *The Lost Girl* as a book, but to minor discardable figures in it.

He was keen after money, was Arthur. . . . (LG 69)

He was rather stout, frail in health, but silent and insuperable, was A. W. Jordan. (LG 100)

She was the clue to all the action, was Kishwégin. (LG 183)

These sentences end on an expanded type of appositive. They deliver backhand epithets, with verb and noun tagging along superfluously. The only example in *Kangaroo* comes in the essay-chapter "Harriet and Lovat at Sea in Marriage," where the locution occurs in metaphor: "She had some awful weather, did the poor bark *Harriet and Lovat*" (K 173; Lawrence's italics). That the figure comes from idiomatic speech is indicated by a comment once made by the second-most-dangerous character in *Kangaroo*, Jack Callcott, about its most dangerous character: "He's a wonder, is Kangaroo..." (K 114). The phrasing has a very "homey" sound. But for the very reason that difficult people like Jack and Kangaroo are *not* discardable, we will not find Lawrence lightening his prose by this method in the main narrative of *Kangaroo*.[9]

DICTION: SOME MORPHEMIC STYLE MARKERS

If Lawrence bedevils his readers with repetitions, some deserve attention because of the chance they offer for relieving tiresome effects. A passage describing Harriet Somers's annoyance with her husband begins and ends as follows:

> But she saw by the shut look on his face that he was not going to tell her: that this was something he intended to keep apart from her: forever apart.... Yet she hated the hoity-toity way she was shut out. (K 93)

We have been conditioned to several things here: the short paragraph-ender, the "but"/"yet" redundancy, the simple repetition of "apart." And of course the last sentence swings around to reconfirm the first. The repetition of "shut," however, requires some small adapting by the reader, for the verb-derived adjective has changed back to verb form. One moves from the idea of "shutness" (a quality) to that of an action. The shift conveys Harriet's own process of apprehension: seeing the look, feeling "shut out."

Another passage gives Somers's reaction to schools of fish "swimming in a shudder of silver fear. That is the magic of the ocean. Let them shudder the huge ocean aglimmer" (K 138). Again the values alter as "shudder" changes from noun to active infinitive. A related move would be to classify with a noun, then make the noun work adjectivally: "Alvina's sphinx was an old, deep thoroughbred, she would take no mongrel answers. And her thoroughbred teeth were long and sharp" (LG 271). Or, reversing the process, an exotic dance may make its entry as an adjective: "Then [Madame] waved for a partner, and set up a tarantella wail. Louis threw off his coat and sprang to tarantella attention. [On his mandoline] Ciccio rang out the . . . tarantella, and Madame and Louis danced in a tight space" (LG 225). The dance, though it has its own name, is nonetheless "made flesh" only when the word is used to qualify first a sound and then an attitude (the "tarantella wail," "tarantella attention"). This sort of repetition is peculiarly Lawrentian.

While these examples involved straight changeovers of parts of speech, the main device a writer like Lawrence uses to modulate his diction is morphemic substitution that changes the class or degree of a word. There can be an obvious side to such practice, when the author's tone becomes very "knowing":

> . . . [Miss Pinnegar's] voice . . . seemed almost like a secret touch upon her hearer. Now many of her hearers disliked being secretly touched, as it were beneath their clothing. (LG 19)

> . . . Harriet had learned to cook during war-time, and now she loved it, once in a while. This had been one of the whiles. (K 29)

Besides the obvious class shifts ("secret touch" to "secretly touched," "once" to "one"), note also how both versions employ degree shifts, as "hearer" becomes "hearers" and "while" becomes "whiles." But the changes are not always so crisp:

> She enjoyed glimpsing in through uncurtained windows, into sordid rooms where human beings moved as if sordidly unaware. (LG 39)

> Again she stretched out her long white arm from the sudden blue lining of her wrap, suddenly, as if taken with desire. (LG 312)

Another writer would probably have cut "sordid" from the first example and "suddenly" from the second, for the power of the sentences comes from the odd associations of "sordidly unaware" and "sudden blue lining" (each acting in the manner of transposed epithets in poetry). But it is not Lawrence's way to get that much compression in his sentences. His dependence on partial repetition (here, by twice adding an "ly" suffix) is what is symptomatic. Substantives can likewise be modified by affixes:

> It was Victoria's high moment; all her high moments would have this Bacchic, weapon-like momentaneity: since Victoria was Victoria. (K 143)

> [The sea] had a language which spoke utterly without concern of him, and this utter unconcern gradually soothed him of himself and his world. (K 154)

As the root "moment" produces the coinage "momentaneity" and the root "concern" produces "unconcern," we follow the workings of Lawrence's mind—the more so because the new nouns attract demonstrative "this" as well. Morphemic variation becomes the source of

Lawrence's inclusiveness, helping to put themes into focus. (The two sentences just given embody the main themes of *Kangaroo:* the "momentaneous" [K 148] shortcomings of Australians and the natural restorative values of Australia.)

The most recurrent morphemic habit of Lawrence is his favoring of the "-ness" suffix. A sample of it coming into play is this description of the least appealing of Alvina's suitors, Albert Witham of Oxford: "He was tall and thin and brittle, with a rather dry, flattish face.... His impression was one of uncanny flatness..." (LG 75). When Alvina considers marrying Albert, she thinks how "dishuman" he seems (LG 96); the next time she lays eyes on him, "his dishumanness came over her again like an arrest..." (LG 97). The order is not always predictable—that is, it does not always proceed from adjective ("flattish," "dishuman") to noun ("flatness," "dishumanness"). When another suitor, Mr. May, shrinks from Alvina, the order is inverted and a noun coined in advance: "If he had seen the least sign of coming-on-ness in her, he would have fluttered off in a great dither. Nothing *horrified* him more than a woman who was coming-on towards him" (LG 120; Lawrence's italics). Regardless of order, one recognizes that Lawrence continually reponds to the qualities of things, and abstracts those qualities to create nouns of them. Although Josephine Miles in her *Style and Proportion* has rated Lawrence among the "verbal" as opposed to "nominal" writers (her comparisons made mainly against nineteenth-century stylists), it seems to me that his most striking vocabulary patterns make a nominalizer of him.[10]

Even with concrete nouns in the foreground, one finds Lawrence working toward abstractions derived from them. This passage about "Celts" defines his practice well:

> And perhaps, in the true Celtic imagination slumbers the glamorous king as well. The Celt needs the mystic glow of real kingliness. Hence his loneliness in the democratic world of industry, and his social perversity. (K 68)

While the last fragment is composed only of abstract nouns, a really odd process is at work before this. Note that the general concept "Celtic imagination" hatches a concrete king, and that, as Lawrence envisions a concrete "Celt," he moves to the notion of "kingliness." This requires a two-stage morphemic substitution: first the adjective "kingly" must be fashioned, and to it added the "-ness" suffix customary to Lawrence.

We are really witnessing a double habit of his. While I have not made a quantitative study of Lawrence's adjectives, it is noticeable that he has a predilection for adjectives ending in "y" (themselves noun derived), of which some of the more singular usages follow in italics:

The Lost Girl

a green-white, *mouldy* pony (15)
soft, *drossy* coal (25)
an *airy-fairy* kind of knowledge (56)
the rather *stumbly* railroad (80)
James's *coppery*, *grimy* fingers (125)
Ciccio's *velvety*, suave heaviness (182)
really *toney* women (304)
foot-hills with *twiggy* trees (348)
white-fiery now in the dusk sky (358)
the *sappy*, shut, striped flames (370)

Kangaroo

bushy with stars (10)
a *sheeny* sea-green back (84)
very clean and *steely* (142)
immensely *sniffy* (149)
dozy as ripe pears (151)
queer *glittery* creatures (154)
their *notchy* little trunks (179)
a *slobbery* affair (230)
the *scrappy* amorphousness (353)
rushing, *clayey* water (360)

"Clayey water" may seem about as far as one can go—adding "y" to a long vowel. Yet Somers even describes the ocean as "so very seaey" (K 280). Other oddments include the "green-white, mouldy pony" of *The Lost Girl* reappearing as a "greeny-white pony" in Australia (K 278).

A related way of showing the pervasiveness of nouns is to mention a smattering of noun-derived adverbs. They also mark a double morphemic operation: first an adjective formed from the noun, then an adverb from the adjective. Striking examples include these:

shadowily (LG 26)   hoarily (K 8)
sprightlily (LG 39)   gawkily (K 30)
ghastlily (LG 161)   bushily (K 80)
stonily (LG 201)   fierily (K 123)
slipperily (LG 354)   flirtily (K 278)

If morphemic choices affect patterns of repetition, it is also true, as these later examples suggest, that Lawrence is drawn to certain forms of words even when there is no question of repetition. His attraction to the "-ness" suffix can be borne out by a count of nouns thus formed as distinct from those employing "-ity" suffixes (the other basic way of deriving nouns from adjectives). In *The Lost Girl* there are 252 "-ness" nouns and 175 "-ity" types, the former occurring half again as often, while in *Kangaroo* the "-ness" nouns appear nearly twice as often (390 "-ness" to 229 "-ity"—see table 3.5).

The fact that "-ness" is an Anglo-Saxon form and "-ity" is Latinate goes some way toward explaining Lawrence's preference for the plain rather than learned suffix. Since some adjectives offer a choice between these endings, perhaps some subtler reasons for Lawrence's usages can also be suggested. In summing up the antisocial attitude of the Celt, Lawrence used the word "perversity" (K 68), whereas Alvina's private decision to take up nursing was done out of "curious perverseness" (LG 38). Similarly, as Alvina emerges from the coal mine she is struck by the "luminosity" of the "glossy, svelte world-surface" (LG 57–58)—the word is used three times; at a certain compelling moment between her and Ciccio, however, what strikes her is

Table 3.5   Noun Formations in "-ness" and "-ity"

	Number of "-ness" Nouns	Number of "-ity" Nouns	Ratio of "-ness" to "-ity"
The Lost Girl	252	175	3 : 2
Kangaroo	390	229	2 : 1
Lawrence aggregate	642	404	5 : 3
Howards End	137	169	1 : 1.2
A Passage to India	140	166	1 : 1.2
Forster aggregate	277	335	1 : 1.2
Tarr	273	297	1 : 1.2
Self Condemned	179	352	1 : 2
Lewis aggregate	452	649	2 : 3
Back	19	17	1 : 1
Concluding	52	36	4 : 3
Green aggregate	71	53	5 : 4

NOTE: The sheer number of nouns he uses makes Lewis stand out even more than Lawrence. Both total over 1,000 (whereas Forster, in nearly the same space as Lewis, uses about 600). Forster and Lewis (in *Tarr*) both favor the "-ity" suffix slightly. Lawrence's preference for the "-ness" suffix comes across most strikingly when *Kangaroo* and *Self Condemned* are compared, for there the ratios are inverted! (Green hardly uses abstract nouns, so his totals are of little value in this comparison.)

the "dark luminousness" of his face (LG 324). There is a sense here of something collective having luminosity, of something private and interior giving off luminousness.

In *Kangaroo,* Lawrence displays an intense aversion for "humanity." The word occurs 25 times, in almost every instance pejoratively. We hear of "this lit-up cloy of humanity" (K 137), "this sub-normal slavish humanity" (K 150), "humanity [scratching] its own lice" (K 287), and so on. But, when in a rare moment Somers is refreshed by England (in the "Nightmare" chapter), he locates there "a sweetness and a humanness that he had never known before" (K 256).

I would suggest that the "ity" ending, aside from being Latinate, has a distancing quality about it traceable to another source. The normal multisyllabic adjectives in English are dactylic or trochaic ("lúmĭnoūs," "húmān"). To create nouns of them via the disyllabic Latin ending, one must alter the accent of the stem word, and, as a result, the original sound of the adjective is lost ("lūmĭnósĭty," "hūmánĭty"). This never occurs when the "-ness" ending operates: the "húmān" of "húmānness," the "lúmĭnoūs" of "lúmĭnoūsness," and every other stem of a "-ness" noun retains its sound and structure as an adjective. It is my feeling that this retentive effect is probably the strongest lure to Lawrence as he fashions his nouns. By means of it he can remain in the grip of the felt experience, trying to convey the "whatness" of states that are, to him, deeper than mere personalities.

Once this is sensed, his characters' motivations become somewhat more palpable. When we are informed of the "dishumanness" of Albert, the "coming-on-ness" of Alvina, the "luminousness" of Ciccio, the "kingliness" longed for by the Celt, we are being apprised of factors in their makeup over which they have no control. In Lawrence's responsiveness to such upwellings in people's natures— connected with growth, process, atmosphere, climate, and place—can be found the sources of his pronounced nominalizing habit that works through this one morphemic election.

Perhaps it is no surpirse that the noun of this type that appears most often in the two books is "darkness" (37 times in *The Lost Girl,* 35 in *Kangaroo*). Out of a condition of darkness come most of the triumphs in Lawrence's novels. In *The Lost Girl* the agent of darkness is of course Ciccio, given also the quality of "duskiness" (LG 212, 303), of "remoteness [and] southernness" (LG 235), even (his eyelashes) of "sootiness" (LG 148). Coming under his power, "the loveliness of his passion" (LG 358), Alvina must yield, though "for all her wistfulness and subjectedness" (LG 228) she has periodic recoils, as when we learn that "Somewhere in her soul, she knew the finality of his refusal to hold discussion with a woman" (LG 368). (Note how it is an "-ity" word that initiates a recoil.) In *Kangaroo,* it is withdrawal *back* to darkness that Somers needs to manage. So, for him, the states of "aloneness," "apartness," "separateness" (K 334) need to be maintained against the lures of commitment offered by the busy Australians. To the kingpin Kangaroo, inspirer of the Diggers' movement, Somers says at the novel's first climax that it is against his "ponderousness" that he is reacting, and "against the whole sticky stream of love, and the hateful will-to-love" (K 213). The outburst precipitates Kangaroo's near-attack on Somers. The Australians are that wayward— though their continent is not. Considering all the wilfulness against which Somers is set, it is worthwhile indicating how a subdivision of the "-ness" construction comes into play. It is induced by a "spirit of place" that outlasts human wilfulness: the morphemic resource in this case is the noun formed from the negative adjective that ends in "-less". For Lawrence there are paradoxical positive values to words so formed though lexically they seem to deny value.

Where in *The Lost Girl* such words effect an interaction between Alvina and Ciccio at certain key moments,* in *Kangaroo* the language strains to record not an *effect* of something on Somers, but rather a cosmic sort of non-effect. The constructions approach absolute negativity. Somers leaves wartime England "with a feeling of expressionlessness in his soul" (K 264); he ponders his "friendlessness" as he dissociates himself from Jack Callcott's offer of brotherhood (K 104); on both occasions these feelings are to be judged as good. Later the "innermost symbol" of humanness, for Somers, takes shape as "man: alone in the darkness of the cavern of himself, listening to soundlessness of inflowing fate" (K 287). And one reason he is able to steel himself against the deathbed appeal of Kangaroo is that, just beforehand, the Australian land had communicated to him "the reality of timelessness and nowhere":

> No home, no tea. Insouciant soullessness. Eternal indifference. Perhaps it is only the great pause between carings. But it is only in this pause that one finds the meaninglessness of meanings. Only in this pause that one finds the meaninglessness of meanings, and the other dimension, the reality of timelessness and nowhere. (K 341)

---

*Alvina's sensual breakthroughs are accomplished through Ciccio's shamelessness and recklessness. In her first submission to him, Ciccio "was awful to her, shameless so that she died under his shamelessness, his smiling, progressive shamelessness" (LG 227). In her second, "White, and mute, and motionless, she was taken to her room. And at the back of her mind all the time she wondered at his deliberate recklessness of her" (LG 260). Note that by using the prepostion "of," Lawrence comes close to the original sense of the noun. Another writer probably would have said "recklessness with."

The point remains that all these constructions and the relaxing of the will they endorse are positive in value. They culminate with perhaps the strangest noun formation of all at the end of *Kangaroo* when, along with the "motionlessness" of the Australian bush, Somers perceives its "manlessness." This leads straight to an epiphany, as he discerns "a stillness, and a manlessness, and an elation, the bush flowering at the gates of heaven" (K 362–63).

In keeping with this, it seems proper that Lawrence categorized the quality he distrusted in Australia as "momentaneity." Not that "-ity" words automatically denigrate; that would be expecting a too rigorously disciplined behavior of words. Plenty of combinations rise up in *The Lost Girl* and *Kangaroo* to check such a suspicion:

> Purity and high-mindedness (LG 44)
> dowdiness, obscurity (LG 59)
> liveliness and conviviality (LG 222)
> animosity or coldness (LG 303)
> familiarity and heartiness (K 54)
> sheepishness, stupidity (K 223)
> madness and insanity (K 302)
> their curiosity and their inquisitiveness (K 352)

Heavy concentrations of "-ity" nouns, however, do tend to reveal something. *Kangaroo,* for instance, will in its "preaching" interludes often marshal such nouns; this is the voice of Lawrence, breaking through rather than remaining refracted through Somers. Such an occasion comes up in the tirade against "mate-trust" (in the chapter "Willie Struthers and Kangaroo") and in the digression on mobs (in the chapter called "A Row in Town"). In the latter instance, as Lawrence winds up a ten-page treatise on mobs, it is interesting to watch what happens when he returns to his hero and the actual "row in town." In a peroration of seven brief paragraphs, *Lawrence's* voice produces the following sequence: "relativity," "positivity," "authority," "stability," "surety," "superiority," "nullity" (K 309). Not one "-ness" noun intervenes during this sequence. Lawrence then makes his transition, bringing Somers's name back to prominence: "What Richard wanted was some sort of a new show . . ." (K 309). Here, all in the one paragraph, we discover the following nouns: "dreariness," "highness," "lowness," "weaknesses," "loveableness," and "nothingness" (K 309–10). And not another sign, either here or in the next ten paragraphs, of a noun that ends in "-ity."

There seems to be an opposition here between a dialectical class of words ("positivity," "nullity") and their emotive counterparts ("dreariness," "loveableness"). Has Lawrence been committing an act of cerebration from which he is able to recover only when he returns to Somers's feelings? (Do we rightly recall his dictum to trust the tale and not the teller?) Certainly he seems overly cerebral in his warnings on mate trust:

> Ah no. This individuality which each of us has got and which makes him a wayward, wilful, dangerous, untrustworthy quantity to every other individual, because every individuality is bound to react at some time against every other individuality, without exception—or else lose its own integrity; because of the inevitable necessity of each individual to react away from any other individual, at certain times, human love is truly a relative thing, not an absolute. (K 201)

A sentence like this is almost impossible to read; indeed, Lawrence has lost the thread of it. Here he may be cerebrating at his worst. In *The Lost Girl*, though, he has the ability to show Alvina cerebrating. Now his use of the "-ity" noun becomes judicious (abetted by a rare syntactic balance). He deserves applause on these occasions. Once, when it is Alvina's turn to "react away," she is glad a storm prevents Ciccio from coming to her house: "She was relieved by the intermission of fate, she was thankful for the day of neutrality" (LG 198–99). These clauses are balanced even down to their syllable count, with a neat interchange of short and long nouns at the concluding points. A Johnsonian touch—in Lawrence!—but it mirrors the conscious assuredness felt by Alvina. When she later "reacts away" from the Natcha-Kee-Tawara troupe, we hear the same accents: "She was a spoke to their wheel, a scotch to their facility" (LG 233). In both these sentences the "-ity" noun helps produce a cursus ending (of the 6-2 and 7-2 varieties: see conclusion of chapter two).

Alvina's "assured" feelings are most emphasized right after the "Honourable Engagement" chapter, in which she has become betrothed to Dr. Mitchell. She has gained a full measure of self-respect (a blow to the book's theme of "lostness"), yet is nettled at becoming "pigeonholed" by the engagement.

> In this northern town Alvina found that her individuality really told. . . . And into the bargain she was a personality, a person.
>
> Well and good. She was not going to cheapen herself. . . . [The engagement] cast a slight slur of vulgar familiarity over her. . . . Apart from Dr. Mitchell she had a magic potentiality. Connected with him, she was a known and labelled quantity. (LG 304)

Alvina is celebrating individualism that is ultimately spurious to Lawrence, but, luckily, she is at the brink of a last healthy downward plunge. For the chapter begun by these paragraphs is a raffish one, and saves her. It is called "Allaye Is Also Engaged"; in it Ciccio reappears to reclaim "Allaye" (her troupe name) and recommit her to the pull of downwardness.*

A CONDONING VOICE AND A RAILING VOICE

At the start of this chapter I referred to a stylistic device in *The Lost Girl* not present in *Kangaroo,* and to one given heavy use in *Kangaroo* but used more sparingly in the other novel. For purposes of expediency I shall label these the "preempted question" and the "déjà vu" devices.

While authorial intrusion is common to both novels, the sharp distinction between author and character in *The Lost Girl* and the close identification between them in *Kangaroo* cause intrusions of different sorts. For example, there is a much higher incidence in *The Lost Girl* of the imperative mood, as in the novel's first words: "Take a mining townlet like Woodhouse...." There is also a heavier use of the first-person plural, joining author and reader in the role of alert spectators. (Again from the first page: "Here we are then.... But let us go back a little." The second sentence combines imperative mood and first person plural.) The effect of these asides is to keep the audience informed that a story is in progress. The audience is presumed to be detached and intelligently approachable. Incidentally, over three middle chapters ("Ciccio," "Alvina Becomes Allaye," "The Fall of Manchester House"), all varieties of the editorial "we" drop out, a fact clearly related to the involvement begun between Alvina and Ciccio. There is a 152-page gap (LG 138–290) until, in that mentally conscious chapter "Honourable Engagement," we have this reprise: "For this year of our story is the fatal year 1914" (LG 291).

From the first page of *Kangaroo* we get a different sort of audience involvement, an implicit sort. The first paragraph describes some workingmen of Sydney, who "had that air of owning the city which belongs to a good Australian." The second paragraph gives a related description of the Somers couple: "Well-dressed, and quiet, with that quiet self-possession which is almost unnatural nowadays." In both we find the "déjà vu" construction to which I referred. Comments on "self-possession" or "that air of owning the city" are given as if already assimilated—as if there is a preexistent understanding be-

---

*When Julian Moynahan writes of *The Lost Girl* that it "celebrates the triumph of low-mindedness and attempts to replace the old metaphors of moral strenuousness ... with fresh metaphors of downwardness and underneathness," he is attesting to Lawrence's morphemic standards by his own prose style. (*The Deed of Life* [Princeton, N.J.: Princeton University Press, 1963], p. 122.)

tween narrator and reader that both are knowledgeable (even experienced) about Australia, and already in basic rapport. The effect, found in *The Lost Girl*, of unfolding a narrative to an interested spectator, has been changed, in *Kangaroo*, to the effect of sharing ruminations.

The device in *The Lost Girl* to which I would like to turn is not that of imperative mood or plural pronoun, but is derived from them. It is the odd practice of preempting question marks. Altogether Lawrence creates 34 questions without punctuating them as such. (He almost never does this in *Kangaroo*.) Half of these questions in *The Lost Girl*, like the following, end with exclamation points:

> Iridescent golden—could anything be more fascinating! (LG 57)
>
> There!—why had she not seen it before! (LG 93)
>
> Whatever could she be thinking of herself! (LG 234)
>
> How could a man's movements be so soft and gentle, and yet so inhumanly regardless! (LG 321)

That these seem highly conventional is to the point. They are typical highpoints of any heroine's narrative (only the last is thematic Lawrence). They punctuate a story. When, though, in the other 17 instances, Lawrence deletes the question mark and supplies only a period, he causes the final inflections to be depressed:

> But what is the good of saying acid things to those little fiends and gall-bladders, the colliery children. (LG 15)
>
> But why, once more, drag it out. (LG 21)
>
> To sit still—who knows the long discipline of it, nowadays, as our mothers and grandmothers knew. (LG 51)
>
> What *had* all this to do with her. (LG 86)
>
> Could anything be more *infra dig* than the performing of a set of special actions day in day out, for a life-time, in order to receive some shillings every seventh day. (LG 96)
>
> How could she bear it. (LG 198)

Excepting the last example, these uninflected questions have a distinctly shrugging quality about them (as did the sample given earlier, "but why enumerate"). The narrator's voice, though present, is only making declaratives, offhand categories, of his items. They are only blocking his progress for a moment, he wants to shrug them aside—why drag it out, what *had* it to do with her. The indiscipline of the colliery children, the discipline of our mothers and grandmothers, are taken as a matter of course. (The clustering of these examples toward the front of the book is instructive, as the author leads us around the obvious.) The last example is a striking departure—a moving sentence that, by undercutting the question form, domesticates the unbearable (Alvina's "unbearable feeling" when she is in the throes of love for Ciccio). The last sentence is atypical but still falls within the "preempted" syndrome. The main contrastive feature of all of them (as opposed to trends in *Kangaroo)* is their unpretentious way of engaging the reader. There is no rhetorical question posed to which the reader must address himself. These sentences and also the exclamatory ones are, in the parlance of the theater, "throwaways." There is, consequently, no inveigling of the reader. The effect of the "déjà vu" construction in *Kangaroo* is just the opposite, at least in my judgment.

For there is a subtle upgrading of the reader involved in exposing him to assertions that are esoteric and at the same time assumed to be recognizable. That does amount to a form of inveigling. As Richard Hoggart has said, "The reader may appear to be invited to collaborate by the suggestion that he, like the author, has seen this kind of thing before."[11] Here is a new pitch of didacticism—possibly an unconscious process in Lawrence—that is a means of taking knowledgeability for granted, something that was seldom resorted to in *The Lost Girl.*

Statistically, accounting even for borderline examples, there are no more than 30 "déjà vu" constructions in *The Lost Girl* and at least twice that number in *Kangaroo* (making for one every six pages). The latter reveal a "having weighed" quality that is more insistent than in *The Lost Girl* (see table 3.6). The term "déjà vu" derives from the presence in these sentences of demonstratives without antecedents— most are variants of the "one of those who" and "that [noun] which" constructions. A selective list follows:

    a. "one of those who"

    He was one of the proletariat that has learnt the uselessness of argument. (K 3)

    ... they settled themselves right at the front, in one of those long open second-class coaches with many cane seats and a passage down the middle. (K 71–72)

    Richard Lovat was one of those utterly unsatisfactory creatures who just could not. (K 217)

    He was one of those with the big, heavy legs, heavy thighs and calves that showed even in his trousers. (K 281)

    b. "that ... which" (present tense)

    The persimmons were good big ones, of that lovely suave orange-red colour which is perhaps their chief attraction.... (K 66)

And Somers had that shrinking feeling one has from going to see the doctor. (K 83)

And he moved quickly down the stairs, though still not apparently in flight, but going in that quick, controlled way that acts as a check on an onlooker. (K 215)

So alert and alive and with that loveableness that almost hurts one. (K 281)

c. "that . . . which" (past tense)

[Kangaroo] It was that kangarooish clownishness that made a vicious kind of hate spring into Somers' face. (K 129–30)

[Jack Callcott] He just leaned back and stretched himself in that intense physical way which Somers thought just a trifle less than human. (K 183)

[Willie Struthers] He looked rather shabby, seedy; his clothes had that look as if he had just thrown them on his back, after picking them up off the floor. (K 196)

[the women of Sydney] . . . like madwomen the females, in their quasi-elegance, pranced with that prance of crazy triumph in their own sexual prowess which left little Richard flabbergasted. (K 312)

I broke the categories up for a special reason. My feeling is that tenses do not affect the group (a) examples. The force of generalization seems about the same whether we are apprised of "one of the

Table 3.6   The Déjà Vu Construction

	Number of "Déjà Vu" Items	Number of Pages	Incidence per Page
The Lost Girl	30	372	.081
Kangaroo	67	367	.183
Lawrence aggregate	97	739	.131
Howards End	25	315	.079
A Passage to India	14	300	.047
Forster aggregate	39	615	.063
Tarr	13	291	.045
Self Condemned	18	386	.047
Lewis aggregate	31	677	.046
Back	4	180	.022
Concluding	2	200	.010
Green aggregate	6	380	.016

NOTE: The only outstanding figure here, aside from that for *Kangaroo* (where the device is salient), is that of 25 for *Howards End,* making it comparable to *The Lost Girl.* The authorial intrusion of Forster's narrator seems responsible. As usual, Green eschews the device.

proletariat that has learnt" or "one of those utterly unsatisfactory creatures who just could not." But in the other, more compact "déjà vu" form, the reader is made more of a referee where present tense appears. His corroboration is requested beyond the immediate context. The narrative flow is arrested when one is reminded of the "feeling one has" before seeing the doctor; likewise, the "loveableness that almost hurts one" can make an appeal on its own terms. Statements like these give a kind of world authority to the narrator, and indeed, when extended, begin to sound like Homeric similes (*Kangaroo* by such means does attain to epic sprawl). Conversely, with the past tense, the episode at hand is made more compelling. That is why I have a separate group (*c*). The situations there deal with Australian people who threaten or confuse Somers; the first three involve the important males with whom he comes in contact (identified in brackets). For Jack Callcott alone—who befriends Somers at the start but threatens him virtually throughout—there are reserved seven "déjà vu" constructions. Such accumulation serves to emphasize the need Somers has to characterize his potential foes, even to the point of inventing sobriquets for them ("that kangarooish clownishness"). By use of these tags he retains his authority and superiority in the reader's eye. He can anticipate the recurrence of traits, perhaps even when he cannot cope with them on the spot—in "The Nightmare" he could identify "that instinctive regard and gentleness which he usually got from men who were not German militarist bullies" at a time when, consequent to his military call-up, he had to endure some nasty English bullying (K 218). Meanwhile we get the sense of Lawrence's being caught up with Somers when, no longer stepping from context to philosophize in present tense, he instead fixes his character's memory on "this or that" manifestation given off by the Australians.

In either case Lawrence-Somers keeps command, though, and this need informs the style of *Kangaroo*—except when the god-concealing "outback" interrupts that self-sufficiency. The voice in the novel declaims and "knows" at virtually all other points. It even produces a rare variant of "déjà vu," what I would call a genitive form,* comprising such authoritative plays on words as "his tub of a summerhouse" (K 7), "that sharp weapon of a voice" (K 132), "the great insect of a thing" (K 195), "the little terrier of a sergeant" (K 223), and, appropriately, "that barking white dog of a Richard" (K 359). Lawrence describes whole human movements in similar phraseology: "this sub-normal slavish humanity of democratic antics" (K 150); "the monster of humanity, with a Scylla of an ideal of equality for the head, and a Charybdis of industrialism and possessive conservatism for the

---

*There are 33 of these, as opposed to 22 in *The Lost Girl*.

tail" (K 303). The best indictment of stylistic "knowingness" comes from Lawrence-Somers when we read, "He preached, and the record was taken down for this gramophone of a novel" (K 286).

To conclude our differentiating of the books' styles, I would like to return to those rare fragments of Lawrence that are not noun derived but, rather, verb derived. If the novels' main differences are tonal—*The Lost Girl* revealing a more condoning narrator, *Kangaroo* offering more space for hectoring or railing—it may be of interest to discern whether *Kangaroo*'s higher ratio of verb-derived fragments lends to the distinction.

Earlier I quoted a powerful infinitive fragment that ended a paragraph in *The Lost Girl*, "To go down in the débâcle" (LG 59). The context was Alvina's descent into the mine, noted by some critics as an event almost in violation of the novel's tone, because it evoked such depths. It is provocative to find only four other infinitive fragments in the novel:

> And then to find Miss Pinnegar! (LG 19)

> To sit still, for days, months, and years—perforce to sit still, with some dignity of tranquil bearing. (LG 51)

> Cling like a bat and sway for ever swooning in the draughts of darkness——— (LG 57)

> And then, to be taught to ride a bicycle by Albert Witham! (LG 77)

The exclamation marks indicate ironic shock. Only in the other fragments is Alvina seen in testing circumstances (watching at her mother's deathbed and sensing the lure of the mine). The point is that the sardonic positions she is placed in are much more the rule, whereas Somers, in *Kangaroo,* is consistently tested in depth. Thus the incidence of infinitive fragments rises (because of their irresolution), and these examples typify it:

> To have oneself exultantly ice-cold... and to have all the terrific, icy energy of a fish. To surge with that cold exultance and passion of a sea thing! (K 124)

> Drift, drift into a sort of obscurity, backwards into a nameless past, hoary as the country is hoary. (K 179)

> Just to keep enough grip to run the machinery of the day: and beyond that, to let yourself drift, not to think or strain or make any effort to consciousness whatsoever. (K 185)

> To cut himself finally clear from the last encircling arm of the octopus humanity. To turn to the old dark gods, who had waited so long in the outer dark. (K 271)

There is a sleight of hand operating in these examples (and in the two or three significant ones in *The Lost Girl*). If one thinks of a bat that actually *is* clinging, a fish that *is* surging isolated, a man who *is* drift-ing, one recognizes the essential mundaneness of these states. Law-rence, however, is exhortative, trying to endorse the states passionately, so what is actually passive in them is made a matter of energy because it is kept in potential by the infinitives. Note, too, how an active quality is striven for in subsidiary ways—through reflexives, for instance: "to have oneself," "to let yourself," "to cut himself"—all evocative of decision. Dropping the anterior "to" from the infinitives "cling" and "drift" suggests the quality of finite predicates, yet the structure remains nonfinite.

The same holds for participial fragments. One assumes that the simplest of all ways to concoct sentence fragments would be to supply the participle in place of the verb. Yet only five examples represent the pure form in *The Lost Girl*. Of these, two involve ironic exclama-tions; a third, Alvina's exposure to "slum cases" as a nurse, is serious: "A woman lying on a bare, filthy floor, a few old coats thrown over her, and vermin crawling everywhere, in spite of sanitary inspectors" (LG 41). The other two are run together and generate power, as Alvina leaves her homeland:

> England, beyond the water, rising with ash-grey, corpse-grey cliffs, and streaks of snow on the downs above. England, like a long, ash-grey coffin slowly submerging. (LG 328)

In *Kangaroo* Lawrence uses the same coffin image of English cliffs receding (though not in a fragment). In *The Lost Girl*, for Alvina to become truly lost means being taken to the fastnesses of the Abruzzi. On the way, the sight of England receding delivers a last and pro-tracted wrench: a coffin submerging—and then she is free of it.

In *Kangaroo*, just as with the infinitives, one may equate the far greater incidence of participial fragments with the sense of things being permitted their lingering impact on the protagonist. The bulk of a paragraph given over to the coastal spot Wolloona illustrates the method well:

> On the bay one lone man flinging a line into the water. . . . And many white gannets turning in the air like a snow-storm and plunging down into the water like bombs. And fish leaped in the furry water, as if the wind had turned them upside-down. And the gannets dropping and exploding into the wave, and disappearing. On the sea's horizon, so perfectly clear, a steamer like a beetle walking slowly along. (K 279)

The switch to a full predicate, two sentences from the end, refur-bishes the technique and helps defamiliarize what could become over-familiar. Meanwhile Australian *things* have their day through this "continuous" register of their activity:

And all lying mysteriously within the Australian underdark.... (K 8)

The great sea roaring at one's feet! (K 78)

A huge, brilliant, supernatural rainbow, spanning all Sydney. (K 156)

The old psyche slowly disintegrating. (K 183)

The huge figure, the white face with the two eyes close together, like a spider, approaching with awful stillness. (K 215)

These half-formations have a sense of allure that can swing over to hypnotism when the thing described conveys terror (as in the last instance). Most importantly, the structure predominates at the novel's climax, the end of the chapter entitled "Kangaroo Is Killed." At the hospital Somers has refused the dying leader's plea for a declaration of love. From hospital to zoo he goes, where two actual kangaroos elicit tenderness from him. That same night a full moon takes him to the shore, and, as he has empathized with the nonhuman kangaroos (in defiance of a human plea), so will he empathize with the inanimate. It is thus virtually a two-step climax. A kinship with the beasts makes him acknowledge deeper mystic isolation—or, put more positively, makes him respond to the non-alive—as though animals were intermediaries. They comfort by being acknowledged in similar mute predicaments, but they themselves have to be dispensed with as intermediaries before a final vision can come, a vision of decomposition that is all-consuming and epiphanic. The waves under the moon that bring on this vision are described in the metaphor of radium. I omit the middle paragraph of the three climactic ones, but want to point out that in it, in a sentence fragment, some bush ponies are encountered near the beach: "Only, when he came past the creek on the sands, rough, wild, ponies looking at him, dark figures in the moonlight lifting their heads from the invisible grass of the sand, and waiting for him to come near" (K 348). The first and third paragraphs follow:

A huge but cold passion swinging back and forth. Great waves of radium swooping with a down-curve and rushing up the shore. Then calling themselves back again, retreating to the mass. Then rushing with a venemous radium-burning speed into the body of the land. Then recoiling with a low swish, leaving the flushed sand naked.

Richard rocking with the radium-urgent passion of the night: the huge, desirous swing, the call clamour, the low hiss of retreat. The call, call! And the answerer. Where was his answerer? There was no living answerer. No dark-bodied, warm-bodied answerer. He knew that when he had spoken to the night-half-hidden ponies with their fluffy legs. No animate answer this time. The radium-rocking, wave-knocking night his call and answer both. This God without feet or knees or face. This sluicing, knocking, urging night, heaving like a woman with unspeakable desire, but no woman, no thighs or breast, no body. The moon, the concave mother-of-pearl night, the great radium-swinging, and his little self. The call and the answer, without intermediary. Non-human gods, non-human human beings. (K 348-49)

The first paragraph reenacts the meeting-and-withdrawing pattern that has been in evidence throughout the book. By now withdrawal has become the dominant of the two motifs. Richard, isolated to a "little self," has become a kind of wind harp, allowing a deity to manifest itself in him: something spoken to and through, "The call and answer, without intermediary." What warrents stylistic notice is that the intermediary ponies, which had come to the scene in a fragment the paragraph before, are here referred to in past-perfect tense, their potency taken away: "He knew that when he had spoken a word to the night-half-hidden ponies. . . ." That construction clears the way for the resumption of the participial and other fragments as the nonhuman gods are at last in process of being reached.

Remembering Lawrence as mainly a noun-fragment writer, we may remark in conclusion that *Kangaroo* also surpasses *The Lost Girl* in the other kind of verb-derived fragment, the unattached adverbial clause. An extra word—the subordinate conjunction—is required to make a clausal fragment: these are the only kind that depend on addition rather than deletion or substitution. The difference between this type of fragment and the participial/infinitive type is that those are exhortative and these logical: both extremes being more common to *Kangaroo*. The following examples, however, show that some similarities exist and that a certain drastic tone informs such fragments, especially because they are rare:

> When what was wanted was a Dark Master from the underworld. (LG 58)
>
> Since *willing* won't do it. (LG 73)
>
> Till he could almost touch the bird. (K 84)
>
> If the stillness suddenly broke, and he struck out! (K 215)

Where *Kangaroo* takes a departure is in the area of "because" clauses. They help increase its declamatory tone—only twice in *The Lost Girl* are fragments headed by this word. In *Kangaroo* Lawrence fashions 16 such adverbial fragments, all remarkably similar, as the following samples attest:

> Because Harriet *really* disapproved, and he didn't know what was inside that rose-and-brown-purple cloud of her. (K 185-86)
>
> Because she felt that it was *she* whom these authorities, these English, hated, even more than Somers. (K 242)

Because men were *compelled* into the service of a dead ideal. (K 269)

Because *we* are the second generation, and it was our fathers who had a nice rosy time among the flesh-pots of this newly-glutted globe of ours. (K 290)

The italics in these examples—all Lawrence's—are giveaways, showing how "forcing" he has become. The italics are paralleled by other rhetorical heighteners on other occasions—inversion, for example: "Because, without the polarised God-passion to hold them stable at the centre, break down they would" (K 202); and emphatic verb: "Because in truth he did love the working people, he did know them capable of a great, generous love for one another" (K 204).

Perhaps in this single variant of a sentence fragment Lawrence's didactic purpose can be demonstrated to affect *Kangaroo* more than *The Lost Girl*. If the impact of Australia was meant to appear through the nonfinite verbals, now Lawrence will make the Somerses' beliefs resound through these irrefutable "becauses." After such logical hammering the author's distance from the main character has shrunk to virtual nonexistence.

I would say emotions operate more ventrally in *The Lost Girl*, so that explanations for them need not attempt persuasions that violate grammar. A passage describing the young doctors' pursuit of nurse Alvina illustrates the point: "And so the doctors put their arms round Alvina's waist, because she was plump, and they kissed her face, because the skin was soft" (LG 45). That Lawrence can generate power from conventional sequence like this is attested by a passage from *The Lost Girl* on which I would like to conclude. It describes Alvina's acknowledgment of her love for Ciccio, in the chapter "Alvina Becomes Allaye":

> She locked the door and kneeled down on the floor, bowing down her head to her knees in a paroxysm on the floor. In a paroxysm—because she loved him. She doubled herself up in a paroxysm on her knees on the floor—because she loved him. It was far more like pain, like agony, than like joy. She swayed herself to and fro in a paroxysm of unbearable sensation, because she loved him. (LG 198)

This, I think, is great writing. Her reaction I would call ventral. True, in this passage there is a fragment, but it is a noun-derived fragment endemic to Lawrence, and onto it he has grafted the subordinate: "In a paroxysm—because. . . ." Afterwards there occurs one of the most sensitive modulations to be found in Lawrence, the kind of thing that can rescue repetitive writing and confer on it perhaps inadvertent greatness. It is a shift from the heavy dashes preceding the "because she loved him" clauses to a more domestic comma before the last one.

The comma makes Alvina's sensation of her love simpler at this point, having borne it now for a little, enabling a less stark acceptance of it, even in the midst of her paroxysm.

How accidental was this? Possibly not accidental at all. Any writer knows the value of a dash to heighten an end effect, and Lawrence may have deliberately depressed the effect at this great moment by electing the alternative approach. Only a few pages later, when satire rather than empathy was his aim, he induces a crescendo effect through the opposite movement, from comma to dash: "In truth, Woodhouse was in a fever, for three weeks or more, arranging Alvina's unarrangeable future for her. Offers of charity were innumerable—for three weeks" (LG 215). Thus the fecklessness of Woodhouse is caught through a deliberate heavy emphasis, and the enduring quality of Alvina's love through a deemphasis.

If *The Lost Girl* and *Kangaroo* are pseudo-novels, the latter, being prophetic, has a much greater sense of freightage about it. *The Lost Girl,* by contrast, is more appealing because less stoked up with doctrine. Its false Indians, the Natcha-Kee-Tawaras—creations of a free-wheeling story-teller—strike the reader with greater verve than (to make another comparison) the Indians Lawrence counted so much on for message in that much more "worked up" book, *The Plumed Serpent.* His gift, perhaps, lies best exposed in books where he is least a taskmaster. One thinks of Saul Bellow's judgment, made in an interview, in which he gave real measure to the range in Lawrence by saying, "I take his art seriously, not his doctrine. But he himself warned us repeatedly not to trust the artist. He said trust the work itself. So I have little use for the Lawrence who wrote *The Plumed Serpent* [would Bellow have included *Kangaroo?*] and great admiration for the Lawrence who wrote *The Lost Girl.*"[12]

4 E. M. FORSTER: *HOWARDS END, A PASSAGE TO INDIA*

Aided as he is by the preservative of style . . . his fine distinction will survive some more strident originalities of our day.
AUSTIN WARREN

APHORISMS AND EXEMPLA

Making intrusions into his own works is so recognizable a practice in E. M. Forster that one of his critics, George Thomson, actually characterizes the hero of the Italian novels as the narrator himself.[1] In fact, Thomson holds that Forster does not write novels, but romances. The involvement of the narrator does tend to recede in the later work, but even as Forster's myths deepen in complexity, the governance of his fiction remains tinged with the designs of the romancer.

It makes good sense to approach Forster on these terms, especially in light of Northrop Frye's distinction between romances and novels. In romances a clear attachment is made to protagonists; in novels a scrutiny is made of their character. The former is an introvertive approach, the latter, extrovertive.[2] The voice of the romancer is ready to draw morals, give warnings, and be conscious of peril (a house in *The Longest Journey* is called "Cadover, the perilous house," before any reason for danger is in sight).[3] And of course there is the immanence of allegory in romance, whereby particulars can be equated with ready generalizations. The presence of irony—E. M. Forster is always credited with being ironical—does not disqualify an author from the romance genre, it may only temper somewhat his attachment to his protagonists.

Forster's works move along a scale nevertheless, as Thomson's study implies. *Where Angels Fear to Tread* and *A Room with a View* most nearly qualify as pure romance. The two Cambridge stories, *The Longest Journey* and *Maurice*, might better be labeled quasi-romances, in that the ideal "greenwood," as Forster calls it, remains intact, yet

89

the predicaments of Rickie Elliot and Maurice Hall are to a large degree objectified. Forster may be at his most passionate on behalf of these young men. He understands and defends their pursuing lives without women and without procreation; even so, the pedestrian world remains formidable in these books. An impasse is struck between the Cambridge-bred spirit of uniqueness and the call to order of a society that will not tolerate romance. Finally, there are *Howards End* and *A Passage to India,* where the exigent world is blent with, rather than represented as an alternative to the idealistic. These, in Forster's canon, deserve most nearly the generic term of novel. The "greenwood" sees its last in them. Compared with other modern novels, they do preserve some hallmarks of romance. Thomson does not go wrong in retaining them in that category, for he apprehends the visionary quality that does not desert Forster regardless of how realistic he becomes. But seen alongside Forster's other fiction, they are his genre-pieces—and no less his masterpieces.

Howards End and *Passage* are similar in that each reposes intuitive wisdom in an older woman who disappears from the story before its most significant events take place. Yet Mrs. Wilcox differs from Mrs. Moore in being a "given" character—she is endowed with wisdom that does not undergo "processing." Mrs. Moore's experience of the Marabar Caves unnerves her into self-recognition. It also brings about a sideslip in her personality. She is less stable, and what she knows, she knows less stably, than Mrs. Wilcox. There is a connection between this fact and the fact that Mrs. Wilcox's protégées, Margaret and Helen Schlegel, are more certain of their own means of securing knowledge than are any of their counterparts in *Passage.* These remarks echo a commonplace of E. M. Forster criticism which says that themes unfolded in *Howards End* are more assured than those in *Passage.* What becomes of issue is whether there are stylistic properties that work in anything like a ratio to the assuredness of the one novel and the mystifications of the other.

Through a discussion of some of Forster's romance holdovers, one practice (having to do with compounding) that permits greater intrusiveness to the narrative voice in *Howards End* becomes clear. It leads to the most conspicuous feature of Forster's style, sharing an equal dominance over both novels: his fondness for antithesis. Once this has been examined, some idiosyncrasies are taken up that again point out distinctions. These involve some muted techniques, more to be associated with "novels" than with their romance counterparts.

As for romance, a pair of intrusions reveal a typical Forster mannerism:

> If you think this ridiculous, remember that it is not Margaret who is telling you about it; and let me hasten to add that they were in plenty of time for the train.... (HE 13)

> Visions are supposed to entail profundity, but—— Wait till you get one, dear reader! (PI 203)

Here are interjections making direct assumptions about reader response. They represent the lengths to which Forster will go in buttonholing his audience. Many predictable elements operate here—present tense, vocative mood ("remember," "wait"), and, at varying points, questions, exclamations, Beerbohmisms,[4] and the use of authorial "we." As style-markers these are obvious enough to be hardly worth cataloguing. (In the case of Lawrence, there was reason to point some of them out as affecting the tone of his paragraph endings.)

Out of this intrusive tendency, however, grows a construction that has a pronounced consequential twist to it. In *Howards End,* Forster remarks his grocer's solecism of calling his produce "the best" while arguing that the best cannot be offered at such prices. Of this rationale Forster says,

> It is a flaw inherent in the business mind, and Margaret may do well to be tender to it.... (HE 171)

In *A Passage to India* he makes a similarly pedestrian comment:

> Most of life is so dull that there is nothing to be said about it, and the books and talk that would describe it as interesting are obliged to exaggerate.... (PI 132)

The relationships in these sentences are interesting. The clausal components break down as follows:

> It is a flaw...
> and Margaret may do well to be tender to it.

> Most of life is... dull,
> and the books and talk... are obliged to exaggerate.

From his generalization, Forster moves to a particular adaptation. What is unique is the transitional "and." It enables the initial aphorism to retain its weight. Forster could have subordinated either insight quite simply ("Since it is a flaw, etc.").

A sizable number of his compoundings take the form here illustrated. Their effect is different from Lawrence's "knowing" relative clauses, which record "that prance of crazy triumph" of the Sydney girls or "that kangarooish clownishness" of Ben Cooley. Those expressions assumed an instant familiarity; Forster, on the contrary, is taking pains to be mediate. Like a helpmeet of the reader's, he seems to aphorize in one clause so as to prepare for what might happen in his narrative in the next.

Two variations help him lead up to an action thus to be expressed. He will either (a) reserve separate clauses for the aphorism and the exemplum, or (b) handle them in separate parts of a predicate:

> a. Passion was possible, and he became passionate. (HE 24)
>
> Practical talk was the least painful, and he and McBryde now told her one or two things which they had concealed.... (PI 191)
>
> b. ... his education had been cranky, and had severed him from other boys and men. (HE 100)
>
> ... she was forty years older, and had learnt that Life never gives us what we want at the moment that we consider appropriate. (PI 26)

These beginnings are not too aphoristic, since each bears immediately on a situation. In fact the last sentence delivers its aphorism late (this type, confined to *Passage,* is discussed later). They all do have in common a general condition attributed through an adjective ("painful," "cranky," etc.), followed by an outcome of that condition. (Observe that "thus" could have come after "and" in each second predication.)

One spots the prospect for a considerable leap from aphorism to exemplum if the present tense leads off.

> The problem is too terrific, and they could not even perceive a problem. (HE 94)
>
> There are moments when virtue and wisdom fail us, and one of them came to her at Simpson's in the Strand. (HE 142)
>
> Shrines are fascinating ... and it amused him to note the ritual of the English club, and to caricature it afterwards to his friends. (PI 45)
>
> Facts are facts, and everyone would learn of Mrs Moore's death in the morning. (PI 247)

When I speak of a leap, I mean one from the author's clairvoyance to his characters' fallible positions. In the samples from *Passage,* the characters are in fatuous stances and the narrator's voice is condescending toward them. In the *Howards End* samples the characters are again at a disadvantage (they can't perceive what the author can), but note the sympathy extended in "The problem is too terrific," and the narrator's inclusion of himself in the phrase "when virtue and wisdom fail us." The tone is more truly romancelike in the *Howards End* pair. At the climax of that novel, when Leonard Bast dies of a blow from the flat of a sword, Forster's empathy is clear. Leonard has perceived that, out of squalor, tragedy can sometimes arise, redemptively. Squalor and tragedy "can beckon," Forster says, setting up the potentiality, "and the knowledge of this incredible truth comforted him" (HE 302). In terms of author involvement (a hallmark of romance), it is a long way from the voice that says "facts are facts" in *Passage* to this voice vouchsafing an "incredible truth" to Leonard Bast about the interplay of squalor and tragedy.

The most frequent occasions for romance (at least in inverted form) occur in *A Passage to India* with respect to the Marabar Caves. Forster often uses his general/particular structure to describe them— three times, in fact, as he introduces them in part two. The sentences follow:

> They are like nothing else in the world,
> and a glimpse of them makes the breath catch.
> Nothing, nothing attaches to them,
> and their reputation . . . does not depend upon human speech.
> It is as if . . . the passing birds have taken upon themselves to exclaim "extraordinary,"
> and the word has taken root in the air, and been inhaled by mankind. (PI 123–24)

These statements are filled with awe; in them one detects a difference from the authorial involvement normal to *Howards End.* Here, and in other examples as well, the second clause remains in present tense. The caves are so extraordinary that there is no inclination for the narrator to bring them over into a context; their amazing qualities (or nonqualities) cover all situations. The narrator is not left so awestruck in *Howards End,* where he carries over from even the gravest statements to applications in the novel. "It is impossible to see modern life steadily and see it whole, and she had chosen to see it whole" (HE 152). For this rather famous kernel sentence there is no close counterpart in *A Passage to India.*

Statistically, Forster shows himself much more inclined toward the device in *Howards End,* where it appears twice as frequently. Using a fairly liberal standard—one requiring a sense of consequence in the "and" connective—we discover 120 compound sentences of the type in *Howards End,* 42 in *Passage* (see table 4.1). When Margaret and Helen are not involved, a mild pomposity tends to creep in, helping to account for the preponderance of *Howards End* examples. The Wilcox males in particular are treated with a certain archness, in sentences like these:

> Calligraphy was the item before them now, and on it they turned their well-trained brains. (HE 93)
>
> There was a concourse of males, and Margaret and her companions were hustled out and received into the second car. (HE 198)

The actions of these males are pretty well muffled; more in control of the sentences are the nouns that "group" the men—the "concourse" they get into, the "calligraphy" they face up to. Sometimes their gadgets get so much the better of them that the cause-effect rhetoric is stretched illogically:

> The car came round with the hood up, and again she lost all sense of space. (HE 186)
>
> Then came a difficulty about a spring-board, and soon three people were running backwards and forwards over the meadow.... (HE 203)

In the first instance, it is unclear that Margaret has actually been helped into a car and is being driven somewhere. In the second, a diving board presents a problem, but we do not see men addressing the problem; the prose only has them scurrying about. There has

Table 4.1   Compound Sentences, Aphorism-Exemplum

	Number of Sentences	Number of Pages	Incidence per Page
Howards End	120	315	.381
A Passage to India	42	300	.140
Forster aggregate	162	615	.263
The Lost Girl	8	372	.022
Kangaroo	11	367	.030
Lawrence aggregate	19	739	.026
Tarr	3	291	.010
Self Condemned	8	386	.021
Lewis aggregate	11	677	.016
Back	0	180	.000
Concluding	0	200	.000
Green aggregate	0	380	.000

NOTE: Henry Green does not use the aphoristic compounds at all, and their use by Lawrence and Lewis is negligible. Examples from *Kangaroo* and *Self Condemned* illustrate a lack of urbanity in the technique when it is employed—in these instances, the "exemplum" is an awkwardly phrased negative:

England was still England, and he was not finally afraid. (K 222)

The species "friend" has no exact definitions and René Harding had no other complete friend.... (SC 79)

been no human command over these experiences. In a sentiment close enough to all these others, Forster sums up his indictment of such commercial people and their gadgetry: "We are reverting to the civilization of luggage, and historians of the future will note how the middle classes accreted possessions without taking root in the earth . . ." (HE 141). The narrator of *A Passage to India* has less zeal for making such pronouncements. Hence the constructions are much less conspicuous there.

In one variant of the pattern, though, *Passage* does equal *Howards End* (surpassing it proportionally). This I would call an inductive variant. Both books have eight of these. What happens is that the concrete issue engages the novelist first, after which he is moved to generalize, as in these illustrations from *Passage:*

> . . . he had surmounted obstacles to meet them, and this stimulates a generous mind. (PI 141)

> It challenged a new conviction . . . and new convictions are more sensitive than old. (PI 151)

> They had frightened him permanently, and there are only two reactions against fright. . . . (PI 288)

These all deal with Aziz. The generalizations come as afterthoughts now, in present tense in the final clause. (*Howards End* offers none of this sort.) The narrator is much more caught up with the experiences of his characters, and only afterwards reflects aphoristically—so we might deduce. In a related way, Aziz ponders upon Fielding and his wife when they go out on the lake at Mau at the novel's end. Here it is a compound predicate that develops the late aphorism:

> Those English had improvised something to take the place of oars, and were proceeding in their work of patrolling India. (PI 301)

The overall incidence of examples may be too skimpy for one to claim that Forster shows a more inductive turn of mind in *Passage*. But locally, at least, we can remark the narrator growing sententious *as a result of* a context, rather than preparing the ground for one. This should be kept in mind in the following consideration of Forster's antitheses.

ANTITHESIS

A couple of examples combining the aphoristic technique with antithesis can serve to introduce Forster's most personal literary signature. In these from *Howards End* and *Passage,* the antitheses work in concessive clauses (though this . . . [yet] that).

> The female mind, though cruelly practical in daily life, cannot bear to hear ideas belittled in conversation, *and* Miss Schlegel was asked however she could say such dreadful things. . . . (HE 120)

> The flame that not even beauty can nourish was springing up, *and* though his words were querulous his heart began to glow secretly. (PI 24)

While these sentences open with present-tense maxims, which are then applied to the action, there is one small difference between them. Not surprisingly, the antithesis in the *Howards End* sample occurs in the aphoristic clause ("life" opposed to "conversation"); whereas in *Passage* "words" oppose "heart" in the exemplum clause. The complexity develops prior to the action in the early book, and as part of the narrative in the later.

However, the two novels chiefly reveal similarities when this figure comes under analysis. For it informs the ground style of all of Forster's long fiction.

In order to give proof of the astonishingly versatile dispositions Forster had in his control, it is necessary to supply data for several sorts of antitheses. Rhetorically, there are two broad classes—range antithesis and emphatic antithesis. Syntactically, elements can be opposed at primitive levels, such as the juxtaposition of mere qualifiers. From here a writer can move to phrasal and clausal opposition, and to opposed sentence pairs as well.

The tabulations that follow begin with three syntactic variants, easy to isolate, after which the focus shifts to rhetorical strategy (and the broad classes of range and emphasis).

The simplest antithesis derives from conceding a quality to a thing and then stressing an opposing quality that nevertheless prevails. The trick can be turned adverbially—

> They advanced to the topic again and again, *dully, but with exaltation.* (HE 84)

> And he handed his papers to Amritrao and left, calling from the door *histrionically yet with intense passion,* "Aziz, Aziz—farewell for ever." (PI 219)

—but it is predominantly an adjectival option:

> Mrs Wilcox, that *unquiet yet kindly* ghost, must be left to her own wrong. (HE 27)

> Events succeeded in a *logical, yet senseless,* train. (HE 307)

> The point she made was never the relevant point, her arguments *conclusive but barren.* . . . (PI 79)

They moved out, *subdued yet elated,* Mrs Blakiston in their midst.... (PI 179)

I would only like to mention the statistical occurrence of this variety—32 times in *Howards End,* 20 in *Passage* (see table 4.2)—and pass on to a related form, the concessive clause signaled by "though" or "although." While, normally, such antitheses are not very arresting, those that follow from *Howards End* have an unmistakable Forsterian ring:

... they cared deeply about politics, though not as politicians would have us care.... (HE 28)

... visions do not come when we try, though they may come through trying. (HE 191)

... business men ... saw life more steadily, though with the steadiness of the half-closed eye. (HE 301)

Here again is the intrusive narrator, pushing each statement toward paradox. He has reversed the normal order of concession, and saved the subordinate element to carry the force of the antithesis. But more than this, he has managed three epigrams, because the key word in each affirmed clause is also the word used opposingly in the concessive clause. Different morphemic options permit this action in each

Table 4.2   Antithetical Adjective Pairs

	Number of Occurrences	Number of Pages	Incidence per Page
Howards End	32	315	.102
A Passage to India	20	300	.067
Forster aggregate	52	615	.085
The Lost Girl	32	372	.086
Kangaroo	18	367	.049
Lawrence aggregate	50	739	.068
Tarr	18	291	.062
Self Condemned	17	386	.044
Lewis aggregate	35	677	.052
Back	4	180	.022
Concluding	7	200	.035
Green aggregate	11	380	.029

NOTE: With each author showing fluctuation (and Green again negligible), the only factor of note here comes from the combined results. Forster's 52 adjective pairings surpass Lawrence and Lewis, though each has more pages than Forster. The ultimate significance of this table is that it marks but *one* area of antithesis in which Forster prevails; that he continues to prevail in this area (tables 4.3 and 4.4) becomes the real factor of moment.

case. Politics are affirmed while politicians denied; the intention "to try" dismissed, but "trying" applauded; and the vital "steadily" dissipated to a noun-class modifier, "with the steadiness of." In *A Passage to India* there is only one construction in which a word's class changes across clauses: "India was certainly dim this morning, though seen under the auspices of Indians" (PI 132). Although we are dealing with only a few special instances, the zeal of the *Howards End* narrator again becomes apparent by contrast. Similar emphases attempted in *Passage* avoid such epigrammatic competence:

> ... besides, though Major Callendar always believed the worst of natives, he never believed them when they carried tales about one another. (PI 104–05)

> And the girl's sacrifice ... was rightly rejected, because, though it came from her heart, it did not include her heart. (PI 238)

> Sir Gilbert, though not an enlightened man, held enlightened opinions. (PI 252)

In these, direct repetition is the only enforcer. There is less wit in play. They seem the offspring of the narrator who was disposed to say, "Facts are facts. . . ."

Statistics again show *Howards End* leading—75 "though" constructions to 63 in *Passage* (see table 4.3).

Directly contrasted sentence pairs are also relatively easy to tabu-

Table 4.3   Concessive-Clause Antithesis ("Though"/"Although")

	Number of Antithetical Concessives	Number of Pages	Incidence per Page
Howards End	75	315	.238
A Passage to India	63	300	.210
Forster aggregate	138	615	.224
The Lost Girl	21	372	.056
Kangaroo	15	367	.041
Lawrence aggregate	36	739	.049
Tarr	21	291	.065
Self Condemned	49	386	.127
Lewis aggregate	70	677	.103
Back	16	180	.089
Concluding	17	200	.085
Green aggregate	33	380	.087

NOTE: Here the only moderate "sport" (aside from Forster) is Lewis in *Self Condemned*. Yet Forster doubles Lewis's output there, meanwhile quadrupling the incidence of concessive antitheses in the other novels.

late. A writer disposed to antithetical constructions might be expected to poise sentences against one another. An early example from *Howards End* shows how a point can be thus driven home—here, a fact about Mrs. Wilcox: "High born she might not be. But assuredly she cared about her ancestors, and let them help her" (HE 22).

Some of the tentative force is gained by the inversion of "high born" in the first element. Then, in the second, the weight of the whole declaration pivots on the adverb "assuredly." This brings up a point about *Howards End* juxtapositions in general.

> They were not "English to the backbone," as their aunt had piously asserted. But, *on the other hand*, they were not "Germans of the dreadful sort." (HE 28)
>
> The practical moralist may acquit them absolutely. He who strives to look deeply may acquit them—*almost*. (HE 94)
>
> One little twist, they felt, and the instrument might be in tune. One little strain, and it might be silent *for ever*. (HE 115)

The emphases are made in all three "accomplice" sentences by the adverbials just italicized. The most ingeniously qualified is the second, for there the weak adverb "almost" usurps power from "absolutely" through use of the dash. Still, it is true that the forms of all three are nearly letter-perfect in their duplication of an original syntactic arrangement. The first pits similar quotations against each another; the second supplants "practical moralist" with someone "who strives to look deeply"; and the third invokes point-by-point contrasts till the clinching "for ever." It is in this way that the adverbs get their pace.

These habits hint of something mechanical about *Howards End,* especially early in the book. Portions of other sentence antitheses illustrate this as well:

> ... the native hue of resolution. The pale cast of thought.... (HE 63)
>
> Yesterday.... Today.... (HE 94)
>
> To the Schlegels... he was.... But they to him were.... (HE 116)
>
> Some day.... At present.... (HE 152)

In *A Passage to India,* which again registers lower numerical incidence (32 sentence pairs to 50 in *Howards End*), there is much less syntactic reiteration. Consider the early description of the Indian sky, treated in a pair of sentences that begin and end "By day" / "by night." The first, 30 words long, describes the gradations by which the blue pales to white, orange, even "tenderest purple." Then comes the short antithesis: "But the core of blue persists, and so it is by night" (PI 10). It is not so much the chiasmus "By day" / "by night" that enforces the dominance of blue; more, it is the yielding of a tortuous description of the daytime to the simple "and so it is by night." At times even briefly, what was turgid becomes clear, as in a sentence pair like this one:

> The court, the place of question, awaited her reply. But she could not give it until Aziz entered the place of answer. (PI 222)

The scene is the crucial one at the trial. Adela is about to break through her obsession about Aziz. He will not enter that "place of answer," namely the cave in which she thinks he assaulted her. Consider what would have happened if Forster had inverted the nouns at the very beginning and written, "The place of question, the court, awaited her reply." We would have had full chiasmus, "place of question" as subject anticipating "place of answer" as object in the next sentence. Instead, with the court kept as the ground of the scene, Forster has retained the integrity of the first sentence, by making "place of question" merely a dispensable appositive. Not so its echo: "place of answer" conjures up those caves, and when Adela cannot locate Aziz there, a sudden vision has come to her in the antithesis. Forster has preserved the integrity of that sentence, too, by not mentioning "caves" to offset "court." Adela's psyche cannot realize the rapist in a way that would offset the actuality of the courtroom. ("Place of answer" comes to have no objective correlative, for there *was* no scene of rape.)

One leaves some *Howards End* passages with the impression that the second sentence of an antithetical pair may have already been "set" in the process of writing the first. But in *Passage* the likelihood seems to involve the seizing of a contrary notion suddenly at odds with an utterance that has just been made. Mechanical echoes, even when they do appear to be operating, support no mechanical syntax at all in *Passage:*

> There, games, work, and pleasant society had interwoven, and appeared to be sufficient substructure for a national life. Here all was wire-pulling and fear. (PI 103–04)

> When Aziz arrived, and found that even Islam was idolatrous, he grew scornful, and longed to purify the place, like Alamgir. But soon he didn't mind, like Akbar. (PI 292)

"There" and "here" in the first passage and the late allusions to Moslem rulers in the second appear to "set" these antitheses. But as with the earlier example of the blue of the sky, a turgid syntax is supplanted by something definite and all-inclusive. "All was" takes over from that opening series of nouns that "appeared to be sufficient"; and in the Aziz example, five positive verbs ("arrived," "found," "was," "grew," "longed") suddenly give way to a single negative. What is more, that negative is relaxed by being contracted. *A Passage to India* has many long-short antithetical movements like this; *Howards End* has some. And since I alluded to a certain rigidity early in *Howards End,* it may be well to say that Forster seems to wean himself of such infelicities toward the book's close. *Howards End* may have learned its way, so to speak, into making contrasts that sound less ringing and militant. Over the final twenty pages in which the story is resolved, there are only two antithetical pairs of sentences. They are these:

> One usen't always to see clearly before that time. It was different now. (HE 313)
>
> Logically, they had no right to be alive. One's hope was in the weakness of logic. (HE 316)

These mark the only uses of the impersonal "one" in this novel. By itself it lends a subdued effect. This is furthered by the absence of a connective, and by the homeliness caught through a contraction in one case and a possessive in the other. The accents here are reminiscent of the simplicity of Joyce's prose at the end of "The Dead." Forster's sententious narrator, as the novel sheers away from its past—all that being settled—has, with the slackening of his militance, slackened his rhetoric. The writer of *A Passage to India* may have come to fill his shoes.

In the three forms of antithesis covered so far, the figures for *Howards End* (32-75-50) always have exceeded those for *Passage* (20-63-32), and this will continue as we mention other forms. The total thus far for *Howards End* (157 in 315 pages) represents one usage for every two pages, with *Passage* having something less than that ratio (115 in 300 pages). The categories of range antithesis, emphatic antithesis, and a complex combined form—all now to be dealt with—yield the following figures:

	Howards End	*Passage*
Range antithesis	167	160
Emphatic antithesis	206	190
Complex antithesis	53	38
Subtotal	426	388
Already tabulated	157	115
Total	583 (315 pages)	503 (300 pages)

101

The *Howards End* incidence of 1.85 per page remains slightly higher than that of 1.68 per page in *Passage,* with the similarity rather forcibly evident. There is also the astonishing fact that Forster averages five antithetical devices for every three pages of text in these books (see table 4.4).

A note to make in passing is that the Schlegel sisters (especially Margaret) are given to using such structures in their own writing and speech.* That, I believe, is because Forster is so readily identified with them, whereas, though he sometimes seems near in thought to Fielding in *Passage,* in the long run Fielding is dismissible as Forster's spokesman; neither he nor any other character in *Passage* talks in antitheses like their creator.

The point of course is not to recur to the engaged narrator in *Howards End* and the detached one of *Passage,* but to concentrate on the "why" of antithesis itself.

The device is, in brief, an index of moral clarity. It represents a voice that vigilantly seeks out alternatives and limits, and that will not fail to put the reader in mind of shades of differences. It offers an eternally rebalancing process. As it envisions a quality on one side, it seeks, and expects to find, some counterpart on the other; when it does this it is involved in range antithesis. But when it summons up a contrary quality only to *deny* that quality's force, it is then involved in emphatic antithesis. In either case, it illustrates a thing by its opposite.

William K. Wimsatt illustrates range and emphatic antithesis in his *Prose Style of Samuel Johnson.* He points out that enumerating two properties of a thing can produce "illustrative range"—suggested boundaries within which a thing may be conceived as existing. Quoting a Johnsonian sentence describing "the vehemence of desire which presses through right and wrong to its gratification," Wimsatt indicates how range can extend as well as delimit: "Right and wrong are antithetical, yet here, where both are affirmed in the same respect, their expressive value is that of a pair placed at extremes of range and so emphasizing its length."[5] Range antithesis may set up limits like this (right and wrong) to show that neither applies and both are transcended; it may set up limits in order to focus some third quality

---

*At age thirteen Margaret said to her relatives, "To me one of two things is very clear; either God does not know his own mind about England and Germany, or else these do not know the mind of God" (HE 30). Another time she reminded them of an axiom of her father's, carried from girlhood: "the confidence trick is the work of man, but the want-of-confidence trick is the work of the devil" (HE 41). Or consider her admonition in the letter to her sister: "Don't brood too much on the superiority of the unseen to the seen.... Our business is not to contrast the two, but to reconcile them" (HE 98).

Table 4.4   Incidence of Antithesis (All Forms)

	Number of Antitheses	Number of Pages	Incidence per Page
Howards End	583	315	1.85
A Passage to India	503	300	1.68
Forster aggregate	1,086	615	1.77
The Lost Girl	229	372	.62
Kangaroo	256	367	.70
Lawrence aggregate	485	739	.66
Tarr	200	291	.69
Self Condemned	352	386	.91
Lewis aggregate	552	677	.82
Back	92	180	.51
Concluding	129	200	.65
Green aggregate	221	380	.58

NOTE: Besides the overwhelmingly higher incidence of antithesis in Forster, there is also near-parity between *Passage* and *Howards End* (as there is between the other authors' novels). Forster's habitual double perspective seems to make the others sound different from him even when they use antitheses. Of all the other novels, it is in *Tarr*, I would say, that Forsterian accents are sometimes heard. I suspect this is true because of the artist-activist conflict that is at the heart of *Tarr*.

midway between the extremes; or it may illustrate that while one thing approaches one limit its opposite nears another. Pope's couplet about those who scorn crowds ("if the throng / By chance go right, they purposely go wrong")[6] is a good example of range antithesis, whereby two affirmations are made. Here the several counters (crowd/individual: by chance/purposely) of one category are set up against those of the other and the crowd and the individual are mutually illuminated. Emphatic antithesis, on the other hand, would tend to represent something as "not right, but wrong," whereby nothing that was "right" would be affirmed.

Forster is found often enough using range and emphasis in a single sentence. Portions of two sentences from *Howards End* and *Passage* show range antithesis commencing the ideas—

He thought Helen wrong and Margaret right.... (HE 260)

Fielding saw that something had gone wrong, and equally that it had come right.... (PI 66)

—but just where these portions stop Forster continues; pivoting each sentence around "but," he persuades that the right and the wrong are immaterial, so that an emphatic antithesis results:

103

He thought Helen wrong / and Margaret right, // but the family trouble was for him what a scene behind footlights is for most people.

Fielding saw ... wrong, / and ... right, // but he didn't fidget, being an optimist where personal relations were concerned. . . .

Here are two other specimens (there are almost a hundred in all) showing Forster's readiness to devise complex antitheses out of variant patterns:

If he was a fortress / she was a mountain peak, whom all might tread, / but whom the snows made nightly virginal. (HE 172)

There was the problem of [Godbole's] food, / and of ... Godbole and other people's food—two problems, / not one problem. (PI 127)

Complex antitheses are discussed more fully later; the categories of emphasis and range need to be pursued here, because Forster's practice in the second of these does show variance that can be related to divergent themes in *Passage*. In both novels, emphatic antithesis helps Forster align his *dramatis personae* with assurance.

[Mrs. Wilcox] She seemed to belong not to the young people and their motor, but to the house, and to the tree that overshadowed it. (HE 22)

[Helen] The truth was that she had fallen in love, not with an individual, but with a family. (HE 23)

[Margaret] Margaret hoped that for the future she would be less cautious, not more cautious, than she had been in the past. (HE 102)

[Leonard] Leonard seemed not a man, but a cause. (HE 290)

[Fielding] He had no racial feeling—not because he was superior to his brother civilians, but because he had matured in a different atmosphere. . . . (PI 62)

[Adela] ... she was no longer examining life, but being examined by it; she had become a real person. (PI 238)

[Ralph] Hastily [Aziz] pulled away, feeling that his companion was not so much a visitor as a guide. (PI 308)

[Stella] He could assure Aziz that Stella was not only faithful to him, but likely to become more so. . . . (PI 314)

There is an element of definition in all of these; and, through this emphatic form, concepts may be clarified as well. Witness the definitions of "cynicism" and "regret" in the novels:

Cynicism—not the superficial cynicism that snarls and sneers, but the cynicism that can go with courtesy and tenderness. . . . (HE 89)

One touch of regret—not the canny substitute but the true regret from the heart. . . . (PI 50)

Logic, we are made to feel, is at work at high intensity. So of this form
of antithesis we may say that it spots Forster at his most didactic.

Less so with range antithesis. Sometimes this serves as a simple
scanning device. Forster pretends that Jacky, mistress of Leonard
Bast, poses a problem in description. "As for her hair ... one system
went down her back, lying in a thick pad there, while another, created
for a higher destiny, rippled around her forehead" (HE 49). Here we
have standard illustrative range (in each clause, participial and prepositional phrases are "ranged" against their counterparts). Leonard's
options after marriage are similarly bracketed off: "He could not
leave his wife, and he did not want to hit her" (HE 116). And the same
is true for the London that contains Leonard and Jacky: "Electric
lights sizzled and jagged in the main thoroughfares, gas-lamps in the
side streets glimmered a canary gold or green" (HE 115).

All this makes for a very neat moral and physical geography.
Practices in *A Passage to India* do not match it, and nothing so easily
capturable emerges from descriptions like "houses trees, houses
trees" (PI 35) or "Mosque, caves, mosque, caves" (PI 306). These are
examples of illustrative range that fail to suggest any complacency at
all. The hodgepodge grows in *Passage* as the following question gets
answered:

> Where was the procession going? To friends, to enemies, to Aziz's
> bungalow, to the Collector's bungalow, to the Minto hospital where the
> Civil Surgeon would eat dust and the patients (confused with prisoners)
> be released, to Delhi, Simla. (PI 227)

The element about the Minto hospital is deceptive in that it has no foil
like the others in the series, yet its "where" clause has an interior
duality of its own (surgeon: patients). Here is the kind of
displacement-within-formula that is characteristic of the prose of *A
Passage to India*. It testifies to the great strains posed by that novel, but
also to a resourcefulness in Forster that is equal to them—the strug-
gling up of formlessness, of "a hundred Indias" threatening to
occlude vision, and the capacity of prose to retain semblances of favored forms, the writer's voice still remaining audible.

The theme and epigraph of *Howards End*, "Only connect," assumes polarities that have a way of guarding their separate integrities.
That is probably the reason for the novel's many range antitheses,
which rate things in pairs and keep placing them at odds. It is over-
simplifying to say that Forster wishes a triumph of one set of qualities
(let us say, humane) over another (imperial). For what he openly
champions, through Margaret and her liaison with Wilcox, is a connection and a blending—a choice *now* of poetry, *now* of prose—a
fluctuation that wisely continues, to the benefit of both. As Margaret

says, "Our business is . . . to reconcile." (Conversely, in the Hindu world of *Passage,* great achievements come *against* the pressure of fluctuation.)

It is true that sometimes the antinomies seem too fixed in *Howards End,* the dialectic set down in ironclad terms. As a result some readers mistake aversions in *Howards End* for intransigence. Syntax does not allow for much connection in statements like these:

> They were—she saw it clearly—Journalism; her father, with all his defects and wrong-headedness, had been Literature. . . . (HE 60)

> It was . . . the good, the beautiful, the true, as opposed to the respectable, the pretty, the adequate. (HE 160)

The Schlegel sisters often measure off distinctions as firmly as this; yet when Forster once went to a limit with one of them—the time he said Margaret chose to see life whole (not steadily)—he went too far. For Margaret's actions belie the firmness of her choice, and like Mrs. Wilcox before her she can sometimes follow a prosaic line and set aside the demands of wholeness. The best precedent for the prosaic occurs at the King's Cross station when Mrs. Wilcox accidentally meets her husband and daughter and reneges on her invitation to Margaret to accompany her to Howards End. Forster had praised Margaret's belated acceptance of the invitation—"But imagination triumphed"— only to write on the same page, a few lines down, "Before imagination could triumph, there were cries of 'Mother! mother!' and a heavy-browed girl darted out of the cloakroom . . ." (HE 82). This represents Margaret's last chance of becoming intimate with Mrs. Wilcox, but the older woman has all the same "connected," because she proves as able to respond to the prosaic demands of her family as she is to the "poetry" of her house. Later Margaret matches Mrs. Wilcox in this ability, choosing to remain at her aunt's house (prose) instead of visiting Howards End with her fiancé, Henry, all because her aunt's feelings would be hurt if Margaret suddenly curtailed the traditional visit. ·

Thus is the spirit of connection fostered in *Howards End,* though the actual management of "connection" proves difficult. Stylistically, to implement this management a sort of range antithesis is called into play that either attempts a compromise between polarities or indicates that extremities are not to be depended upon for solutions—not even the extremity of "seeing life whole."

The following propositions from *Howards End* illustrate the second of these gambits:

> To the insular cynic and the insular moralist [the chance collisions of human beings] offer an equal opportunity [for sneering]. (HE 25)

> The business man who assumes that this life is everything, and the mystic who asserts that it is nothing, fail, on this side and on that, to hit the truth. (HE 182)

> We are evolving, in ways that Science cannot measure, to ends that Theology dares not contemplate. (HE 225)

Where two of the antithetical statements have a context to help show their application, the last does not. It gives a good example of *Howards End*'s optimism, through an axiom that finds both the material and spiritual methods of approach wanting. Syntactically it is splendidly early-Forsterian, with the predicate "are evolving" modified twice by phrases identical in pattern: "in ways that," "to ends that. . . ." The earlier antitheses are making the same thematic statements. The "insular cynic" (that is, scientist) and "insular moralist" (religionist) both go wrong in making easy assumptions about human emotional contact; the businessman and the mystic equally fail when they measure according to their preconceptions. That assertion leads to one of the great thematic utterances in *Howards End,* which is that truth is to be found "by continuous excursions into either realm, and though proportion is the final secret, to espouse it at the outset is to insure sterility" (HE 182). This last is true because proportion cannot be secured without the testing of experience; it is not as though it can be charted mathematically.

In the novel, Henry Wilcox is the businessman, Helen Schlegel the mystic, and Margaret the connector. "How wide the gulf between Henry as he was and Henry as Helen thought he ought to be! And she herself—hovering as usual between the two, now accepting men as they are, now yearning with her sister for Truth" (HE 215). Where the first of these sentences places Henry and Helen apart in basic range antithesis, the second sets them as shuttle points between which Margaret vacillates. This is the sort of antithesis that *Howards End* upholds as a thematic motif—an embracing of two extremes made possible be intermittent excursion from the claims of one to the claims of the other. Neither is wholly cancelled, neither becomes ultimately ascendant. The novel's solution in this respect is different, as we shall see, from solutions offered by *A Passage to India.*

Tenderness—D. H. Lawrence's word—is what can weld the antinomies in *Howards End,* and help build

> the rainbow bridge that should connect the prose in us with the passion. Without it we are meaningless fragments, half monks, half beasts, unconnected arches that have never joined into a man. With it love is born, and alights on the highest curve, glowing against the grey, sober against the fire. (HE 174)

107

"Without it," "with it"—so range the sentences, with the final pair of images even affecting that rainbow, making the everyday "glowing" and the passionate "sober." Lacking tenderness, men are ranged into partitions, "half monks, half beasts." (Later Forster reaffirms "the tenderness that kills the Monk and the Beast at a single blow" [HE 205].) Since *Howards End* is a novel about place, it is out at the house, shadowed by the English wych-elm, where the connection is built—by means of the "comradeship, not passionate, that is our highest gift as a nation . . ." (HE 250). In a series of antitheses, the author announces his faith in this comradeship, house-and-tree fostered. (The paean is totally different from the "houses trees" interchanges of *Passage*.) First Forster tells what the wych-elm is not.

> It was neither warrior, nor lover, nor god; in none of these rôles do the English excel. It was a comrade, bending over the house, strength and adventure in its roots, but in its utmost fingers tenderness. . . . (HE 192)

Having established its consanguinity with the house, Forster produces another emphatic pairing, insisting that house and elm remain within human scope:

> House and tree transcended any similes of sex. . . . Yet they kept within limits of the human. (HE 192)

If one recalls, from the previous chapter, Lawrence meditating about "sex in trees" or being driven by the call-and-answer of "non-human gods," one will see that in *Howards End* Forster is distinguishing an altogether more accountable tenderness (and here is one reason Lawrence is a nonantithetical stylist; Forster appeals to a more temperate sort of composure). At last, ending this section that condenses all the optimism of his novel, Forster produces first an emphatic, then a range construction:

> Their message was not of eternity, but of hope on this side of the grave. As [Margaret] stood in the one, gazing at the other, truer relationship had gleamed. (HE 192–93)

The house here can be connected with shelter and the flesh, the tree with exposure and the spirit. And the house is *made from* the tree.[7] Like the hay that lives since it is past dying—a symbol well detected by George Thomson[8]—so the house is in the state of being past dying: a reservoir, while the tree is in the dying state. Their differentness as well as their comradeship is finally extolled by Forster. On the night spent at Howards End by the Schlegel girls, he emphasizes how the "house had enshadowed the tree at first, but as the moon rose higher the two disentangled, and were clear for a few moments at midnight" (HE 293). This differentness is anticipated a page before by Margaret, who says of Mrs. Wilcox, "She is the house, and the tree that leans over it. People have their own deaths as well as their own lives, and even if there is nothing beyond death, we shall differ in our nothingness" (HE 292).

Here *Howards End* records the deepest imprint death makes on Forster's mind: that with death something unique leaves the earth. On this side of the grave, a loyalty to what has gone can be forged by this fact; yet it is a remorseless fact. Mrs. Wilcox, who is both house and tree, is the preserving house because she has exhibited the retentiveness owed to the dead, to ancestors, to death itself—the knowledge of the irreplaceableness of the unique. As the tree, she is herself both unique and uniquely lost. The passage describing her own manner of death is probably the greatest in the novel, certainly from the stylistic point of view, and reflects Forster's feelings about death and the unique personality. It is a gloss, in fact, upon Helen's insight (which came from Michelangelo): "Death destroys a man: the idea of Death saves him" (HE 223).

In this paragraph, aside from its opening and one short medial ("She had kept proportion") every sentence is antithetical in some way. It begins with Margaret's musing on the impact of Paul Wilcox and the larger impact of his mother, and goes on to evaluate Mrs. Wilcox's way of dying.

> She was parting from these Wilcoxes for the second time. Paul and his mother, ripple and great wave, had flowed into her life and ebbed out of it for ever. The ripple had left no trace behind: the wave had strewn at her feet fragments torn from the unknown. A curious seeker, she stood for a while at the verge of the sea that tells so little, but tells a little, and watched the outgoing of this last tremendous tide. Her friend had vanished in agony, but not, she believed, in degradation. Her withdrawal had hinted at other things besides disease and pain. Some leave our life with tears, others with an insane frigidity; Mrs Wilcox had taken the middle course, which only rarer natures can pursue. She had kept proportion. She had told a little of her grim secret to her friends, but not too much; she had shut up her heart—almost, but not entirely. It is thus, if there is any rule, that we ought to die—neither as victim nor as fanatic, but as the seafarer who can greet with an equal eye the deep that he is entering, and the shore that he must leave. (HE 97)

No paragraph in Forster better reveals his way of assaying his thoughts by ranging for boundaries to frame them. In passing over the early portion we may note one odd reversal of an emphatic structure. Margaret thinks of the sea (death) "that tells so little, but tells a little." Usually "but" will diminish the first half, and strengthen the second, of an antithesis. Yet here the power remains in the earlier "tells so little." It is a way of admitting how, to the survivor, only a glimmer is afforded of death's import and what it meant to the dying one. The paragraph is not truly consolatory. Of the three long sentences ending it, the first and last may be classed as the "pivotal" kind: they range to extremes that do not yield wisdom, and then express a middle course that does. Both sentences carry overtones of the futile positions, sentimental and scientific, that were discussed earlier. ("Some leave ... with tears, others with ... frigidity"; "we ought to die—neither as victim nor fanatic.") The richest sentence is the next-to-last, a sentence of "connection." Two emphatic antitheses produce a range of their own. Against the first disclosure about Mrs. Wilcox ("She had told a little ... but not too much") is ranged the obverse ("she had shut up her heart ... but not entirely"). One movement of her nature attests the uniqueness of death (calling for the tight-lipped attitude); the next attests its universality (calling for openness). With the pairing we have Forster's accolade for Mrs. Wilcox, who is faithful to self and others in the process of dying: "She had kept proportion."

The resolutions in *Passage* that are managed by way of range antithesis do not rely on the kind of shuttling, proportion-keeping, espoused in *Howards End*.[9] The reason is that the boundaries normally workable for range have opened out too far. To compare Forster's distaste for motor cars is enlightening here. He may make them ludicrous in *Howards End*, or even pernicious, but in *Passage* they are merely petty. The accident on the Marabar road causes the English passengers to inspect their tire tracks. "Steady and smooth ran the marks of the car," writes Forster, "... then all went mad" (PI 87). Such range antithesis shows what India can do. The opposition is not between steady and whole, but between steady and mad.

In India, when a situation *is* resolved, the solution does not stabilize gradually across a pivot. Rather, the effect is meteoric—complete—and then the moment dissolves.

Fortunately, within the Hindu conspectus of the book, salvaging can come right out of the chaotic upheavals themselves. At the trial of Aziz we have the saving moment conveyed through the theme word itself—a "complete" antithesis, Forster calls it. Typical of resolutions in *Passage*, it has been led to by a recantation. In a sort of trance, Adela admits that Aziz could not have come into the cave, and Fielding sees that his friend is saved. Forster then writes,

> Here were the English, whom their servants protected, there Aziz fainted in Hamidullah's arms. Victory on this side, defeat on that—complete for one moment was the antithesis. (PI 224)

But the crux lies in what he is obliged to write next: "Then life returned to its complexities, person after person struggled out of the room . . . and before long no one remained on the scene of the fantasy but the beautiful naked god [the punkah wallah]."

Now, happy people "struggle"—as opposed, in the suspended moment, to the defeated parties being "protected"—such is the shift of mood away from the perfect and complete.

In the Hindu version of things, the advent of good (tantamount to the awakening of the dormant god) is felt in a pulsive way, and, as Godbole explains, all partake of that good. Thus antitheses like the last can only be captured entire—no shuttling possible or desirable— after which such moments recede. Several examples of this kind occur during the Hindu festival in the "Temple" section. The "Complete-ness, not reconstruction" (an emphatic fragment) resultant from Godbole's dance, when he impels the images of Mrs. Moore and the wasp to the realm of God as it were, sets up a whole series of them. A page later, "All sorrow was annihilated, not only for Indians, but for foreigners, birds, caves, railways, and the stars . . ." (PI 283). Likewise, in the cavorting at the palace, "All spirit as well as all matter" (inclusive terms) "must participate in salvation . . . [or else] the circle is incom-plete" (PI 284). At the climax of the procession, when the boats of the non-Hindus collide on the lake, Forster again insists on this com-pleteness, but, importantly, will not recapitulate it. "Whatever had happened had happened, and while the intruders picked themselves up, the crowds of Hindus began a desultory move back into the town" (PI 310).*

Characteristically, low moments ("desultory," and so on) succeed the highs; as for those highs, the prose will either act as described above, or it will go further through a paradoxical *cancelling* of an-tithetical pairs. The achievement of a "passage" itself (when "emblems of passage" are thrown, at the time of the boats' collision) is reported through multiplied negatives, the ultimate recourse for the writer driven to paradox: "a passage not easy, not now, not here, not to be apprehended except when it is unattainable . . ." (PI 309).[10] Through this strategy Forster attains two goals. He keeps ineffable experience inchoate; he also reverses the nihilistic paradoxes of "Caves"— summed up in Mrs. Moore's terrific visions—with benedictions that are managed *through the same structures.* For those antivisions had also depended upon cancellations of conflicting ideas. From the start of the ill-fated journey to the caves, all the way through the late reflec-tions of Mrs. Moore on her experience, doubled negatives (or the negating "boum") equate extremes to evoke the spiritual abyss. Note

---

*This sentence echoes the dispersion at the end of the trial, right after the novel's situational climax. It also anticipates the conclusion of the story, where we are told, "The divisions of daily life were returning, the shrine had almost shut" (PI 316).

how every one of the following structures collapses a once-valid set of antitheses:

> Nothing was explained, and yet there was no romance. (PI 139)
>
> If one had spoken vileness in that place, or quoted lofty poetry, the comment would have been the same—"ou-boum." (PI 147)
>
> ... all its divine words from "Let there be Light" to "It is finished" only amounted to "boum." (PI 148)
>
> But in the twilight of the double vision ... we can neither act nor refrain from action, we can neither ignore nor respect Infinity. (PI 203)
>
> The unspeakable attempt presented itself to her as love: in a cave, in a church—Boum, it amounts to the same. (PI 203)

There is strict employment of range antithesis in each of these, stretching the bearing of meaning (as Johnson did the meaning of right and wrong) until self-cancellations occur and no meanings or antithetical pairs exist.

However, in "Mosque" and "Temple"—"Mosque" tentatively and "Temple" triumphantly—this "muddledom" is obliterated and mercurial good replaces it. We have seen how this could be expressed in "Temple," through something that could be completed though not reconstructed. It resists being sought, as well. In the "Mosque" section there are foreshadowings of possible fields for harmony. (Since the harmony cannot be willed, the potentialities are handled by way of negatives.) One has to do with Aziz, of whose personality Forster writes,

> Nothing stayed, nothing passed that did not return; the circulation was ceaseless and kept him young, and he mourned his wife the more sincerely because he mourned her seldom. (PI 55)

The first paradox here lays the ground for the second. Nothing stays to "fix" Aziz's personality, yet everything does return. Thus his mourning of his wife is freshened and made sincere by the surprisingness (yet sureness) of its return. While Aziz's character is expressed here, there is also an ingredient present that defeats echo, which is the same as defeating the negative message of the caves. Aziz does not fall into a false echoing bewailment of his loss. Another key sentence from "Mosque," employing a pair of quiet negatives, offers the best early instance of this positive motif. It ends the scene of the discordant tea party at Fielding's house, when Godbole sings his inconsequential song. The sentence may seem to use simple illustrative range ("No ripple disturbed the water, no leaf stirred" [PI 78]), yet it marks the defeat of echo. Just before it, "Ronny's steps had died away, and there was a moment of absolute silence." The god invoked in the song does not come—Godbole is serene about that—yet complete silence, non-reverberation, signals a moment of perfection. Discord has "died away" and a field has replaced it—perhaps the first of the novel's sanctified moments.

On occasions like these, either personal or universal, the key element is a lack of will or wish. A sort of washover of good invests things, and resolutions do not come through dialectical struggle but rather through its lapse. (There is the paradox.) In *Howards End,* where the will is never abrogated, any perception of ultimate good lying outside the pale of immediate concern is achieved always through logical antithesis. There are two moments when a technique alien to *Passage* dominates. By citing these we may end on a note that again underlines difference. Leonard Bast, just before his death, and Margaret Schlegel, just after that death, are accorded visions of greater good in the midst of their entrapment in present evil.

> To Leonard, intent on his private sin, there came the conviction of innate goodness elsewhere. (HE 301)

> As a prisoner looks up and sees stars beckoning, so [Margaret], from the turmoil and horror of those days, caught glimpses of the diviner wheels. (HE 307)

Such statements reveal the essence of Western tragic art, in that the predicament of the sinner/prisoner is not cancelled. Forster said of Leonard's peace that it "arose from his sorrow" (HE 302). Such insights depend on unexpunged evil to give glimpses of good and grounds for provisional hope. *Howards End* is more pessimistic than *Passage.* The triumphs of the latter are less logical, as they are less Western. Evil is ravished away at blinding, or even quiet, pulse moments, moments such as those attesting that "the Lord of the Universe . . . transcends human processes. He is, was not, is not, was" (PI 279). The sentence strategies for these ineffable disclosures still juxtapose opposites, but the strain of logic will not bear the brunt, and the moments that save, redeeming India and Forster's book, are those that cannot be seen into, or held past the instant.

Of Forster's writing, it can be said that the pressure of the alternative, of the not-present, which informs this manner of seeing, makes for a syntactic vocabulary especially his. Just as any writer is the stronger for his command of words, so one might be the stronger for suppleness of relation-perception. One thinks in broad metaphors to account for this kind of writing—metaphors of complex games, or perhaps of the conduct of battle. Take the game of polo: Aziz going onto the Maidan to practice a bit: "He could not play, but his pony could. . . ." A subaltern turns up. "The new-comer had some notion of

113

what to do, but his horse had none, and the forces were equal" (PI 57). And so, as incremental possibilities arrive, this kind of writer moves along with a premonition of structure ahead. Presences become defined by absences: what emerges is a way of overviewing, an "epistemic choice," if you like. It certainly stands Forster to the good. His vision seems to thrive on perceptions that grasp from the start that they are but the first half of something about to receive its fuller shape.*

POSITIVE AND CASUAL NEGATION

Within Forster's sentences, his practices in the actual forming of negations cast special light on his novelistic style. As my foregoing section has implied, an enormous number of negative statements show up in his pages. The epistemic condition of such a writer finds him counting on what is not true about a situation, not present, not applicable. So alert is Forster to negative tendency that he compensates when an issue for some reason appears questionable. He does this by using emphatic modal verbs, as in the first paragraph of *Passage*, where he says, "Houses do fall ... but the general outline of the town persists" (PI 9), or in the final description of Aziz in action, where we are told, "His horse did rear" (PI 316). It is as if we were not to expect such things. Many of his transitions are like the following:

> Just as this thought entered Margaret's brain, Mr Wilcox did ask her to be his wife. . . . (HE 154)
>
> Yet he did alter her character—a little. (HE 164)
>
> Paul did send a cablegram. (HE 240)
>
> It does make a difference in a relationship—beauty, thick hair, a fine skin. (PI 151)
>
> Miss Quested did pull him up short. (PI 176)
>
> . . . he always did possess the knack of slipping off. (PI 188)

The last example here, referring to Professor Godbole, gives mild emphasis to a chapter's conclusion, a device an experienced novelist sometimes avails himself of (see table 4.5 and note). But table 4.5

---

*Even when Forster's vision is ultimately foiled, it will probably have had such an origin. Of his abortive novel *Arctic Summer* he was able to say, "I had got my antithesis right. The antithesis between the civilized man, who hopes for an Arctic Summer, and the heroic man who rides into the sea. But I had not settled what was going to happen. . . ." (John Colmer, *E. M. Forster: The Personal Voice* [London: Routledge and Kegan Paul, 1975], p. 113.)

Table 4.5   Incidence of Positive Modal Verbs ("Do"/"Did")

	Number of Emphatic Modals	Number of Pages	Incidence per Page
Howards End	27	315	.086
A Passage to India	38	300	.127
Forster aggregate	65	615	.106
The Lost Girl	4	372	.011
Kangaroo	16	367	.044
Lawrence aggregate	20	739	.027
Tarr	4	291	.014
Self Condemned	20	386	.052
Lewis aggregate	24	677	.035
Back	13	180	.072
Concluding	5	200	.025
Green aggregate	18	380	.047

NOTE: As was said, the emphatic modal can provide a novelist with a way to end a chapter, especially when he wishes to leave a sense of irresolution in the air. Here are examples of such chapter-endings from *Kangaroo, Self Condemned,* and *Back:*

Yet Jack did want to get at him, somehow or other. (K 34)

Even more than herself René was shocked; and something did find its way into his manner of thinking which was insane. (SC 304)

But he did feel somehow ashamed. (B 176)

illustrates that affirmative uses of "do"-verbs occur more often in Forster's novels than in the others', a tendency I associate with his feeling for what might not, after all, follow.

The section on antithesis demonstrated that portions of sentences were in contention, illustrating what was there by what was not. Simple negation, of course, is more the rule. Even here Forster remains separated from the other writers, and for two reasons. Quantitatively, he makes more negative statements; he also has a way of making them strenuously, employing what I shall call "positive negation" to a greater degree than the others. Tables 4.6 and 4.7 together illustrate why *Passage* in particular is radical; the first compares sheer incidence, and the second, emphatic or "positive" forms of negation—the more important category.

There are two ways to negate statements, the more usual being adverbial, the other, pronominal-adjectival. The following are standard examples of possible options:

He *did not give* anything away. (adverbial)

He gave *nothing* away. (pronominal)

Table 4.6   Incidence of Negations (All Forms)

	Number of Negative Statements	Number of Pages	Incidence per Page
Howards End	830	315	2.63
A Passage to India	875	300	2.92
Forster aggregate	1,705	615	2.77
The Lost Girl	920	372	2.47
Kangaroo	1,000	367	2.72
Lawrence aggregate	1,920	739	2.60
Tarr	738	291	2.54
Self Condemned	1,025	386	2.66
Lewis aggregate	1,763	677	2.60
Back	510	180	2.83
Concluding	451	200	2.25
Green aggregate	961	380	2.53

NOTE: The only items omitted from this table are "neither/nor" combinations and a few partial constructions (such as negative infinitives). The count represents all fully negated statements.

Forster's totals are not strikingly superior to the others in the matter of negations. Nor can much disparity be seen in any writer's practice, except that *Back* rivals *Passage* for highest single incidence. (That could be because *Back*'s stunned hero is neutralized by recurrent statements like "He did not dare go near" [B 62].) Table 4.7 shows an added idiosyncrasy, distinguishing Forster more firmly as a negator.

> He *would not commit* any money to the enterprise. (adverbial)
>
> He would commit *no* money to the enterprise. (adjectival)

What happens in the one class of examples, of course, is that the predicate is negated in a standard way, through an auxiliary plus the adverb "not." In the other situation the predicate remains positive: we are faced with a nonexistent substantive that does all the work. Negating the predicate is both natural and logical because the action itself is made null; in the other case, illogically, the affirmed verbs set up expectations that are then denied. Instead of having an action negated, one finds an absence affirmed.

One might call the "pronomial-adjectival" technique a time-honored poetic form of negation. (When, in Forster's prime, the death of Kitchener in the North Sea called forth many schoolboy poems, two students at St. Cyprian's, George Orwell and Cyril Connolly, joined the competition. Here are the respective opening lines of their poems: "No stone is set to mark his nation's loss," and "No honoured church's funeral hath he."[11] I offer them as examples of why the term "poetic" roughly suits.) Resourceful prose writers have

Table 4.7   Ratio of Simple to Forcible Negation

	Simple Negatives[a]	Forcible Negatives[b]	Total	Percentage of Positive Negation
Howards End	480	350	830	42
A Passage to India	495	380	875	44
Forster aggregate	975	730	1,705	43
The Lost Girl	575	345	920	37
Kangaroo	600	400	1,000	40
Lawrence aggregate	1,175	745	1,920	38
Tarr	435	303	738	41
Self Condemned	566	459	1,025	45
Lewis aggregate	1,001	762	1,763	43
Back	330	180	510	35
Concluding	284	167	451	37
Green aggregate	614	347	961	36

NOTE: In this table, Green's *Back*, which came closest to rivaling Forster in overall negative statements (table 4.6), falls farthest behind in the fashioning of forceful negatives. Forster is nearly matched in "positive negation" by Lewis, both surpassing Lawrence. Where Forster outdoes Lewis is in the strongest usages of all: "never" and "nothing." For him, these words appear 325 times in 615 pages; for Lewis, 301 in 677 pages.

It is the combination of high general incidence (table 4.6) and high "positive" negation (table 4.7) that seems to me to set Forster off as a rhetorical "nay-sayer."

[a]Simple negatives were compiled from negatives made with "not" and its contraction.
[b]Forcible negatives were compiled from negations made with "never," "no," "nothing," and "none."

no problem wresting negatives from verb to substantive when it suits them. Forster, to a greater degree than our other stylists, relies heavily on this "positive negation." His verb constructions have their way of achieving comparable results.

One device he makes use of frequently is negating a verb forcibly with "never." In *Howards End* this adverb occurs 97 times, in *Passage*, 89, an average of more than once every four pages. If "never" is combined with the pronouns "nothing" and "none" and the adjective "no," one discovers that the resulting forcible negations occur more repeatedly in Forster than in the other writers. In other words, he exceeds them in negative statements, but even more convincingly in *emphatic* negations (see table 4.7).

From *Howards End*, some typical uses of "never" can show the sort of variance that has all along been in force between that novel and *Passage*. In each of the following cases some form of inversion has been employed to strengthen the placement of the already strong adverb.

> In all the variable years that followed she *never* saw the like of it again. (HE 25)
>
> ... for a wife may be replaced; a mother *never*. (HE 88)
>
> *Never* before had her personality been touched. (HE 155)
>
> Of her own tragedy Margaret *never* uttered a word. (HE 291)

The inversions do differ. Where prepositionals retard the first and last sentences, the "never" itself gets special end-positioning in the other two. In a less rhetorical way, typical sentences from *Passage* muster their force through combinations. In each of the following, the "never" clause, syntactically normal, is followed by a clause that negates a noun.

> In her ignorance, she ... *never* surmised that his outlook was limited and his method inaccurate, and that *no* one is India. (PI 71)
>
> ... he *never* knew beforehand which effect would ensue: he could discover *no* rule for this or for anything else in life. (PI 103)
>
> ... for the pattern *never* varies, and *no* carving, not even a bees'-nest or a bat, distinguishes one from another. (PI 124)
>
> ... the universe, *never* comprehensible to her intellect, offered *no* repose to her soul. ... (PI 148)

So the strong "never's" are reinforced in the late portions of these sentences, and it would seem as though Forster, having canceled his verbs, is driven on to cancel nouns that might have accompanied them (no rule, no carving, no repose). The nouns have a way of pressing their attention (or their nonpresence) on him. Were *Howards End* to "double up" an effect like this, it would be in a more formal way. Observe what happens in a pair of sentences that record Margaret's experiences of love, past and present. (We shall work off the keyword "nothing" here.)

> Others had loved her in the past ... young men who had *nothing* to do, old men who could find *nobody* better. (HE 155)
>
> *Nothing* in their previous conversation had heralded [Henry's passion], and, worse still, *no* tenderness had ensued. (HE 172)

Here, true, we have doubling up, "nothing" followed by a cancelled substantive. Notice, though, how range antithesis has formalized all this. Consider how much more baffled are a pair of sentences about the caves in *Passage:*

> *Nothing, nothing* attaches to them, and their reputation—for they have one—does not depend on human speech. (PI 124)
>
> ... if mankind grew curious and excavated, *nothing, nothing*, would be added to the sum of good or evil. (PI 125)

Here Forster is impelled to repeat "nothing" and let it stand at that. In the *Howards End* samples, Margaret was able to reflect on the inadequacy of past and present love; here "human speech" and "mankind" have no powers of penetration, and the double use of "nothing" serves as a compensation, as though the narrator had reached an impasse. Certainly the abrupt repetition takes away from any eloquence or decorum in the presence of the caves.

Thus Forster is prone to negate things more forcefully in *Passage*—the last examples illustrating only some of the possibilities. There remains to be examined perhaps the oddest discrepancy between *Howards End* and *Passage,* having to do with contractions. The point at issue is this: if a practice informs a book, as forceful negation does *Passage,* will it not be puzzling to find a *contrary* tendency also in force when the texts are compared? Consider, then, that the most casual way to form a negative, by contracting the verb plus "not," is a method encountered 85 times in *Passage* and only 10 times in *Howards End*. I gave the final instance from *Howards End* earlier—"One usen't always to see clearly before that time" (HE 313)—and tried to prove that it marked a nonsententious advance for the Schlegel sisters. The other contractions are negligible, except for one, in which Forster expresses a downright contradiction of one of Henry Wilcox's views. "No, it wasn't," says the narrator, "and if he did not understand it, the artistic crew would still less . . ." (HE 192). This kind of thing is done often in *Passage*. A contraction will deliver a sharp fact while a character is left laboring in the wake of a formal construction like "did not understand it." The casualness takes precedence, and admits a kind of preemptive force into the texture of *Passage*. Where its people try to keep faith in reason, Forster's narrative voice will steal up to subvert their rationalizing, often by way of contractions.

Early in the novel, Forster had used this device archly, when writing from the point of view of the British. Mrs. Turton "trusted," for example, that Miss Quested "hadn't been brought out to marry nice little Heaslop," concluding later that "Mr. Fielding wasn't pukka, and had better marry Miss Quested, for she wasn't pukka" (PI 29). These are really moments of indirect dialogue and are discountable. The first solid example of the contraction vying with the full negative occurs when Godbole hints of the enormities of the caves. First Forster describes Aziz's mind going under, as it were: "a power he couldn't control capriciously silenced his mind." Against this is placed Adela's inept response: "She did not know that the comparatively simple mind of the Mohammedan was encountering Ancient Night" (PI 74). The example epitomizes, in itself, the device at hand. Both sentences treat of Aziz's mind, but the contracted verb refers to the unconscious

119

force taking it in control, while the formal verb registers the mental frustration of Adela in the presence of that force. The declension can work in the opposite direction, as in the well-known description of the punkah wallah: he "did not understand why the court was fuller than usual, indeed he did not know that it was fuller than usual, didn't even know he worked a fan, though he thought he pulled a rope" (PI 212).

Note that the punkah wallah's thought (what there is of it) is conveyed in the uncontracted form, his action in a different way. The latter suggests his real submental existence, which is less accessible to slow-paced, formal scrutiny. The same holds true for the reaction of Fielding when he hears Aziz accused of rape.

> He repeated "Oh no," like a fool. He *couldn't* frame other words. He felt that a mass of madness had arisen and tried to overwhelm them all; it had to be shoved back into its pit somehow, and he *didn't* know how to do it, because he *did not* understand madness.... (PI 160)

There is something tragic in this incapacitation. Fielding's actions are short-circuited—"couldn't frame," "didn't know how"—sheer intellectual blockage because of referral to the logical mind ("did not understand"). In the most important passage about Fielding, when he is sure that evidence will clear Aziz, he is suddenly shaken by a moment of fleeting beauty he realizes he is missing. Forster's conclusion joins a contraction to a pair of "never's."

> What was the "echo" of which the girl complained? He *did not* know, but presently he would know. Great is information, and she shall prevail.... the cool benediction of the night descended, the stars sparkled, and the whole universe was a hill. Lovely, exquisite moment—but passing the Englishman with averted face and on swift wings. He experienced *nothing* himself; it was as if someone had told him there was such a moment, and he was obliged to believe. And ... suddenly, [he] wondered whether he was really and truly successful as a human being. After forty years' experience, he had learnt to manage his life and make the best of it on advanced European lines.... A creditable achievement, but as the moment passed, he felt he ought to have been working at something else the whole time,—he *didn't* know at what, *never* would know, *never* could know, and that was why he felt sad. (PI 187)

Despite "forty years' experience," this generic Englishman experiences "nothing" as the benediction descends. Which causes his early assurance ("He did not know, but presently he would") to be transformed to "didn't know ... never would." The fact that the verb "to know" is repeated throughout is most depressing; the final insight is shortened into an instinctual sense of failure. It is almost as if Fielding's insides (with Forster's verb) contracted with this bitter knowledge.

Mrs. Moore's worst moment likewise employs this style-marker. The paragraph recalling her panic in the cave begins in past perfect tense, then suddenly refocuses in simple past (the experience now direct), at which point Forster begins his contractions. They introduce the panic.

> A Marabar cave had been horrid as far as Mrs Moore was concerned.... Crammed with villagers and servants, the circular chamber began to smell. She lost Aziz and Adela in the dark, *didn't* know who touched her, *couldn't* breathe, and some vile naked thing struck her face and settled on her mouth like a pad. She tried to regain the entrance tunnel, but an influx of villagers swept her back. She hit her head. For an instant she went mad, hitting and gasping like a fanatic. For *not only did* the crush and stench alarm her; there was also a terrifying echo. (PI 145)

The final sentence here, begun with a formal inversion, returns the experience to the conscious mode that tries to get perspective on it and grapple with it. Hence in the ensuing pages we see Mrs. Moore attempting (through formal, neutral negotiations) to regain her balance. Aziz, smiling, approaches her,

> and she *did not* want him to think his treat was a failure, so smiled too. ... *Nothing* evil had been in the cave, but she *had not* enjoyed herself; *no,* she *had not* enjoyed herself, and she decided *not* to visit a second one. (PI 146)

She sets out to write her son and daughter in England, but soon desists. In the paragraphs that end this undermining chapter, the cause of her growing laxity is signaled in different ways, for first she remains consciously trying to right herself.

> She took out her writing-pad, and began, "Dear Stella, Dear Ralph," then stopped, and looked at the queer valley and their feeble invasion of it. Even the elephant had become a *nobody.* Her eye rose from it to the entrance tunnel. *No,* she *did not* wish to repeat that experience. (PI 147)

This modulates, in the last paragraph, to:

> Then she was terrified over an area larger than usual; the universe, *never* comprehensible to her intellect, offered *no* repose to her soul, the mood of the last two months took definite form at last, and she realized that she *didn't* want to write to her children, *didn't* want to communicate with anyone, *not even* with God. (PI 148)

However, this end of ratiocinative thought marks a necessary descent into the void, and is thematic in Mrs. Moore's progress toward spiritual regeneration. Terrifying though it is, her caving-in marks her salvation as well. In the end, Forster wants this renunciation to overtake his Englishmen and Englishwomen. When it is Adela's turn to be so "taken," she has her own saving moment, which turns the trial around. Trancelike, she overcomes her rehearsed answers to the counsel's questions, and Forster's negatives sanction her way of arriving at the truth.

> But as soon as she rose to reply, and heard the sound of her own voice, she feared *not even* that. A new and unknown sensation protected her, like magnificent armour. She *didn't* think what had happened or even remember in the ordinary way of memory, but she returned to the Marabar Hills, and spoke from them across a sort of darkness.... (PI 221)

It is thus that the trial's momentum is reversed, as a "new and unknown sensation" intercedes and the girl, bypassing mental process with "didn't think what had happened," actually *says* what happened: "Dr. Aziz never followed me into the cave" (PI 223).

So Forster at last vouches for the upwelling of subconscious knowledge (even when that tapping of depths causes alienating attitudes). For the *will* to do things logically and constructively and positively is worse (and more alienating) than the yielding to the dictates of the depths. Thus, sensing his ultimate sanctions, we are able to say that all the contractions that pile together at the end of the novel can be looked on benignly—how Aziz "didn't want to meet Stella and Ralph again, knew they didn't want to meet him," for instance; and "Hadn't he wanted to say something else to [Miss Quested]?" (PI 315). What he says is something beautiful—that he will henceforth connect her in his mind with Mrs. Moore. And then the novel ends with contractions, apparently divisive, actually benign:

> But the horses didn't want it—they swerved apart; the earth didn't want it, sending up rocks through which riders must pass single file; the temples, the tank, the jail, the palace, the birds, the carrion, the Guest House, that came into view as they issued from the gap and saw Mau beneath: they didn't want it, they said in their hundred voices, "No, not yet," and the sky said, "No, not there."

For the instinctual is certain of its way in those negations. Forster would consider it otiose of us to tax our brain and lament that we do not understand.

5 WYNDHAM LEWIS: *TARR, SELF CONDEMNED*

Mr. Lewis is the greatest prose master of style of my generation.
T. S. ELIOT

PRELIMINARIES: ROOMS

The major difference between *Self Condemned* (1954) and *Tarr* (1918; revised 1928) lies in the fact that the hero of *Self Condemned,* René Harding, compounds the experiences of both the anti-hero and the hero of *Tarr,* Otto Kreisler and Frederick Tarr. Harding, a historian, shares with the artist Tarr a distrust of the forces that have made history and society what they are. Like Tarr, René has parried life by dealing with it in a semiprotected way; he has carved out a perch for himself that is immune to the competitive urgencies both men equate with the death drive of living things. (This may sound reminiscent of Forster in *Howards End*—of the refuge symbolized there by house and hay, things gone beyond the flux of living. But *Howards End* mellowness has no part in René's and Tarr's scheme for protection; they set themselves up as enemies rather than connectors.)

Tarr arrives at his perch under the aegis of the artist, nourishing his sense of reality through deliberate proximity to "the intoxication of the merry-go-round" (T 34). This phrase he uses early in the book, and he has not budged near the end when he says, "My passion for art has made me fond of chaos" (T 217). These are the criteria of the vorticist artist who, from the still center, the eye of the hurricane, as it were, observes the components of the chaos and creates art from them. Making art is really an arresting process, an abstracting of ultimate reality (which is gritty and hard) from a passing "reality" that seems exciting. In Wyndham Lewis's formula, this is done not in a time scheme (not by tracing motives or foreshadowing outcomes), but by breaking up actions as they unfold, and externalizing their souls—along with the souls of their perpetrators—in a kind of minute-by-minute changing frieze.[1]

Accordingly, the worst enormity of Kreisler in *Tarr* (the killing of his rival Soltyk at a dueling ground) is no more ruthless and cumulative in its impact than is the opening description of Kreisler admitting a woman to his room while he is dressing: "He did not take his eyes from the glass, spotted blue tie being pinched into position by finicky finger-tips, at the end of lanky drooping hands, with extended high-held formal elbows and one knee slightly flexed. Above and around his tie the entrance of a young woman was considered with a high impassibility" (T 70). In several stylistic ways (the woman's arrival passively "considered," while Kreisler's appendages follow their separate routines, with both descriptions grammatically dependent from a bow tie) a total incapacity for interchange is established for Kreisler. Repeated "friezes" of this type are Lewis's forte. His gift lies in his manifold resources for arranging them, making it possible for him to form narrative textures that are "unprecedented in fiction," as Hugh Kenner has said.[2]

These resources are the subject of this chapter. Meanwhile, to get back to resemblances between René Harding and Tarr: when Lewis has Tarr say, "all effectual men are always the enemies of every time" (T 216), he strikes the chord that will attune the two. For just as Tarr affirms that chaos (or the vortex) supplies the artist immemorially, so does René affirm that what passes for history has been a continuous honoring of deeds of violence and uncreation, a Dunciad that deserves exposure by the true historian. In a volte-face from Forster's or Lawrence's condonings of instinct, René Harding remarks all about him "the functional coma of the animal world" (SC 211), and marvels that a mircle should have taken place in spite of it. For

> No one could imagine why man had abstracted himself and acquired the sanity of consciousness; why he had gone sane in the midst of a madhouse of functional character. —And History: with that, René's central tragedy was reached. History, such as is worth recording, is about the passion of men to stop sane. [Ideal history, René means, not the usual kind.] Most History so-called is the bloody catalogue of their backslidings. Such was René's unalterable position. (SC 212)

Those two conflicting propositions about history cause the action of *Self Condemned*. On the brink of the second War, René has written *The Secret History of World War II*, and has employed his discipline against itself in doing so. It is a creative act exercised on the record of the past (as Tarr's is one exercised on the life of the present): both men thus appear as Lewisean "enemies." However, because *Self Condemned* is told from a late perspective of Lewis's, we follow René into a stage beyond Tarr's. If René has worked to acquire a reputation and a chair in history, his idealism causes him to discard his honors and, together with his wife Hester, to retreat from war-expectant Europe to Canada. An aggressive act against his own intelligence is attempted here, something not encountered in Tarr or in other early Lewis protagonists. Tarr undergoes no development at all, so a word like "stage" is irrelevant to him. (This is not unlike the earlier distinction made between Mrs. Wilcox and Mrs. Moore. At least, the late visions of Lewis and Forster depend on a similar erosion of once-firm views.)

One might say that Tarr and Harding begin as "self-conditioned" men. René's lot is to go further and be self-condemned. Yet he'd begun just like Tarr, and had "drilled himself into tolerance of the Absurd," as Lewis says (SC 60).

Lewis's strategy in his first novel had left a jauntier prospect for Tarr, because here it was Kreisler who would plunge into the vortex and be driven to mad acts like rape and murder, and, eventually, self-murder—acts considered natural by Lewis. They result when an uncreative ego is subjected to delusions of grandeur, and, after that, to envy and humiliation. Where Kreisler enacts that cycle in *Tarr*, it is left for René to bring destruction on himself, but by acting from wilful insight rather than absurd whimsy. Some of the stylistic differences between the two novels derive from this presence of hubris in *Self Condemned*. Many of them may be grouped together under a heading of "rooms." It is in rooms, Lewis could well say, that the civilized man hews out his perch of observation, rooms being both workshops and symbols for the protected mind.

Tarr living in Paris and René in London make a concession to what they regard as the absurd by choosing domiciles that are fairly intractable, and making them "do." There is an element of living in danger that they initially share, a sort of rent they pay that keeps them in mind of their own finiteness. In Tarr's case this is seen twice, because his first conflict in the novel arises out of his compromising situation with Bertha Lunken, who has extracted a proposal of marriage from him. It is her room as much as Bertha that threatens to stupefy Tarr.

Lewis records Tarr's approach to this place, and to the studio he later hires, in comparisons that are markedly similar:

> Tarr examined the room as you do a doctor's waiting-room. (T 46)
>
> ... with Tarr a new room had to be fitted into as painfully as a foot into some new and too elegant shoe. (T 185)

Both introductions then give way to assessments. Of Bertha's room, Lewis continues,

> It was really more serious than it looked: he must not underestimate it. It
> was the purest distillation of the commonplace: he had become bewitched
> by its strangeness. . . . So much was it the real ordinary world that for him
> with his out-of-the-way experience it was a phantasmagoria. (T 46–47)

The "it" is repeated often enough to create a disturbing mag-
netism.[3] Somewhat in the manner of Joyce, the declaratives lead to
colons, and by the second one, Tarr is unable to fend the room off.
When the "out-of-the-way" life of the artist is threatened in this manner, he must break away: but the point is that Tarr placed himself in
jeopardy by trafficking with such banality, and he furthers it by not
removing to England, but only to a more remote quarter of Paris,
engaging a new studio. This he in turn has to grapple with and sub-
due.

> This large studioroom was worse than any desert: it had been built for
> something else, it would never be right. . . . Once he had packed this place
> with consoling memories of work it would improve and might become
> quite perfect: he would see, time would tell. (T 186)

Even tighter compounding appears in these sentences. In both,
comma-spliced statements occur. The anticipation that the room had
been "built for something else, it would never be right" quickly
modulates to "he would see, time would tell." Tarr's work ethic has
taken charge. It is thus no surprise to read that "A half-hour after
entering into possession he left it tired out and swam out into the
human streams of his new Quarter..." (T 186). The swimming
metaphor (endemic to the novel) indicates what a short time has been
required for Tarr to get control. Starting a new project (after coping
with the disorder), he creates a sanctum, and he swims out. Such a
room becomes the sally port for the artist, since genuine work helps
him convert it to a creative "still space," important because it is so
proximate to the vortex.

Kreisler, whose room serves only as an address where his monthly
allowance from his father may be received, has no such aptitude for
making a space into a refuge of work and meditation. Isolation is
terrifying to a fraud of an artist like him. "And it was this room, yes,
this room that cut him off from the world: he gazed around as a man
may eye a wife whom he suspects..." (T 73). If Tarr's first reactions
had also been given in similes, those had been businesslike (doctor's
waiting room, tight-fitting shoe), whereas Kreisler's simile is one of
suspicious dread. He is thus *propelled* out into the world to one place
or another—it might be the circle of German ladies collected around
Fräulein Liepmann: " . . .next moment he was walking on obstinately

in the direction of the Liepmann's house. . . . His weakness drew him on, back into the vortex. . . . His room, the Café, waited for him like executioners" (T 115–16). At the Liepmann's he creates a vortex of his own, deliberately disgracing himself (he whirls an old woman around in a mad and exhausting dance, among other things). Lewis's vorticist position is clarified in the distinction between Kreisler, driven from the still center "back into the vortex" on account of having no centrality of his own, and Tarr, able to make excursions to and from the vortex, by virtue of having furnished his hired room "with consoling memories of work."

This notion of conquered space associates René Harding with Tarr because of René's decision to pass his London life in "the House that Jack Built," despite his architectural good taste, which is demonstrated when he visits a wealthy relative's house, "beautifully unlike the House that Jack Built. Nothing absurd about *this house*. How excellently abstract wealth was after all: it got rid of the idiosyncratic, the absurd!" (SC 46). Better yet is René's response to the room of his academic admirer, "Rotter" Parkinson. "It was really a fragment of paradise," thinks René (SC 76); yet he understands "why he preferred to stop where he was":

> He occupied a separate flat, a flat for work only; it was inviolable. No one had ever ventured to disturb him. . . . So he did not envy Parkinson his work-room: dimly perhaps he realized that men like himself always were to be found in Houses that Jack Built, working in a book-lined area the size of a bathroom . . . while for the Parkinsons there was always more amenity, more comfort, more space—which is not to scorn the Parkinsons but to define how these things are allotted, for one purgatory, for the other paradise. (SC 78)

René has an inkling to the fact that he requires "purgatory," or near access to the vortex, as it could also be called. In the flat across the hall from his "inviolable" study René lives with Hester; this flat is invaded by a charlady, Mrs. Harradson, her life symptomatic of the violent and the absurd (which are also commemorated by the fact that houses like these will get bombed in the blitz and wild cats will breed in their cellars). By the time of the report of Mrs. Harradson's death—in wartime, but absurd since she has simply fallen downstairs—René and Hester are in a new locale, Canada. And they have spent the first three years of war there, in a twenty-five by twelve-foot room. Here is a stage the early Lewis of *Tarr* could not have foreseen. René's existence in the house that Jack built may have paralleled Tarr's, and allowed for a refuge near chaos where the work of thought could go on; but in *Self Condemned* that room in Momaco,

Canada, is capitalized to "Room" (as was Tarr's "Reality" capitalized) and is accorded different thematic and stylistic treatment from what was given the eye-of-the-storm retreats mentioned up to now.

"The Resignation," "The Room," and "After the Fire" are the titles of *Self Condemned*'s sections, the middle one devoted to the Hardings' three-year seclusion in a room in Momaco's Hotel Blundell, a confinement terminated by fire. The fire produces some social interaction at last: overtures are made to René by a Canadian university, and his response makes his wife grow desperate, as she sees him accept this déclassé substitute for the chair he resigned in England. His backsliding will cause her suicide, the most tragic event of the book. The earlier confinement to the room, desperate enough in its own way, produces the kind of oppression that forges human bonds (as distinct from artistic/intellectual ones). This middle section thus receives special stylistic treatment, most effectively as it begins.

The hallmark of the new treatment is its tremendous sense of recapitulation. One could never say that Lewis's style becomes "temporal" (it never does), but its segmentations do become extraordinarily repetitive and demonstrative. Reliance on demonstrative pronouns and adjectives for simple reference, in fact, becomes the most obvious style-marker when the "Room" is presented to us.

At the outset, that singular tic of the Lewis hero, of the man who hunts for his perch, is described:

> It was René's habit to place an upended suitcase upon a high chair and drape it with a blanket. He stood *this* between his wife and himself, so blotting her out while he wrote or read. He could still see, over the crest of *this stockade*, a movement of soft ash-gold English hair, among which moved sometimes a scratching crimson fingernail. *This minimum* of privacy, *this substitute* for a booklined study, was all he had for three years and three months.... (SC 169)

Four returns to the upended suitcase are managed, without the word repeated, the atmosphere created by means of "this." Immediately afterwards, a group of comparisons also employ demonstratives. As in *Tarr*, similes help give impressions of a room, but here the treatment is unusual. The formula "that of" appears four times within the span of a page:

another glare, that of the Canadian snow (SC 169)

a coldness as great as that of the ice-pack (SC 170)

a smell, as distinct as that of a hospital (SC 170)

[prison-like] gases, those of a place where people are battened down (SC 170)

Farther on, sentences unstandard for Lewis summarize the Canadian weather. One paragraph ends with the explanation, "It is the wind that does it," precipitating two other paragraphs. Each starts normally enough, but notice the follow-up sentences:

> Bad as is the wind, in the periods of great cold, there is something even more disagreeable. That is the ice. (SC 186)

> There is perhaps something more than the ice, the glaring snow, and the pulverizing zero wind. That is the mud. (SC 186)

It sounds as though Lewis is writing a textbook for primary grades. Referring to the things he has just detailed, the wind and so forth, he tells his pupils to expect something worse now: "That is the ice," "That is the mud." It is hardly necessary to remark how unsophisticated such writing is. In the same fashion, irrelevant appositives occur. They label the Hardings as residents of the room, but we know all the time that no one else is being spoken about.

> They never left this Room, these two people.... (SC 170)

> ... for the Hardings, husband and wife, it stank of exile.... (SC 170)

> So they conversed, these two inmates of this lethal chamber. (SC 174)

In *Tarr,* there were several images of the hero swimming the Parisian streets like a fish. This whorling symbol carries over to other people's bodies, minds, even their emotions.* In *Self Condemned* only the eerie "Room" is given aquatic properties.

> Its depths were dark. Looked into from without... the Hardings would have seemed (as they moved about their circumscribed tasks, or rested sluggishly upon the bottom as it were) provided with an aquatic medium.... Of the six windows, three... resembled very closely the plateglass sides of a tank in an aquarium.... Green blinds latticed with use further contributed to this effect of water, thickening the blooming cavity. (SC 174)

What really has happened, thematically in *Self Condemned,* is that the "Room" for the Hardings has become not a sanctum but the vortex itself, and while in it—for three years—they live the mindless life of the animal kingdom. In this respect their experience mirrors Kreisler's rather than Tarr's. Lewis does a sizable about-face as well, because there is something salutary about this *ur*-existence undergone by Hester and René. Only after the fire, in the final movement of the

---

*For example: Anastasya's "powerful body swam in the fluidities of [her clothes] like a duck" (T 90); Bertha's "silence swarm[ed] with unuttered thoughts, like a glassy shoal with innumerable fish" (T 163); Soltyk's "blood ... hurtled about in him ... like a sturgeon in a narrow tank" (T 252).

book, does the experience in the Hotel Blundell become detrimental; the cause given is the professor's return to ratiocination. While pent up in the room, and in spite of its awfulness, Hester and René had become deeply knowledgeable of one another—a gain attested to in the chapter "Vows of Hardship." A new idea is here accepted by Lewis, one of the value of life minus a sanctum. No other chapter of his (unless it be the final one of *The Human Age*) reveals him so humanized. Hester's suicide follows the breach between her and René when they are freed from the room, a breach described retrospectively:

> Up to the period of the fire he had informed her, from day to day, of everything he was doing, or intending to do. As castaways upon Momaco they had lived together, in an idyllic communion in which it was unthinkable that they should hide anything from one another. Now he would consult her upon nothing of serious moment. So they went back to a régime which had obtained for some years before his resignation of his professorship. (SC 347)

The difference between the room's value to the Hardings and the disastrous life of Kreisler in *his* vortex is dependent, of course, on the fact that Kreisler cannot share anything with anyone. Not before *Self Condemned* was Lewis able to make much virtue of intermingling. A writer who could always discount intimacies nurtured through time, Lewis felt the need to prolong time hyperbolically in "The Room." This perhaps amounted to a gesture of relinquishment for him, in that no ordering, no control would be forthcoming from René. The following passage even suggests that saurian state we discussed in Lawrence.*

> In the Rip van Winkle existence of René and Hester—of suspended existence so that they might as well have been asleep—a thousand years is the same as one tick of the clock. It was a dense, interminable, painful vibration, this great whirring, agelong, thunderous *Tick*. (SC 170)

Note the seriate adjectives modifying the last nouns and imparting tension to this stretch of vibrating time. A different technique is reserved for Suzanne, the early visitor to Kreisler's room, called "this small indifferent and mercenary acquisition" (T 72)—a series which, by clumping qualities together, prevents any possible escalating effect. (I mention this habit of *Tarr*'s style later.) On the same page, Kreisler is described as unaffected by any prolongation of time. "He leapt the

---

*See chapter three. Lawrence, of course, would have accepted the vortex, and we have already seen Richard Somers wishing "To surge with that cold exultance and passion of a sea thing!" (K 124).

130

hour. . . . Then [the clock] struck twelve. He at once absorbed that further hour as he had the former. He lived an hour as easily and carelessly as he would have lived a second" (T 72).

At the end Kreisler will pay for his apathy and his gymnastics with time. For Kreisler ends up in yet another room—a cell at the French-German border, to which he has fled after his murder of Slotyk. Of this place he becomes fond, for in it his death wish surfaces and he begins to play a diverting game. Those "hours" of the past become a sort of mounting indictment, nudging him to suicide.

> It had all the severity of a place in which an operation might suitably be performed. He became fond of it. He lay upon his bed: he turned over the shell of many empty and depressing hours he had lived: in all these listless concave shapes he took a particular pleasure. (T 264)

Lewis, great enemy of Time that he was, always had a faculty for transforming temporal into spatial entities. Kreisler here finishes his "shell game" and impassively hangs himself. The opposite—the temporal—prevailed in the Hardings' room at Momaco. One could argue that Lewis made his peace with Time in this section: old enemy of Bergson though he was, it was Bergsonian *durée* that the Hardings lived through. The only day of the week they could retain was Sunday, and actually, that was marked by benign duration, when the Jack Benny and Fred Allen programs brought them "vigorous joy . . . and in the end the war-bulletins began to fade, and like all good Americans they came to realize that it was only the comic that mattered" (SC 246). As William Pritchard has pointed out, such passages in the "Vows of Hardship" chapter redeem the whole moribund situation of *Self Condemned,* and are not ironic.[4]

How, then, can René's experience be compared to Kreisler's? The "After the Fire" section of *Self Condemned,* in which René enters a shell of a life (imaged by the shell of the burnt-out hotel), holds the answer. Near the end, after his wife's suicide, René retreats to a cell not unlike Kreisler's—the cell of a Catholic monastery. Here he muses about his experience at the Blundell, endured for a principle, and his present seclusion, aimed at assuaging the ghost of Hester. He is right only on the first count, the period of the room having "had for its rationale a great moral issue"; wrong to judge "his second exit . . . a sacrifice, an emotional act of propitiation . . ." (SC 385). It is belated and false, the comfort he accepts in the cell at the College of the Sacred Heart, and it is not long before he gravitates from there to a post at an American university. From here on he sets blame elsewhere—does what Kreisler does—and is heard roundly condemning the tragic Hester at the end of the book. Thus *Self Condemned's* denouement confirms him as "a glacial shell of a man" as we reach the final sentence. His compromising all through the third section—fatuity on a scale great enough to cause his wife's death—leads to a state of soul caught in the final chapter title, "The Cemetery of Shells." It could have served as well to epitomize Otto Kreisler's last hours.

"PELTING" PROSE

As early as the Atlantic crossing to Canada, when René wore the ribbon of the Legion of Honour to the ship's dining saloon, he was able to recognize fatuity in himself of the type the room would soon help him avoid. "An individual," he reasoned, "who has repudiated publicly the compromise of normal living must thereafter be careful never to use compromise, or half-compromise, under whatever circumstances" (SC 163). Both René and Tarr make firm rejections of compromise. René's intolerance is toward civilization itself, for the reason that it begets wars, whereas Tarr must avoid what *individuals* have to offer. Anastasya Vasek, the heroine of *Tarr,* must not enlist the hero's commitment because "Surrender to a woman was a sort of suicide for an artist" (T 194). Thus Tarr marries Bertha, knowing she is carrying Kreisler's child, because that way he can remain immune from the "intense life" and the dark "unconsciousness" of Anastasya. (If Lawrence's Alvina Houghton were an artist, Lewis might say she would have had to marry Dr. Mitchell, not Ciccio.) Tarr ends his novel uncompromised. René ends his compromised, for a singular reason. He has also impugned an authentic woman, Hester. This is a grave mistake, since it is not an artist's integrity he needs to preserve, but a man's. He becomes a "glacial shell" after he disregards his wife's appeal that he not become an Americanized academic.

Words like "surrender" and "compromise," while anathematic to protagonists in these novels, continue to exert their pressure. Lewis's prose continually harks back to the conditional nature of any plan a man may seek to live by. When Lewis collected his early stories under the title *The Wild Body,* he named the agent that makes plans conditional, and it accounts for his radical style. The "wild body" is responsible for a certain *entity*-factor in Lewis's descriptions. It is not simply that men's and women's bodies are ungovernable, a fearful enough idea. It is more that the body's components are entities that run little contests of their own. And while these threaten to discompose their owner from one direction, his nature is subject to abstract forces that discompose him from another: forces like "personality," "indifference," and "violence." Such intangibles bid to control the wild body just as its organs and appendages do. Lewis's people are caught between a set of pincers, the abstract and the minutely concrete, each operating in a manner that his style has little reason to differentiate.

At the end of *Self Condemned,* a twofold resumé subjects Harding's personality, and afterwards his carcass, to physical laws that seem inescapable. The verb "emptied" sums up the mental defections of Harding; afterwards, the verb "dropped" shows a sort of physical consequence:

> If the personality is *emptied* of mother-love, *emptied* of wife-love, *emptied* of the illusions upon which sex-in-society depends, and finally *emptied* of the illusions upon which the will to create depends, then the personality becomes a shell. (SC 400)
>
> ... He *dropped* back upon the sofa, where he had been sitting, as if *dropped* by somebody who just now had violently snatched him up, as if a supernatural being had whipped him up into the standing position ... and had now *dropped* him back on to the sofa with a gravitational thud. (SC 404)

The emptiness could not be more complete. In *Tarr,* too, the hero's personality is purged of illusions in language like this—with one notable exception. The last item snatched from René above was the illusion "upon which the will to create depends." Nowhere in *Tarr* does Lewis suggest that the will to create depends on illusions. Rather, it depends on reality. Thus one element of autonomy remains in the first novel, keeping its hero at that early "stage" that saw him, for instance, coping with his studio room. Hence, even while the style in both novels credits those "entities" that take over a man from within and without, we never see Tarr placed at the mercy of absolute gravity—he is able to "swim"—whereas in *Self Condemned* the motif of gravity has been insidious from the start.

Two of these prior instances are revealing. One has to do with René early on, capable of dominating Hester; the other with Hester after the fire, capable of disloyalty to René.

> He fastened a hard stare upon her, as though he had dropped something into Essie and were waiting to see it emerge. (SC 35)
>
> He said this so categorically, that she recoiled as though something heavy had fallen upon the table between them. (SC 360)

The significant feature of the style is the notion of something being dropped "into" a person, or a voice causing something to fall "between" people. During the three-hundred-page gap here the rapport between husband and wife has gone. Hester, recoiling, has resolved at last to change her husband's course, and somehow get him back to England, even if it means sacrificing herself. Though she fails, her act is based on her conviction that he can be rescued. All this is tragic. When, in *Tarr,* the time comes for the heroine Anastasya to see through Tarr, the syntax is the same but the image is different.

> Anastasya looked blankly into him, as though he contained cheerless stretches where no living thing could grow. (T 297)

The passages describing the women sitting across from the men at tables are similar in that the Lewisean formula is borne out: Anastasya looks into Tarr, he contains stretches of something. The fact that he supports no living thing is an admission by Lewis, true to form, that life is to be sacrificed if art is to be created. This is not as stern a matter as the gravitational pull that works on the Hardings, on Hester toward England, on René toward glacial stupor.

Played off against Tarr's "standing army of will" (T 46),* the uses of gravity in *Self Condemned* help make it a great realistic novel. From the time of Mrs. Harradson's "plunge" down the stairs of the house that Jack built (SC 14) to the moment Hester throws herself under a moving truck (SC 370), Lewis is alert to the possibilities of the body truly gone out of control—and not some gesticulative wild body that can serve as the source of vorticist art. Images of rolling, slipping, and stumbling abound in the novel. The most powerful prefiguring of Hester's suicide is the act performed by René's sister Helen, who jumps off a train, having prolonged her goodbye to him. As she does, Lewis says,

> The human body is not a square object like a trunk, and when it falls it tends to roll. In her case it rolled towards the train. But a porter seized her shoulders and stopped the roll.... Helen, now no longer a rolling body, but in command of her limbs once more, sprang to her feet.... (SC 139)

There is an ultimate loyalty paid here: the body's danger is a testimony to Helen's tenacity of mind, and, most important, both are real. René, before he compromises, recognizes the utter contingency of things, physical and mental, while on shipboard in a storm; here mind and body reconfirm one another:

> Sometimes rolling upon the floor of the stateroom, as he lost his balance, at the severest of the sub-polar storm, he analysed all of this down to the bedrock. (SC 163)

But the theme can work another way, if the mind once begins to theorize its way out of impasses. So, when René is reinvigorated by

---

*The standing army of will—like the swimming images in *Tarr*—is countergravitational. Once in that novel Lewis went so far as to have Tarr make "a perpendicular bed" for Bertha, yet refuse to console her while she leaned against him (T 52).

contact with a Canadian professor (this happens in "After the Fire"), the danger of ignoring the body carries warning instead of praise:

> Heading rather precipitately down the hill, the author of *The Secret History of World War II* was in a mental turmoil; and the more chaotic the brainstorm grew, the more his speed increased, until he was in imminent danger of slipping upon the ice, and rolling down the hill instead of walking down it. (SC 324)

All of Lewis's work is founded on the Cartesian division between mind and body,[5] but the later work recognizes better the equal claims of the body. In *Tarr*, where the hero is permitted greater self-control, he is often able to substitute mental alacrity for physical sluggishness. "The backwardness of his senses was causing [Tarr] some anxiety: his intellect now stepped in, determined to do their business for them" (T 270). Even *in extremis* this kind of determination can work, as when poor Soltyk, unnerved at the dueling ground, is at last galvanized by an insult from Kreisler: "will was at last dashed all over him, an arctic douche and the hands become claws flew at Kreisler's throat" (T 252). Now and then a substitution like this will appear with respect to René: "when the sterner side of his nature had attempted to intervene, he pushed it away with a ho-ho-ho" (SC 32). More often the emphasis is on a *transition* from one sphere to another:

> René, who had been laughing, rubbed his face, and came out of the rub purged of mirth. (SC 38)

> "Well!" He spoke with fists raised to the dirty heaven of the Hotel apartment.... His stretch took him forward several thudding paces, like a man with locomotor. (SC 198)

In sentences like these, one finds a real advance in the way Lewis admits the consequences of physical actions. A rub and a stretch (unlike so many other detached actions of the wild body) are positive aids to thought, yet they have their own physical momentum, which finally infects that thought. When, toward the end of the novel, René loses his wife's allegiance, he tries a ploy to win it back. He gets himself spruced up—scented with pine soap, dressed in a striped shirt—to launch a "corporeal and sartorial attack" on Hester. This neat abstraction is countered by her equally exact resistance: "The demonstration was unheeded—by nostrils closed against pine, and eyes blind to a Bengal-stripe" (SC 361). Her organic will power is what is noteworthy, so different from Tarr's "intellect now stepping in" or Soltyk's will power "dashed all over him." Hester's physical response does not come from some disembodied source. The parallelism helps underline this: nostrils closed against ... eyes blind to. If Lewis's novels lack drama in the standard sense, they are certainly dependable for this kind of micro-drama. Here, on the eve of Hester's suicide, Lewis's powers reach their highest level and work in the service of genuine, body-and-soul human conflict.

Dealing thus far with diction primarily—with the "entities" Lewis concocts from bodily parts and abstract notions almost interchangeably—we have not yet made out his "ground style," and are not actually close to it in pursuing René and Hester through uncharacteristic high moments. (The vigorous parallels just mentioned, for instance, are themselves uncharacteristic.) The normal syntactic arrangements of the "entity" language produce a disjunctive effect for which Lewis is well known. His hero Tarr once reflected on the "sturdy optimism shown by . . . inanimate objects" (T 185). Following this clue leads to a discovery of some ways of seeing that are shared by *Self Condemned* and *Tarr* (especially when true drama is not in prospect). For instance, a pair of hats sound much alike across a span of three decades:

> His bowler hat bobbed, striking out clean lines in space as he spoke. (T 24)
>
> . . . he watched with elation the disembodied clerical hat gaining speed as it skimmed along the top of the hedge. (SC 113–14)

Both hats perform their main action participially ("striking" and "gaining"); both sentences end with an "as" clause reporting another simultaneous action. Discreteness results. That is to say, coordination is eschewed—the satirist in Lewis does not value it—and if we add the opening verbs ("bobbed," "watched"), we find that three different simultaneities are registered, each in an unrelated verb action.

It is a scattershot style, once described by a critic of Lewis as "pelting,"[6] and curiously enough it finds Lewis at his most relaxed. When any idea or thing bids for its own autonomy, Lewis can phrase the issue effortlessly. The owner of the clerical hat, Robert Kerridge, one of three brothers-in-law of René who are set up as straw men in part one, offers a good example of this autonomy. A sentence refers to him as "the wicked giant within, alecking away at his smartest" (SC 114), and similar participles attach to Percy Lamport and Victor Painter:

> . . . [Percy] stood in profile, the one eye amusedly and with infinite knowledge simmering away all to itself. (SC 50)
>
> This being Victor, it may be imagined that it was in no way to be in *his* society, René had arranged this party. (SC 67)

In its descriptions of disposable characters like these, *Self Condemned* most nearly approaches *Tarr* in style. Note that, in both trailing and leading positions, absolute participles have been used. Here is a device, one might infer, to which Lewis would be partial. It is inherently disjunctive. Out of scores of absolutes in Lewis, I examine here a few of one type, present participles that conclude sentences. They deserve an epithet like "pelting," I think, for the way they can initiate anticlimaxes, whereas a contrary "pelting" technique, involving expletives, tends to be climactic.

There are 46 trailing absolute phrases in *Tarr* (291 pages), 69 in *Self Condemned* (386 pages). These figures represent better than three occurrences every twenty pages, by far the highest incidence among our writers (see table 5.1). Here are three of the most bathetic from *Tarr:*

> She disengaged her arms wildly and threw them round his neck, tears becoming torrential. (T 50)

> "Ah yes," he sighed heavily, one side of the menu rising gustily and relapsing. (T 92)

> ... he tramped slowly off in his short jacket, his buttocks moving methodically just beneath its rim. (T 292)

Bathos comes about because the trailing actions seem self-generated: the tear ducts and buttocks and even Kreisler's menu seem to pick up the action on their own. Upside-down subordination can get involved, also. Bertha's "tears becoming torrential" should clearly not be rele-

Table 5.1   Trailing Absolute Participles

	Number of Trailing Absolutes	Number of Pages	Incidence per Page
Tarr	46	291	.158
Self Condemned	69	386	.176
Lewis aggregate	115	677	.170
The Lost Girl	42	372	.113
Kangaroo	24	367	.065
Lawrence aggregate	66	739	.089
Howards End	22	315	.070
A Passage to India	12	300	.040
Forster aggregate	34	615	.055
Back	12	180	.067
Concluding	12	200	.060
Green aggregate	24	380	.063

NOTE: Lawrence, Lewis's nearest competitor, produces only half as many final absolutes. The others decline from there. When Forster's total of 34 for 615 pages is placed against Lewis's 115 in 677, the differentiation is tripled.

137

gated to subordinate status. More often, the humor stems from the long-drawn-out final element. "Gustily" and "methodically" help the last two in this way. *Self Condemned* offers specimens of both types.

> Hester . . . listened to the screams of the woman in the apartment beneath theirs, it being the husband's nightly habit to half murder her. (SC 230)
>
> . . . the two Professors disappeared into the barbaric mêlée, Laura waving her posteriors expertly in the embrace of René. (SC 367)

Here the first example has upside-down subordination; the second, prolonged as it is, rates attention as one of the last terminal absolutes in *Self Condemned*. Laura McKenzie's posteriors waving to rumba music are paralleled by Tarr's buttocks moving underneath his jacket's rim—and that item marks the last terminal absolute in *Tarr!* Consider that, in novels written nearly forty years apart, the author seized on a satirist's favorite target, the human buttocks, for some culminating uses of a syntactic form. (Here may be a case of diction suggesting syntax, and quite pointedly. All would have seemed less pseudo-elegant with finite verbs: if Tarr's buttocks had "moved" methodically, or Laura's posteriors had "waved" expertly.)

Interestingly, Lewis is kinder to Hester when she rumbas with Professor McKenzie. "Hester, less disposed to borrow from the buttocks of the Black, wobbled her own a little mournfully" (SC 367). The finite verb, even though it is "wobbled," carries no bathetic overtones. Hester, here, is not utterly depressed—she does, after all, dance on this occasion, a Christmas party—but she is preoccupied with thoughts that have her only pages away from suicide. Lewis is fair to her with "wobbled her own a little mournfully."

With nonfinite constructions so often ending Lewis's sentences, his prose can continue to be sardonic, but occasionally he gains the same effect by means of an opposite strategy. This happens when his expletive constructions, again, very numerous, create a climactic order not supported by content. Two simple expletives, working off adjectives, illustrate the point:

> . . . it was natural, perhaps inevitable, that he should compare her arms to bananas. (T 177)
>
> . . . it was impossible to communicate with that stylistic owl man. (SC 324)

A term like "pelting," if assigned here, would owe more to diction than to syntax: extreme adjectives ("inevitable," "impossible") leading to comparisons made with bananas and owls. A different kind of expletive has more inherent *syntactic* power than this, and Lewis makes much use of it, too, for serious as well as sardonic purposes. I mean the expletives that work off nouns or even adverbs—followed up with clauses—which create a high sense of expectancy as the adjectival kind does not.

Again, a count places Lewis well ahead of the other writers in employing expletives. Table 5.2 has been devised to record his overall lead, and it also isolates the forceful expletives just referred to, which deserve passing attention.

To begin with, these expletives can work as plot intensifiers. So, when Kreisler's pilgrimage ends on the steps of a French jail, Lewis writes, "it was in the doorway of this building that Kreisler now stood" (T 260). The periodic sentence can thus end on the verb, whereas suspense would have been lost from normal arrangement ("Kreisler now stood in the doorway"). To adduce such crises, a construction usually takes the form of expletive plus noun (not adverb). So it is when Kreisler slaps Soltyk, precipitating their duel. In passages fifteen pages apart, we are told,

> ... it was the hapless Soltyk that Kreisler had eventually run to earth, and had just now publicly smacked.... (T 229)
> ... it was a contemptuous laugh of Soltyk's that brought [Kreisler] to his feet. (T 244)

The adverbial expletive, denoting place or manner in advance, operates more truly like the scattershot devices we have been discuss-

Table 5.2   Incidence of Expletives, Including Forceful Types

	Number of Expletives[a]	Number of Pages	Incidence	Forceful Expletives	Incidence
Tarr	96	291	.330	41	.141
Self Condemned	294	386	.762	113	.345
Lewis aggregate	390	677	.576	154	.227
The Lost Girl	95	372	.255	36	.097
Kangaroo	80	367	.218	37	.101
Lawrence aggregate	175	739	.237	73	.099
Howards End	82	315	.260	27	.086
A Passage to India	67	300	.223	28	.093
Forster aggregate	149	615	.242	55	.089
Back	79	180	.439	36	.200
Concluding	47	200	.235	21	.105
Green aggregate	126	380	.332	57	.150

NOTE: The Lewis figure of .576 overall means that with him an expletive occurs more than once every two pages. Note that with each other writer the percentage falls off with the later book, whereas the incidence for *Self Condemned* more than doubles that of *Tarr* (high itself).

[a]All the expletives computed derive from "it" plus the verb "to be."

ing. Note how manner and place clutter up these sentences at the outset, sentences that end with italicized absurdities:

> It was as a protest against this strangeness that he uttered his customary *pfui!* (T 107)
>
> It was in the piano that anybody would have had to look really for her *geist.* (T 121)

These bear the real Lewis signature that helps account for the inordinate number of "strong" expletives in his pages. In *Self Condemned,* the condemnations of René are sometimes placed in adverb phrases following hard upon expletive openings:

> It was with exquisite hard-boiledness that Rotter spoke of the departure of his friend. (SC 99)
>
> It was with a mad wrench that he dragged himself away from a new surrender. (SC 391)

Tactics like these I tend to equate with the trailing absolutes discussed earlier; here, too, all of the force has gone into the subordinate elements: "exquisite hard-boiledness," "mad wrench," these are what we remember from the sentences, not their ultimate predications. When adverbs of *time* are used, though, more normal periodic power is regained. In *Self Condemned*'s most serious plot sequence, leading to the suicide of Hester, Lewis employs time expletives to chart a terrible demise. The incipient moment comes when a friend makes Hester think back to England; after that, the plot links augment:

> It was at this idyllic moment for Hester that Laura McKenzie felt impelled ... to speak of the English countryside.... (SC 334)
>
> It was in May, when, one morning, a very portentous-looking envelope arrived by mail. (SC 359)
>
> It was half-way through the meal he was called to the telephone outside in the hall. (SC 369)

Even the timeworn devices of ominous letter and phone call (the call telling René that Hester is dead), even these are enhanced because they are cast into expletive form—suspension results.

Once this climax is reached, René is doomed; with that "mad wrench" we spoke of, he tears himself from the recognition that Hester's act was done on his behalf. He condemns her and becomes a shadow of a man. Here, too, Lewis traces his demise through a pair of expletives (one in the last sentence of the novel), though these are sinisterly cast in negative form. René resumes professorship and even joins an American college.

> It was not, of course, at all as a wreck, or as a gutted shell or as an empty hangover of himself, that he appeared to himself or to anybody else. (SC 402)

> . . . and the Faculty had no idea that it was a glacial shell of a man who had come to live among them, mainly because they were themselves unfilled with anything more than a little academic stuffing. (SC 407)

A final *intension*—a last contributor to the "peltingness" of the style—may be found in the reflexive pronouns that appear in these indictments ("hangover of himself," "appeared to himself," "they were themselves"). These pronouns convey activity in little closed circles from the doer back to the doer. In *Self Condemned* there are 350 "-self" pronouns in 386 pages, a 90 percent incidence, while in *Tarr* there are more reflexives than there are pages (320 in 291—see table 5.3). Figures like these are rather formidable. When used in Joyce (see chapter two), the reflexive habit was the sign of acute intelligence. By contrast, Lewis's pages are overrun by the device, and it creates in his protagonists an obsessive isolation, a "high impassibility"—to use his phrase.

They run the risk of ridicule, too. As Lewis said of Kreisler, "those

Table 5.3   Incidence of Reflexive/Intensive Pronouns

	Number of Occurrences	Number of Pages	Incidence per Page
Tarr	320	291	1.10
Self Condemned	350	386	.91
Lewis aggregate	670	677	.99
The Lost Girl	294	372	.79
Kangaroo	404	367	1.11
Lawrence aggregate	698	739	.94
Howards End	164	315	.52
A Passage to India	192	300	.64
Forster aggregate	356	615	.58
Back	128	180	.71
Concluding	161	200	.81
Green aggregate	289	380	.76

NOTE: The order here imitates that of table 5.1, with Lawrence most closely approximating Lewis, and Forster the farthest from him. The anomaly in this tabulation is *Kangaroo*. Like *Tarr*, it has more than one "-self" usage per page, whereas *The Lost Girl* drops back to a rate nearer that of Green and Forster. *Kangaroo*'s hectoring passages, in my judgment, explain its surplus of reflexives. Sometimes a litany effect develops, as when a set of paragraphs repeat this single phrase: "The man by himself." Here ten reflexives appear on one page (K 287); such clusters help account for the high total.

who keep to themselves awaken mirth as a cartwheel running along the road by itself would" (T 84). Both halves of the simile are reflexive; this mirth is awakened "at the expense of the solitary."

When something is so automatically reflexive, the chances of sharing in something else are precluded. Thus in *Tarr*, experiences are often kept from being mutual just because these pronouns are present. Tarr's feeling for Bertha, for instance, derives from her having transposed some of his essence onto herself:

> Then [Tarr's] tenderness for Bertha was due to her having purloined some part of *himself*, and covered *herself* superficially with it as a shield. (T 66)

And one narcissistic state can replace another. Various Kreislers conduct the rape of Bertha. "The figure [of Kreisler] talked a little to fill in an interval," says Lewis; next,

> it had drawn: it had suddenly flung *itself* upon her and done something disgusting: and now it was standing idly by the window, becalmed, and completely cut off from its raging *self* of the recent occurrence. (T 178)

Not merely estrangement, but self-estrangement results. Lewis's protagonists are continually *finding* themselves in situations, *flinging* themselves into actions; they *propel* themselves, *assert* themselves, to end by *reproaching* or else *resigning* themselves; an enormous amount of transitive activity is handled in this confining mode. In *Self Condemned*, a meeting between René and his mother has to lose all intimacy when their bodies respond reflexively:

> His fingers entangled themselves in hers, and sometimes with both hands he would crush her small brown fists. (SC 16)

> The mother smiled, and as she did so the furious and bony accents of her face arranged themselves almost with a click in what was a miniature of his own characteristic mask. (SC 19)

There are ways to make these exchanges meaningful, but I think the reflexives prevent that. And if bodily components can "reflex" this way, Lewis grants abstractions the same properties. The verbs involved then will be chiefly idiomatic. Here are a few from *Tarr:*

> the indecency most plainly declared itself (T 37)
>
> a colossal relief announced itself (T 113)
>
> the traditional solution again presented itself (T 148)
>
> a jellyish diffuseness spread itself (T 293)

In spite of galvanic appearances, the verbs only record semblances of action. In a Lewis novel, "there is very little story apart from shifting prose constellations of gesture and attitude," as William Pritchard has said.[7] *Self Condemned* does not vary much from *Tarr* in this respect:

> a compensatory emotion gradually made itself felt (SC 152)
>
> the seasons made themselves visible (SC 184)
>
> the national excitement at the invasion of France communicated itself (SC 365)
>
> reason began to assert itself once more (SC 389)

All the same, the verbs can get uncomfortably dynamic when human beings do ordinary things. The casual way we manipulate our bodies, the fact that all our actions may be viewed as nauseatingly reflexive, is driven home by Lewis in statements about people having the simplest beginnings:

> Hobson resurrected himself.... (T 16)
>
> Lowndes undulated himself.... (T 37)
>
> Bitzenko curled himself up.... (T 245)

It remains for Kreisler to furnish the most harrowing instances of these usages. Could anything sound more onanistic than Kreisler "escorting himself, self-guarded siberian exile, from one cheerless place to another" (T 131)? Yet aren't we forever in the process of "escorting ourselves," Lewis might wonder. To be so self-guarded leads, inevitably, to being self-condemned. And monstrous as Kreisler is, at the time of his duel it is left for a walk-on to receive the worst indictment for solipsism. This "self-appointed second" becomes vicariously aroused by the impending duel. He goes to make the arrangements with his face lighted by "an internal grin, as it were—an exultant tightening in the regions out of sight where all his passions had their existence for himself alone" (T 242). He might be regarded as an Everyman, hugging himself to himself, a gratified onlooker at the scene of others' jeopardies.

THE WIZARD OF AS

The many absolutes in Lewis point to his avoidance of coordinate structures, a tendency that might also be detected in his odd way of changing end punctuation in the revised version of *Tarr*. In the 1928 revision he frequently joined sentences that in 1918—one assumes according to original impulse—had kept their own integrity. He would contrive compounds like "It was the purest distillation of the commonplace: he had become bewitched by its strangeness" (T 46), and other arbitrary linkages. Such late tamperings suggest his lack of incentive, originally, to frame ideas in equally weighed clauses (as Joyce and Lawrence would often do, as well as Forster). In some ways the preceding commentary has already borne this tendency out, in noting Lewis's fondness, say, for clausal similes ("as you do a doctor's waiting-room") and for other comparatives ("as distinct as that of a hospital"). Looking back to the example of the "second" with his internal grin, we notice an "as it were," a familiar comparative use of the subjunctive.

My reason for reverting to these various passages is to point to the presence of the conjunction "as." "As it were" occurs 15 times in *Tarr* and 15 times in *Self Condemned*. That strikes one as a relatively high incidence, since it could easily have been avoided (especially by so metaphoric a writer). The fact is that structures beginning with "as" seem to hover about, available to Lewis's mind's eye, and that his way of seeing perhaps preempts the word. Again we approach unsurvey-able terrain—does the way of seeing produce the word, or does the word—at certain intervals—lead the eye? As elsewhere in this study, one can only beg the question, and go on to exhibit what the writer does.

In nearly all of its manifold uses, "as" yields a spatial connotation. This is even somewhat true of its temporal meaning: "as this happened, that happened." A comparison with its synonym ("while this happened, that happened") makes it apparent that "while" carries a sense of duration which "as" discounts in favor of a more graphic simultaneity. The subjunctive, the positive degree of comparison ("as large as"), the simile—all these juxtapose states of being and are implicitly spatial. Probably the least spatial connotation comes from causal "as," avoided by most writers because it can be ambiguous ("As her lunch was finished, she called the waitress" [T 96]). All these varieties are encountered in high ratios in Lewis, along with briefer "equating" usages, where "as" sounds almost prepositional.

There are quite a number of these latter, including some yoked with prepositions: "as between" (T 55), "as of" (T 71), "as at" (T 91), "as for" (T 223), "as with" (T 265); "as from" (SC 65), "as in" (SC 97), "as against" (SC 171), "as on" (SC 274). There are also many compound adverbials: "as yet" (T 136), "as before" (SC 121), and so on. The variety attests in its own right to a predisposition. The compound Lewis favors is "as to," which occurs no less than 65 times (29 in *Tarr*, 36 in *Self Condemned*). He especially likes to spatialize an idea in advance, and then negate it (a bit Forsterian, this, but Forster would not use "as to"):

As to duelling, he knew nothing at all about that. . . . (T 248)

As to drinking, Furber never did that. (SC 254)

Statistics prove Lewis's addiction to the word. "As" is found more than twice every page in *Tarr* (678 usages, a 2.33 ratio); in *Self Condemned,* the ratio increases to 2.76, with 1,064 usages (see table 5.4, where a vast disparity separates Lewis's contemporaries from him).

There seems to be a general correlation with the other style-markers so far examined in this chapter. The Cartesian drive can claim a large share of the responsibility. "As they talked, their thinking proceeded much as follows" (SC 154). This rather un-novelistic comment oversimplifies the issue, but it does contain the familiar duality. Despite this sentence, Lewis's dualistic thinking does not produce much antithetical balance. He sees two things happening at once, and he is not usually interested in counterpoising them. In fact they are preweighted, with the "wild body's" inertia, when present, usually counting for more than the mind or the heart or the law. This may be revealed through simultaneous "as," or equational "as," or

Table 5.4   Incidence of "As"

	Number of Occurrences	Number of Pages	Incidence per Page
Tarr	678	291	2.33
Self Condemned	1,064	386	2.76
Lewis aggregate	1,742	677	2.57
The Lost Girl	662	372	1.78
Kangaroo	637	367	1.74
Lawrence aggregate	1,299	739	1.76
Howards End	423	315	1.34
A Passage to India	358	300	1.19
Forster aggregate	781	615	1.27
Back	276	180	1.53
Concluding	322	200	1.61
Green aggregate	598	380	1.57

NOTE: The count lists each "as" individually except the comparative ("as . . . as"), which is considered a single usage. The word comes up more than five times every two pages in Lewis, and not nearly as often in the other writers. (Observe that, in only 60 more pages, Lewis employs "as" nearly a thousand times more often than Forster.)

A functional word like this, which has no denotative value, comes as close as possible, presumably, to marking a habit not involving choice. In this respect, it is interesting to see how close one book of each author is to his other one. Here, as in tables 5.1 and 5.3, the order of incidence shows Lewis first, then Lawrence, Green, and Forster.

145

causal "as." The underlevels of the sentence run away with Lewis's action, one might say. There is not the resolution of extremes, as there was with Forster; a structure of Lewis's would not provide the assurance of *Howards End,* telling us, for instance, how to die:

> ... neither as victim nor as fanatic, but as the seafarer who can greet with an equal eye the deep that he is entering, and the shore that he must leave. (HE 97)

Such precision fails to mark Lewis's handling of "as."

A couple of paragraphs of representative length (150 to 170 words) will perhaps illustrate the interplay one is more likely to encounter among his constructions.

> "Come in Sorbett" she said, *as she opened the door.* The formality of the terms upon which they at present met must not be overlooked: prerogatives of past times were proudly rejected. *The same depressed atmosphere as the day before,* and the days preceding that, penetrated his consciousness. She appeared stale, in some way she was deteriorated and shabby, her worth *in the market as in his eyes* had dwindled, she was extremely pitiable. Her "reserve" (a natural result of the new equivocal circumstances) removed her to a distance, *as it seemed;* it also shut her up inside herself, in an unhealthy dreary and faded atmosphere, she who was naturally so over-expansive. She was shut up with a mass of reserves and secrets, new and old. One was a corpse, *as Kreisler was one of her secrets.* Mournfully reproachful, she mounted guard over her store of bric-a-brac that had gone out of fashion and was getting musty in a neglected shop: such was her manner, such were her sensations. (T 289)

> They carefully abstained from all mention of the approaching end of the world. Both were tired of talking about it, and also tended to boycott it *as a subject of conversation.* They shook hands at the door. *As René was hurrying up the street* his critical frenzy had one of its regular spasms. He tore his best friend [Rotter] to pieces *and himself as well;* so much devotion was embarrassing; how could one really feel at ease with a parasite, and with what ridiculous assiduity he had encouraged this man to feed upon his brain. He went round there perhaps once a month to be milked, *as it were. As the ideas imbibed in this way were observed to issue from Rotter's mouth,* René would sometimes hang his head. If only Rotter were a shade less dependent!—but he shook off the critical fiend *as he turned round into Marylebone Road.* (SC 105)

The versatility of "as," one should think, rather than the redundancy, comes to the fore here. Simultaneity—notably where René wrestles with his "critical fiend" while negotiating London streets— does dominate a bit. But there are also comparatives ("the same depressed atmosphere as," "himself as well"), easy modulants ("as it seemed," "as it were"), phrasals ("as in his eyes," "as a subject of conversation"), plus one causative ("as Kreisler was one of her secrets"). Incidentally, there are no similes in use in these paragraphs. The more literal resources of the connective are, in my judgment, of greater interest.

Given the range of possibilities, one way to proceed is to show some idiosyncratic doublings within single sentences. For instance, in those below from *Tarr*, I find the "Lewisean" signature not in the "as though" clause, but in the subdued later linkage that develops from it:

> He said this eagerly, *as though* it were a point in his argument—*as* it was. (T 58)

> ... it was *as though* he had considered Ernst *as* in duty bound to remain at the corner. (T 107)

> ... he just stalked round on a tour of inspection, *as though* to see that all was going along *as* it should. (T 142)

> ... Kreisler could hardly believe his ears, *as though* this sound had been going to accompany life, for that day at least, *as* a destructive and terrifying feature. (T 245)

Similarly, the following subjunctive comparisons from *Self Condemned* are noteworthy because they are combined in advance with "simultaneous" clauses:

> *As* his taxi propelled itself into the broad street ending in Broadcasting House, his face wrinkled up *as though* he had been confronted with a peculiarly involved historical problem. (SC 30)

> They were silent for a few moments, *as* she gazed speculatively at him, *as though* at some not very attractive problem child. (SC 36)

> It made him feel a little sick *as* he read a few paragraphs... regarding preparations for war, *as if* it were an international football match which was being staged in an unusually elaborate manner. (SC 43)

> *As* year succeeds year, marooned in Momaco, you become very conscious of the seasons, *as if* you were engaged in husbandry instead of being engaged in wasting your life.... (SC 184)

Occasionally Lewis's reliance on "as" sequences will cause him to begin and end sentences almost absent-mindedly, or at least that is their effect.

> Kreisler *as he looked doggedly up* still saw the expression on the Englishman's face that he had prefigured *as he had prepared to pop the question.* (T 106)

Here Kreisler, raising his head, sees what he had envisioned before raising his head, and no more that that! René can be caught in the same syntactic eddies.

147

As Mary moved away René accompanied her, opening the door *as they reached it*. (SC 24)

Or consider how René's loutish brother-in-law Victor gets satirized by this fore-and-aft treatment:

As a Publicity Agent, *status* was a cardinal factor in the very existence of *such a trade as* his. (SC 68)

Not that "such as" need always denigrate. It simply assumes some property of a thing that will be called to mind. This "given" may be vicious (like the public relations trade), or the opposite:

... women possessed of *such an intense life as* Anastasya always appeared on the verge of a dark spasm of unconsciousness.... (T 194)

... *such successful people as* Anastasya and [Tarr] himself were by themselves: it was *as impossible to combine or wed them as* to compound the genius of two great artists. (T 293)

With these sentences about Anastasya, we are back to Lewis's primary theme. He grants vitality (Anastasya is his symbol for it in *Tarr*), yet sees it as a state forever foreign to the artist. I believe his predilection for arresting life, for "blocking" it out in phrases like "such as," and in the related ways dealt with here, has a great deal to do with his own unwillingness to partake of life. As the enemy, he remains incorrigible.[8]

A final example of duplication—of beginning and ending a statement with an "as" clause—affords us a chance to make a distinction about similes in the two novels. Here is the sentence:

As he reached this point [Tarr] laughed aloud, *as* a sensible old man might laugh at himself on arriving at a similar decision. (T 222)

The point about this redundancy is that the simile seems unduly close to what it purports to describe, and, moreover, its force is undercut by its conditional verb ("*might* laugh at himself"). Counting similes that work in full clauses, we find that of 34 in *Tarr*, two-thirds (23) are expanded through conditionals like this ("might" or "may" or "would"), whereas of 16 in *Self Condemned*, less than one-third (5) use the conditional tense. In the first place, it is interesting to find *Tarr's* similes spun out to such lengths. Some specimens include:

as a man may eye a wife whom he suspects of intercepting his correspondence (T 73)

as a teacher would go over with each new pupil the first steps of accidence or geography (T 120)

as Mephistopheles might sink with suddenness into the floor at the receipt of some affront (T 144) as a person would [regard] some particularly eloquent chief airing his views at a clan-meeting (T 161)

Only two from *Self Condemned* show anything like the elaboration of these from *Tarr,* which represent the norm.* But the main point of divergence is that in *Tarr* there are relatively few occasions on which the conditional tense is used outside the frame of a simile, whereas in *Self Condemned* the reverse is true—true to such a degree, in fact, that conditional expressions create a major tonal effect in the later book. They supply an additive to Lewis's ground style that modifies it importantly, giving us, in my judgment, the one salient departure of that style from the style of *Tarr.* I take up this factor in the next section, and conclude with remarks about the one stylistic additive in *Tarr* that likewise has no true counterpart in *Self Condemned.*

POTENTIALITY AND CERTAINTY: *SELF CONDEMNED* VS. *TARR*

The effect of a conditional verb in a simile is different from its effect in a literal statement, because the simile-maker has assumed a knowing perspective on a situation in advance. Recall a thematic crux from *Tarr:* "those who keep to themselves awaken mirth as a cartwheel running along the road by itself would" (T 84). The final "would" sets only a mild condition, because the "vehicle" is all that is involved. There is no question about the author's surety as regards the "tenor," "those who keep to themselves." His knowledge of the situation is so well in hand that he invites comparison from terms at large. But the author is directing the reader in such instances, for over the initial situation he has given the reader no sway.

A contrary situation obtains when the conditional or probable is relied upon at the beginning. And in *Self Condemned* Lewis seems to have grounds for importing such structures. He has to prevent René Harding, with all his intelligence, from overmastering this novel and its readers.

René is too adroit at recognizing the absurd, too ready to rate his own perceptions ahead of others'; and just as Lewis humanizes him in the room, and in those moments when gravity brings him low, so does Lewis keep the reader at least abreast of René by the use of conditional expressions in the narrative. These grammatical constructions

---

*The two from *Self Condemned* are: "just as he would had he scored a century for his old school and was being congratulated by the Captain of the Eleven or the Headmaster" (SC 51–52); and "as one might keep one's eye upon a ram of notoriously aggressive habits" (SC 111).

cause the reader to appear, as it were, alongside the author momentarily, to be admitted at his level of perception.

Even when at his fairest to René—presenting him in company with Rotter Parkinson, best index of all for proving René's intellectuality—Lewis remains indirect and considers the reaction of someone observing them.

> For instance, provided with such an abstract as the foregoing, a person would undoubtedly be confused in the actual presence of these two men. The first thing this person would notice would be that René's manner was anything but that of a master, of "the boss" in this relationship. (SC 79–80)

This gives the usually condescending René the benefit of much doubt, but the point is that the judgment is left up to this putative "person" to work out. The technique here is analogous to Lawrence's in his late novel *Kangaroo,* which tended to upgrade the reader through the "déjà-vu" device on which we commented at length. Correspondingly, the narrative offhandedness in *The Lost Girl* makes a good counterpart for the assuredness of *Tarr.* Later in his career (the time span for Lawrence is much condensed), each author is in effect muting a tendency toward cockiness, not by being less "knowing," really, but by tacitly giving credit to an equally knowing reader. In *Self Condemned* this reader, by being accorded a higher wisdom, draws level with or actually passes René Harding in insight, because of the provisional style in which many passages of *Self Condemned* are cast.

Significantly, these practices recur in early portions of the novel, and tend to disappear as Lewis begins its turnabout section, "The Room." Of note are some early descriptions of René:

> When he laughed . . . he thrust forward his bristling mouth in *what might be called* the ho-ho-ho position. . . . (SC 6)

> Harding showed *what can only be described as* apprehension where the charlady was concerned. (SC 11)

The second makes for a virtual rather than a pure conditional. A few phrases like this I have taken into account, so that statistically I am giving a rough estimate of conditional expression (see table 5.5). The quantities are striking when we observe that (outside of similes) *Tarr* presents fewer than 80 conditional usages in all, whereas in "The Resignation" section that opens *Self Condemned* (151 pages) there are about 90, better than one every two pages.

Self Condemned contrives, I would say, to start off with small "panoramas," as if to involve the reader in the atmosphere contributing to René's resignation. A pair of sentences near one another in the opening chapters produce a rather pronounced effect:

It might be argued that all the absurdity flowed from the owner of the house. (SC 12)

Could anyone have entered this apartment unperceived, and have stood there observing this agitated group, he would have heard ... phrases in French escaping it.... (SC 15)

These are the two main vectors of the style marker: assuming what "might" be deemed true of a set of circumstances, and reckoning what "would" result if certain conditions had occurred. Given Wyndham Lewis's usual buttonholing practices, these are an interesting departure for him. In effect, an outside party becomes the agent for the irony. René's brothers-in-law catch the brunt of this, as they did with the absolutes. Percy's expression, for example, "*could* with a comic distinctness *be observed* transforming itself into something else" (SC 54). It is the reader as supposed onlooker who is given credit for judging the comic distinctness, and the reader is subtly upgraded in the process. Variations can find the onlooker being characterized as "anyone" or "no one" or even "the average eye":

As [Victor] strolled from one room to another ... it was with so manifest an indifference to the lapse of time, that *anyone could see* he had been born in the top drawer.... (SC 66)

This being Victor, *it may be imagined* that it was in no way to be in *his* society René had managed this party. (SC 67)

Table 5.5   Conditional Constructions

	Number of Conditionals	Number of Pages	Incidence per Page
Tarr	104	291	.354
Self Condemned	193	386	.500
Lewis aggregate	297	677	.424
The Lost Girl	38	372	.102
Kangaroo	37	367	.101
Lawrence aggregate	75	739	.101
Howards End	60	315	.190
A Passage to India	43	300	.143
Forster aggregate	103	615	.168
Back	25	180	.139
Concluding	36	200	.180
Green aggregate	61	380	.161

NOTE: Again the discrepancy between Lewis and the others is considerable. The extreme figure is *Self Condemned*'s, with a conditional occurring every other page. Numerically, the conditionals in Lewis total more than all the other writers' usages combined.

151

But *to the average eye* the hearty straggling of [Robert's] legs and welcoming movements of his arms *would indeed have spelled* good fellowship.... (SC 110)

"A clean pull!" sang Robert and *no one could say* he was averse to others scrutinizing the inside of his mouth. (SC 112)

Lewis here has a way, for once, of getting around the charge of "knowingness." And most important is the fact that René can be scored for his *own* knowingness, when Lewis employs the device against him.

A key occasion concerns his mother. All along René has railed against matriarchs and the marriage bed, finding them at the root of man's absurdity. René thus breaks with his mother as the first step in his self-exile. But just when he has reduced his family to "junk he had no further use for" (SC 144), a passage is brought up against him that makes his mother's point of view superior. The passage begins with a long appositive (reminiscent of Lawrence). It concludes in the conditional mood:

To see him arrive, walk quickly across the room, his face screwed into a certain expression, reserved for old ladies who at one time have changed one's diapers (and earlier of course have given one house room in their intestines) *all that must fill* so intelligent an old woman with amused contempt. (SC 143)

Lewis does not say the mother is contemptuous. He leaves it to the reader to agree that the son's antics "must" induce that attitude. Ultimately, though, Lewis *is* contemptuous of René's probing mind. It is an advance in Lewis's art for him to have become ill-disposed to incessant analysis. (This does not undercut those few "bedrock" analyses René achieves—it is the habitual mind-play that is faulted, while it was not in *Tarr*.) So Lewis provides the reader with the leverage to be raised above René. An early sentence catches the hero isolated:

As soon as he was alone René's face contracted. Glaring down at his glass, he *would appear to be concentrating* for purposes of analysis. (SC 60)

Here it is the conditional, and it alone, that undercuts the would-be austere thinker. In places like this, the *average* intelligence really becomes the judging norm, with the result that Lewis turns and attacks his own practices, his own austerities. This is the kind of thing Hugh Kenner meant when, in his introduction of *Self Condemned*, he said Lewis pressed "on and down through phase after phase of *hubris* ... phases concerning which Dickens or Conrad were fortunate to know nothing" (SC xv). If judged satiric, this practice of Lewis's would correspond only to that highest norm of satire, identified by Northrop Frye in the *Anatomy of Criticism,* wherein the satirist attacks himself.[9]

Toward the end of *Self Condemned,* when the fire at the Hotel Blundell has driven René back into the academic world, one sign of his disintegration is a book he writes. He has become the supercritic of history by now. "Having more fiercely than ever derided the monotonous, unvarying mediocrity and criminality which History regales us with . . . he then proceeded to go over, lock, stock, and barrel, into what Professor McKenzie had called the Party of Superman" (SC 356). At this point in the narrative Lewis gives pause:

> Here *it must be observed* that the violence of thought which was characteristic of René received everywhere an additional edge because of the mental instability developing in him just then. . . . *One might even go a step farther,* and find in his adoption of the Superman position a weakening; the acceptance of a solution which formerly he *would have refused.* (SC 356)

Lewis's air here is most discretionary, making a good contrast to René's stiffening state of mind. But then, after Hester's death, Lewis accomplishes a coup by having René fail to remember he has even written this book, much less sent off the manuscript: "it was just as though no book had been written at all" (SC 385). A relapse like this is really a plus for René. His true or best self is that which reveres Hester dead; and for a time he almost thinks her sacrifice will succeed in bringing him back to England. Only this is a false denouement, for René finally turns against Hester and violates her memory. "The lubricious little beast had got as much out of him as he had got out of her!" (SC 394). Hubris has again intervened.

In testing Hester's position toward the end, Lewis uses the conditional to indicate how she can defy expectations. Here he confers on her an individuality that no one can gainsay. On the matter of René's book, he reports her indifference:

> Before long *it must have been apparent* that he was engaged upon other work than just that [his weekly column in a Momaco newspaper]. As he did not mention what it was, Hester knew that it was *something she would regard with aversion:* and she never asked him anything about it. (SC 348)

Similarly, when René secures the columnist's job, improving "their economic position overnight," Lewis confutes expectations about Hester.

> *One would have supposed* that this last event *would have stirred* Hester into a certain elation. But that was not the case. She even warned René against the dangers of this new prosperity. (SC 340)

It may seem farfetched, yet it is arguable, that just as the conditional can flatter Lewis's audience, so, when the assumption goes wrong, can it raise esteem for a character. There is no question that Hester's is the spirit most admired in this novel: stylistic deviation adds to our apprehension of that fact.

The last scene in which she takes part is not her suicide (related after the event) but a Christmas Party. Her last dramatic act is to refrain from complicity in the toasts her husband and the McKenzies drink to themselves.

> When René's new academic venture was being toasted, *it was noticed* that Hester watched, with an exclusive concentration, the scene on the dance-floor. "And now, René, your book!" exclaimed McKenzie. But even to that she did not respond. This glass that never rose to celebrate, but which got emptied all the same, in toasts that were undivulged, at the last chilled this Christmas Party, and left an uncomfortable sense of something wrong: although, on the whole, the evening *might be described as a great success.* (SC 368)

I find that last long sentence perhaps the most haunting in the novel. It is circuitous, as Hester herself is. The "undivulged" toasts allude to her determination, firm by that time, to save René by taking her life. With his compromising she will not traffic—and he had been the one all along to make an issue about compromising. But the success of the sentence lies in its narrator's false assurances at the end; for Hester is not interested in conveying anything histrionic on this occasion. Thus author and audience are implicated in the final, contrary-to-fact conditional—one that certifies the integrity of Hester Harding. Only an onlooker who had been taken in could describe that evening as a success.

Tarr offers nothing so sustained in the way of conditional narration. However, it is of interest to note that in places where Kreisler's character is recapitulated, the device does intrude. That it tends to be clustered only at these times seems to mark something inherent about Lewis's expression. When he wants to intrigue us with an *alazon*, a clod, he has this way of bringing us into a position of superiority. Four times on the page that introduces Kreisler, the conditional appears, first with respect to Kreisler's eye. (The man stares at a Paris street, along which Tarr earlier had walked: hence the transition from Tarr's doings to Kreisler's.)

> Had [the eye] been endowed with properties of illumination and had it been directed there earlier in the day, it *would have provided* a desolate halo for Tarr's ratiocination. (T 69)

If this seems cumbersome, it is not half as elaborate as the description of Kreisler's "funeral chamber" of a room, about which Lewis makes the following conjecture:

> *Imagining yourself* in some primitive necropolis, the portraits of the de-
> ceased covering the holes in which they had respectively been thrust, *you
> would,* pursuing your fancy, *have seen* in Kreisler a devout recluse who
> had taken up his quarters in this rock-hewn death-house. (T 69)

Thus is Kreisler's death drive first suggested. Farther down the page
the tone has become less mordant—yet still conditional: "But Cafés
were the luminous caverns where he *could be said,* most generally, to
dwell..." (T 69).

Another concentration of conditionals appears on a page summing up Kreisler as a lover. A sentence beginning *"Much might be
remarked* of a common nature between this honest german and the
drunken navvy on saturday night" leads to this paragraph:

> *A casual observer* of the progress of Otto Kreisler's life *might have said*
> that the chief events, the crises, consisted of his love-affairs.... But, in
> the light of a careful analysis, this *would have been* an inversion of the
> truth. When the events of his life became too unwieldy or overwhelming,
> he converted them into love; as he *might otherwise have done,* had he pos-
> sessed a specialized talent, into some art or other. (T 93–94)

It takes three moves to get to the heart of the matter. Lewis posits a
"casual observer," replaces him with a more careful analyst, and at last
pins down the crucial factor: Kreisler has no talent. Yet it is all done
provisionally. The audience is let into the game.

The final burst of conditionals in *Tarr* confirms Kreisler's death
lust. A paragraph ends disarmingly enough:

> His life *might almost have been regarded* as a long and careful preparation
> for voluntary death, or self-murder. (T 152)

This in turn produces a truly garish paragraph. It is susceptible of
much analysis, but I only want to underscore the method by which
Lewis would have *us* allocate Kreisler to the ranks of murderers, those
who throw "flesh in Death's path" instead of monuments of unaging
intellect.

> Instead of rearing pyramids against Death, *if you imagine* some more
> uncompromising race meeting its obsession by means of unparalleled
> immobility in life, a race... throwing flesh in Death's path instead of
> basalt, there *you would have* a people among whom Kreisler would have
> been much at home. (T 152)

Ostensibly, Lewis asks his collaborators to imagine a race of death-
dealers. Actually, of course, he incarnates that race. He epitomizes
Kreisler as one of a whole class who incessantly pour into the vortex
their own and uncounted other lives, tributes to the elements raging
in them of envy and emulation. (Those who feel there is a way to

eradicate violence in this world would do well to consult Lewis's sentence.)

To conclude, I would like to illustrate from *Tarr* a statement that is only mildly provisional, as it moves from Kreisler's father to Otto himself.

> The father was jealous contemptuous and sulky, Otto the same, if perhaps you substitute "sourly roguish" for "jealous." (T 73)

The style here returns us to Lewis's regular mode of knowingness. That is the real mode of *Tarr.* Though the sentence gives latitude with respect to Kreisler ("if perhaps you . . ."), there is no latitude whatever in the "jealous contemptuous and sulky" accorded the father.

Frequently in *Tarr* Lewis rushes past would-be detaining moments by the use of triplets in adjectival form, like the one just given. The fact that there is no punctuation gives them a capsuled effect. They provide perhaps the only acceleration of pace in this otherwise rock-strewn narrative. Their main effect is of having swept past something quite patent—an effect opposite that of the conditional (and not to be met in *Self Condemned,* nor in any other work we have studied).

Susan Sontag would say that Lewis here is "stylizing" in that he is treating his material (certain portions of it) as being capable of exhaustion.[10] One even occasionally finds nouns treated this way: "Her room dress and manner were a kind of chart to the way to admire Fräulein Liepmann" (T 120); "it could never equal in scope intensity and meaning what he thought he distinguished" (T 262). There are sixteen adjective triplets run together by Lewis in this fashion. Almost all, as in the case of those describing Kreisler's father, refer to dispensable people: to a modiste barely tolerated by Kreisler ("this small indifferent and mercenary acquaintance" [T 72]); to the man he has sponged on ("Vokt had a clean-shaven depressed and earnest face" [T 80]); to one of the seconds in the duel ("His veiled cold and disgusted eyes fishily fastened upon the leg of a chair" [T 237]), and so on. While some vividness may be achieved—"depressed" and "disgusted" ring oddly in their settings here—the flourish is typically early-Lewis; it is meant to disencumber the reader from thinking too hard about these absurd walk-ons.

An instance of how telling this usage can be occurs when Bertha Lunken becomes intrigued with Kreisler. Adjacent paragraphs illuminate what happens:

> Her strange companion's dreamy roughness . . . suddenly captured her fancy. The machine, the sentimental, the indiscriminate side of her, awoke.

She took his hand. Rapid soft and humble she struck the deep german chord, vibrating rudimentarily.... (T 131)

Because of the heavily stopped adjectives, Bertha, however lumbering, is made to seem an arresting character. Each of her "sides," the machine, then the sentimental, and so on, gets a chance to function. The second paragraph just about liquefies her, though.

The culprit is the series "Rapid soft and humble." Is it not odd that nonpejorative words do the damage? They do so because they blur together into the childish sort of response that Lewis hates. Bertha vibrates "rudimentarily," becoming one more piece of flesh to be thrown in death's path (or rape's, the same thing).

Vexed by a keenness of perception that is all too caustic, Lewis mainly wants to take away life in *Tarr*. For all its similar vision, *Self Condemned* yields a grudging respect for life, even when taken away. Deliberately slipshod, run-together series like the ones in *Tarr* do not occur in *Self Condemned*. Its best passages never treat material as being capable of exhaustion. Consider the description of Hester's body on the morgue slab. The punctuation refuses any kind of "liquefying" movement: "At the top, was the long forward-straining, as it were yearning neck" (SC 371). Note an acceleration, something like that in the *Tarr* series, suddenly resisted. The check before "as it were yearning" transfers the emotion to the key word, "yearning." There is likewise, at the end of *Self Condemned,* a memorial to the early René, credited with having possessed "the bright, rushing, idealistic mind of another man" (SC 400)—before his abdication, followed by "the three years in the Hotel Blundell—three mortal, barren, desolating years" (SC 401). Both the early qualities and the destroying experience are given the credit for being real that the stoppages in the adjective series permit. René's friend McKenzie is left to view the wreckage, as far as he can do so. In a nonce usage that is the most forceful adjectival construction in either novel, Lewis records McKenzie's failure. "He could not, naturally, appreciate the full—the massive, the terrible—truth of the position" (SC 406). Here Lewis has made it possible for the rest of us to do so.*

---

*On the last page of Henry Green's *Back,* a book discussed in the next chapter, this same structure reappears: "Then he knelt by the bed, having under his eyes the great, the overwhelming sight of the woman he loved, for the first time without her clothes" (B 246).

6 HENRY GREEN: *BACK, CONCLUDING*

His syntax is his own wild and brilliant secret.
DIANA TRILLING

SHORT WAYS

Some of Henry Green's sentences could have been written by no one else, and hardly seem able to have been written by him. A passage from *Concluding,* telling of the schoolmistress Winstanley's reaction to a kissing episode in the forest, goes a short way toward illustrating Green's specialness. (Winstanley is walking Elizabeth Rock away from the scene she has stumbled across.)

> ... Winstanley, as she bent her head to listen, took her companion's hand in hers as a sort of tribute to this woman's being drenched with love. But after a few yards she let go of that hot hand.
>
> "Would you like my mirror?" she asked, and rummaged in her bag. (C 80)

The only thing odd about the sentences, Henry-Greenish if you like, is the pair of demonstratives: "this woman's," "that hot hand." In all his nine novels Green will refocus on nouns already very much "there" on the page. But two of the normal features of the passage are odd because almost deviant for Green. These are the standard verb sequence ("she asked, *and* rummaged in her bag"), and the standard attribution of nouns to their owners ("bent her head," "her companion's hand in hers," "her bag"). They show up here partly because Winstanley, a lovelorn character consigned to the sidelines, is the novel's most observant person. She proceeds pointedly, for instance, from observing Liz's disheveled state to the remedy that is in her purse. Otherwise, we would have been more likely to encounter verb pairings like these, which are common to *Back* as well as to *Concluding:*

Charley took another gulp, leaned back unburdened. (B 28)

Then the girl leaned right over, stroked that white cat. (C 41)

The verb "to lean" gives the reason in both sentences for the deletion of "and." The actions are done impulsively, with physical objectives accomplished. Logical connection between the predicates is bypassed here, whereas the logical connection was retained, even with the normally impulsive "rummaged," in the opening sample.

Sometimes Green ties in his "impulsive" doubled verbs with well-marked possessives, and sometimes not. Keeping in mind the normal pattern ("*and* rummaged in *her* bag"), we can measure two different results when the verbs are spliced—depending on whether the possessive is retained or not. A pair of sentences from *Back* can be contrasted to a pair from *Concluding* to illustrate the difference:

But he put his hands behind her head, pressed her kissing mouth harder on his own. (B 208)

"There," Nancy said, "there," pressed his head with her hands. (B 247)

"Well, well," he said, rubbed hands together. (C 25)

He rubbed a hand over his mouth, left a cobweb on the corner. (C 165)

As we see, verb sequence has again been subverted: "pressed" and "rubbed" operate without transition, as "leaned" had done. When the pronouns do appear, their role is a strong one.

The examples from *Back* are passionate. Insistent reversions to "his hands," "her head," "his head," "her hands," combined with the asyndetic predicate, show these moments between Charley and Nancy to be concentrated in impulse, yet radiant with individuality: "her kissing mouth on his own." When the possessives disappear, as in the *Concluding* group, the impulses become random and the characters diminished or confused. Not even motive is saved for them, as it would have been had Sebastian Birt been allowed the normal "and rubbed his hands together," instead of "rubbed hands together."

In fact, the two mundane phrases, "Well, well" and "There, there," uttered by a buffoon and by a heroine, reach innocuous or beautiful extremes because of the slight changes that follow in the sentences they begin. And Green's novels thrive on shuttling between these extremes.

While Green has respect for logic—like his hero Mr. Rock and heroine Nancy Whitmore in *Concluding* and *Back*—his eye and ear are most attuned to compulsive behavior, and that is why his sentences so often bend and slip their idiomatic shackles. In his use of language, many varieties of nuance keep the scenes' evolutions "fresh as wet paint"—to use one of his phrases. This has been true of him since his second book, *Living* (1929); and with the exception of the last two, *Nothing* and *Doting*, the novels hardly resemble one another. *Back* and *Concluding* are not necessarily the best pair to examine comparatively, but the fact that they appeared in 1946 and 1948 is no detriment here, since a developing style—which might be detected in another writer by comparing early and late books—is not at issue. Stylistic differences decipherable from any pair of books would be traceable to theme in his case; with him one discovers no direction from book to book, as one finds in late Lawrence (toward "spirit-of-place" fiction) or, say, in late Lewis (toward the condemnation of ego).

Back, though, as a war novel, happens to be the last of Green's "tragic" stories (*Caught* and *Blindness* were the others), and *Concluding*, set in the welfare state of a near future, is his purest example of tragicomedy. The presence of a heroine in *Back* (Nancy) and the absence of a heroine from *Concluding* (the missing schoolgirl Mary) cause a distribution of emotional concern in one place—Nancy shares Charley Summers's burdens—and a concentration of concern onto the scientist Rock in the other. The tensions generated in the books differ because of these circumstances. In order for the repatriated hero Summers to be brought back to sanity, Nancy must be consistent. Since she does not simply dole out compassion, Charley gradually comes to earn it. This steadiness of hers has some counterparts in Green's style, as even my first set of sentences showed. For those who do vacillate in *Back*, there are plenty of occasions for the withheld pronouns that signal disintegration. Here, for instance, is Charley's fellow repatriate, Middlewitch, whose isolate state is made to seem contagious, as pronouns become suppressed:

> ... he piloted [Charley] through the traffic with *a* chromium-plated arm under his black jacket, while Charley dragged *the* aluminum leg in *a* pin-striped trouser. (B 24)

Another vacillator in *Back*, Mrs. Grant (mother of Charley's dead sweetheart, Rose), reveals her dementia more than once, when Green describes how she "screened her eyes with a hand," or "was covering her mouth with a hand" (B 17, 202). This treatment can even undercut the most obvious feminine enticements, as when Dot Pitter, standing by a cabinet in Charley's office, "lowered a forearm down along the green steel front, perhaps so he could notice" (B 71).

When Nancy is involved, though, the distancing technique is dropped. It does not impair love scenes as it does later, in *Concluding*. Relatively similar passages, having comparable images (of an eel and an octopus), can illustrate the difference. In one Nancy kisses Charley; in the other, Liz kisses Sebastian (Green's women are often the initiators):

... [Charley] had again that undreamed-of sharp warmth moving and living on his own, her breath an attar of roses on his deep sun-red cheek, her hair an animal over his eyes and alive, for he could see each rose-glowing separate strand, then her dark body thrusting heavy at him, and her blood-dark eel fingers that fumbled at his neck. (B 208)

... [Liz] turned with a smile which was for him alone to let him take her, and helped his heart find hers by fastening her mouth on his as though she were an octopus that had lost its arms to the propellers of a tug, and had only its mouth now with which, in a world of the hunted, to hang onto wrecked spars. (C 46)

Though both are fervid sentences, the second has not got the power of the first, I think, in part because the octopus simile converts the final possessives. We end on "its arms," "its mouth," whereas with Nancy, Green stayed with the personal to the end: "her blood-dark eel fingers that fumbled at his neck." Liz and Sebastian are not given intact personalities, as Nancy is. They love flounderingly, like that octopus. They are so neutralized, so denatured by the State, that Liz could never have done what Nancy once needed to do, to put Summers straight: "bringing her hand up, she slapped his face hard, and it hurt" (B 101). It is the pronouns that keep demonstrating the integrity.

Overtures of love always seem disturbing in *Concluding,* with pronouns regularly suppressed. These instances are from a single page:

She forced herself on his chest as he stood there, *arms* hard around his neck.

But she gave him a Judas kiss on *the mouth.*

"I love you," he mumbled, against *lips* which were as thin as grass. (C 97)

Compare *Back*: "He just mumbled with his lips at the corners of her mouth. This began to tickle her, and his mouth felt her smile" (B 215). Nor in *Back* would one find the sequence accorded Miss Winstanley after she interrupts the lovers: "... while Miss Winstanley observed, not for the first time, how *a person's* lipstick, when it was smudged ... wounded *the* whole face like a bullet" (C 79).

These examples have presaged some differences between *Back* and *Concluding,* here the result of a single small variable. The point to emphasize—especially as regards Green's shorter sentences—is that his simple methods of modifying idioms bear evidence of a rather remarkable artist. Of all the writers of his generation, he is the one, it seems to me, who comes closest in deftness of language to the early moderns—to Joyce perhaps most of all, but also to the others with whom we have thus far been concerned.

In order to catalogue some of Green's main tamperings with

idiom, I have let ten examples from *Concluding* illustrate different categories. Then, with a similar group from *Back,* I focus on some contexts, show them working in a continuum.

Green alters idioms through compression, nonparallel juxtaposition, and various kinds of transposition. He does not do this whimsically (though that charge has sometimes been made against him). His characters dictate his *modus operandi.* In *Concluding* they are by turns stunned, alarmed, self-protective; their reactions are muffled, devious; they hourly expect the worst to happen on their summer holiday, a long day that runs its course on the grounds of a mansion-turned-state-school, where, as the novel opens, it has been discovered that a student named Mary is missing.

Green's ground style for registering their behavior, in various ways speeded up, parallels their agitation, which stays mostly near tinder pitch. There are opiates for them, too: baths, naps; a drowse-inducing forest and a numbing Founder's Day dance—but these lull only temporarily.

Certain forms of brevity steepen the gradient of alarm and imbalance; statements like the following, for instance, which find Green modifying verbs with adjectives:

> The sage looked blank at his companion. (C 7)

> Sebastian stepped sharp away from his love. (C 46)

These mark a standard method of compression for him (his best-known book, *Loving,* bristles with such usages). The result is a blunting of the action in two ways. The elision of the "-ly" implies the quick cover-up usual to most episodes in *Concluding.* By the same token, with the modifiers squinting toward the subjects, it is Rock who becomes "blank," and Sebastian "sharp," rather than the characters' actions.

Omissions of whole words (rather than just morphemes) equally insure a too-hasty disposal of matters, endemic to *Concluding.* Two samples epitomize Miss Edge, the institution's dominant but "edgy" headmistress.

> Nevertheless she left well alone for a time. (C 64)

> This only proved, so she thought, that the kindest was to pack him off forthwith to an Academy of Science. (C 195)

Here "well" and "kindest" serve as substantives, with the idioms' second halves elided. A packing-off is managed indeed—along with Edge's nice evasion of responsibility.

When the other headmistress, Miss Baker, is upset about Mr. Rock's pig, her alarm gets transferred to Mr. Rock himself, through an odd dangling-appositive embedment:

> "This is your pig, is'nt it?"
> "Daisy?" he enquired, and, *extraordinary man,* she could see he now actually laughed at her. (C 124)

Rock makes the same kind of jump when, upset about a policeman, he suddenly catches sight of his pet goose.

> As he watched the policeman he saw, out of the corner of an eye, his goose come in a rush, *absurd sight,* its neck outstretched, wings violently beating to help cover the ground it had never left. (C 59)

The two appositives ("extraordinary man" and "absurd sight") are generalizations felt *in advance* of particulars. By throwing them forward like this Green provides yet another shorthand way of showing how jumpiness prevails in *Concluding.* While here the transpositions have been syntactic, others may be grammatical; for example, the misuse of "like" and "as":

> "Now what are you getting at?" he enquired, like she were a child. (C 30)
> ... then with the great sun beating stretched earth as a brass hand on a tomtom, they seemed no less than wicked, up to date fairies in a book for younger girls who had just started reading. (C 62)

The slips here, especially in the first instance, are like slips of the tongue when hurry or anxiety cause language to get out of control: "as if she were a child" would have made Mr. Rock a more secure inquisitor than Green wants him to be. In the second sentence, the sun beating "as a brass hand" seems to forget a verb as the sentence tries to keep up with Edge and Baker, two "wicked fairies" driving by in their roadster.

Something else Green often does is leave out the "that" of a "so that" or "such that" conjunction, shortening to record hard impact. He does this in the scene in which Elizabeth sees the effect on Sebastian of a pyjama-clad girl. (This is Merode, one of the missing girls, whom Sebastian has found reposed under a fallen beech tree.)

> "Have my comb, sit here, let me button this up," she was saying ... *so* there might, for not a moment longer, be displayed in full sunlight that expanse of skin how like vanilla ice cream where one of her jacket buttons had come undone. (C 48)

Note that the swiftness of Liz's motive has been caught in the ungrammatical "so there might, for not a moment longer," which ought to read, "might not, for a moment longer." Note, too, the hanging expletive "how like vanilla ice cream," which finds no time to become attached anywhere. It is hard to conceive of this sentence actually being written. To put the matter another way: it would be hard to parody Henry Green. In another example, this one of anger, Green rushes past a "such" clause, and then gets dire results from a misplaced phrase.

> [Mr Rock] made *such* an immense gesture to summon Liz, he almost smashed off his nose the spectacles that reflected reeling chandeliers. (C 186)

The point is that we see Mr. Rock for a moment nearly smashing off his nose.

All these sentences are characteristic. They do not involve a great many varieties of substituting, but they do proffer, in their small ways, "immense gestures," because something alive comes out of them as we are "stolen up upon" and surprised.

The counterparts from *Back* follow. What is unusual about the first pair is the way they drop out an expletive in the course of a series. The others are examined in order of appearance, but these two, dealing with the husband and son of the dead girl Rose, actually frame the whole guilt cycle of the novel. It is instructive that the surprises in these sentences start the novel off (with Charley's guilt at meeting the widower James by Rose's grave), and also conclude its tragic pattern with Charley's pain being passed on to Ridley (whom Charley sees just before he is saved by Nancy's proposal). At first glance these sentences may not look as amazing as they are.

> For of all people, of all imaginable men, and fat as those geese, was James. (B 8–9)
>
> Then, absolutely without warning, stepping out of a surface shelter in the roadway, and not three paces from them, was Ridley.... (B 244)

In these periodic structures, the third unit in each series enables the verb to work, since it is possible to state that "James was fat as those geese" and "Ridley was not three paces from them." Notice, though, that the earlier series members could not have been written without expletive help. Green would have had to say, "For of all people, of all imaginable men . . . it was James"; and "Then, absolutely without warning . . . there was Ridley." Had the sentences actually been written this way, their epiphanic power would have been sacrificed. But Green's ear contrived to have "was James" and "was Ridley" epiphanize the man and the boy, and the extraordinary fact is that he chose to do this twice. Neither predicate leaps out at the reader. The slightly broken parallelism enables Green to slip both bereaved characters onto the page, carrying with them the infinitesimal shock that makes all the difference in his writing, and sets him apart from laboring grammarians. The illustrations that follow roughly help to pace Charley Summers's career in the novel; I place the idiomatic departures in brackets as each comes along, for convenience' sake.

Repatriated, Charley's problems go back to France, his wound, and his imprisonment. His dazed condition is conveyed early, through his thoughts about an artificial leg, plus Green's odd play on words:

> [redundant morpheme] He supposed they would not... make him pay for the new limb waiting there *numb and numbered* in a box. (B 7)

As his numbness wanes and he can even hear the word "rose" without a twinge, Green portrays his new relief this way:

> [omitted modal verb] "Why," she said, "your voice rose," and again, as this word came through, he *not even experienced guilt.* (B 40)

Charley is drawn next to making advances to his secretary, Dot Pitter, but his inexpertise produces confusion:

> [transferred epithets] Yet he found that anything so *simple* as placing his head against a woman's, was not so *ordinary* in practice. (B 52)

Observe that the idiom ought to read, "anything so ordinary... was not so simple in practice." But with this usage Charley's bafflement would have disappeared.

Dot Pitter in her turn, let down rudely by Charley during a weekend at James's ("Charley'd had her down to be gooseberry"), has several ways of saving face through unconcerned grammar:

> ["like"/"as" substitution] Charley'd never come out of himself, he'd stayed *like he was* in the office. (B 144)

Her contractions, along with the breezy "like" clause, dismiss the issue. But, as we saw in *Concluding,* Green resubstitutes "as" for "like"—on one occasion, in order to suit the depressed mood that has befallen Charley:

> ["as"/"like" substitution] He was left, so that... he could not speak, paralysed, for an instant, *as* Mr. Grant. (B 208)

As for Nancy, given her spirited address to whatever may occur, Green lets her mind frame the kind of free appositive that sometimes operates in *Concluding.* But this happens on someone else's behalf with Nancy.

> [noun-phrase embedment] Then, hearing a noise in the kitchen, and thinking it might be burglars, *poor old Dad what a night to choose,* she crept up to the door and looked through the crack. (B 214)

165

It is during this time of Grant's last illness, when he is attended by his unacknowledged daughter, Nancy, that Charley's own crisis comes to a head. While he is bedded below Grant's sick room, he suspects Nancy will come in to him, and is on pins and needles.

> [transposed conjunction] Then he switched on a light, got off the sofa, and opened the door *so,* when she did come, *that* she could get in as quietly. (B 216)

The clause "when she did come" is such an important hope to him that it splits the conjunction that would usher her in. However, Charley guesses wrong. Grant's death is no proper occasion for Nancy to relieve Charley's physical needs. It isn't until after the Ridley episode (when Nancy's resemblance to his mother burns into the child's mind) that Charley's reprieve will come, when he is proposed to by Nancy. The burden of pain will then have shifted. Like Grant's early adultery (from which Nancy was born) Charley's adultery with Rose is never expiated. The consequences of both acts remain, but Ridley bears the symbolic brunt of them in the end. Seeing Ridley, Charley feels "he had never seen such pain on any face" (B 244); one page later Nancy's proposal saves him. Even this release is accomplished through an amazing doubling, one that cancels the deadening effect of "numb and numbered" by butting two hopeful idioms together to convey the wonder of Nancy's offer.

> [idiom overlap] "You really mean it?" he asked, and *for the rest of his life, for the life of him,* he could not remember anything of what passed during the remainder of that afternoon. (B 245)

While the symptoms in the ten last sentences have been of a similar, emergent, sort, Green's "attack" has resulted in a good deal of diversity. The nonce usages are what need underscoring, with statistics not a matter of concern thus far. Before proceeding to Green's longer sentences—since subordination has much to do with the way these augment—it will be useful to note some special clause-types he elects within periods of short scope. Three of them are worth quantifying: delayed causatives (that follow rather than precede a process), remotely attached relative clauses, and relatives that are headed by redundant conjunctions. Though right-branching syntax results, the odd, late placement of these clauses confers on them almost independent status. They are rarely found in the other writers (see table 6.1), but when encountered, they do throw the emphasis on subordinates, as with Green.[1]

By placing results first, ahead of intensives that ought to precede them, Green comes up with a dozen inversions of the following sort in *Back* and *Concluding:*

He almost laughed he was so frantic. (B 57)

Then she took pity on him, he looked so puzzled. (B 234)

Edge had to keep herself from clicking her fingers together she was so exasperated. (C 108)

She smiled through her mood, they looked so serious.... (C 145)

Note that each time the weight swings over to the causative factor. Even an active consequence like "she took pity" becomes subsidiary to what brought it on; due to the nature of the intensive construction, the late-focused word in each case becomes an adjective. Thus Green's inversions make us linger on characters' states, not their actions: "frantic," "puzzled," "exasperated," "serious." Typical of him, affects have asserted control.

Green's latecomer relative clauses work a little differently. They manage to appear independent (because of their remote antecedents), yet a need to recall the headword throws emphasis back upon the sentence's origin. Contexts may be tame enough—as when two women's mild evasions are summed up—but the odd sentences perturb somewhat:

She said this with an easy mind, *who* had a ton and a half stowed safe in the other cellar. (B 35)

"Of course," *Edge* replied, *who* had, in fact, forgotten these decorative birds. (C 87)

Fourteen of this type appear (eight in *Back,* six in *Concluding*). The longer the relative clause is delayed, the more enigmatic is the device. *Back*'s strongest examples are not matched by what is typical for *Concluding:*

He might have been watching for a trap, *who* had lost his leg in France for not noticing the gun beneath a rose. (B 3)

But Charley raised his eyes to *Middlewitch* for the first time, *who* could only stare at what was opened to him in them. (B 133)

... Marchbanks took a wet towel off closed eyes and let her *hand* fall back, *which* still held this towel, over the far side of the armchair. (C 91)

The *Concluding* sample, recording physical unease, just illustrates the awkward surface of that novel. Accordingly, Miss Marchbanks's "hand" is only a short way off from the transposed "which." In the sentences about Charley Summers, though, there is real delay. The retarded placement of "who" imparts an almost Biblical ring to each statement. A reverberance is set up (carrying back to the sentence's beginning), with something of Charley's vulnerability underscored— his deep injuries, which leave him "watching for a trap," and make even the callow Middlewitch "stare at what was opened to him" in Charley's eyes.

The most consistent mannerism of the three covered in table 6.1 involves Green's heading of adjective clauses with redundant conjunctions. Thirteen occasions arise in *Concluding,* eight in *Back.* Fairly standard illustrations follow in italics.

> ... the sound brought home to him a stack of faggots he had seen blown high by a grenade ... *and which* he had watched fall back, as an opened fan closes. (B 4)

> ... she asked in just the voice his mother had used, dead these many years, *and whom* he never thought of, after the doctor put those stitches in his cut. (B 179)

> "But I ..." the girl began, raising limpid, spaniel's eyes to Miss Edge, *and that* were filling with easy tears.... (C 74)

> It was like a prisoner, confined with others to a workshop in which talk is forbidden, *and who* has learned to scream defiance as an unheard ventriloquist beneath the deafening, mechanical hammers. (C 178)

The redundancies occur mostly because of elliptical structures preceding them: ("[who was] dead these many years," and so on). It is true that these contexts are emotion charged. In spite of that, I would say that of all Green's mannerisms, this recurrence of imperfect parallelism is least to be explained by context. It is more a liking for early

Table 6.1 Anomalous Clause Constructions (Adverbial and Adjectival)

	Late Intensives	Remote Relatives	Redundant Relatives	Total	Number of Pages	Incidence
Back	8	8	8	24	180	.133
Concluding	4	6	13	23	200	.115
Green aggregate	12	14	21	47	380	.124
The Lost Girl	6	3	1	10	372	.027
Kangaroo	7	2	3	12	367	.033
Lawrence aggregate	13	5	4	22	739	.030
Howards End	4	1	0	5	315	.016
A Passage to India	1	2	0	3	300	.010
Forster aggregate	5	3	0	8	615	.013
Tarr	2	2	4	8	291	.027
Self Condemned	2	6	5	13	386	.034
Lewis aggregate	4	8	9	21	677	.031

NOTE: The figures for Lawrence and Lewis are about identical. Their tendency to deviate is minimal, and the anomalies in Green occur at four times the rate computed for them. Forster is outstripped at a ten-to-one rate. Still, it is interesting that, out of so many pages, one can find sentences now and then corresponding to Green's.

compression and a need, next, to fill out a further subordinate; here, as with his other "short ways" with idioms, Green finds a method of coping as if but partly thought out. Everything seems owing to his slightly off-line scanning, a knack he has of letting his material emerge on its own, so to speak, while pen and mind concord in their motion. He cannot be pinned down to one or two methods of saving ground. In fact, devices of elision often work together with much more elaborate sentence components, going well past these "and which" clauses of his. Relative clauses do remain the secret in his arsenal, though. His more climactic arrangements, which owe much to them, are the focus of the final sections of this study.

CADENCES AND SYNTACTIC CLIMAX

The first full-dress article on Green bore the title "Henry Green: Dispossessed Poet"; the first "leader" accorded him in the *Times Literary Supplement* was entitled "A Poet of Fear."[2] From any novelist who is considered "poetic," one might expect an answering sensitivity for rhythm. The overwhelming vacuity of *The Good Soldier,* for example, is the result in part of Ford's avoidance of closure rhythms in that novel. Bad rhythms, more even than tonal deficiencies, are responsible for the bathetic narration of *The Good Soldier;* they are appropriate in that they help fix Dowell, the narrator, as a moral cipher. None of the works we have been studying resembles Ford's tour de force, for none are written with as poor an ear for cadence.

Having touched on rhythms earlier, in the *Dubliners* chapter, I have forestalled mentioning them again until now. However, what is now said about Green is said against a background of the others under study, with information given about prose rhythm for all of them.

The compilations deal with endings of paragraphs only.[3] In chapter two Joyce's paragraph closure was surveyed—the way he generated "final" rhythms through accumulations of unstressed syllables. That technique is reapplied here. The count records both falling (cursus) rhythm, with terminals unstressed, and the less common, rising, rhythm, ending on a masculine stress. This masculine form I call the "Henry Green cursus." It involves a sequence of at least three unaccented syllables rising to a stressed ending. This is the pattern of the final sentence of "The Dead" ("upon all the líving and the déad"); it also appears at the ending of *Kangaroo* ("over a cold, dark, inhóspitable séa"). Green has a tendency to favor this ending—so much so that I expected he would outstrip all the others in this regard. It happens that he does not, because of the high incidence in one book, *Howards End*. It creates an anomaly in that about 7 percent of its paragraphs—a high figure—end on the "Henry Green cursus." Otherwise there is a fairly substantial degree of parity among our novelists insofar as cadences are concerned. (See table 6.2. I have included counts for *The Good Soldier* along with the others, to illustrate that the closures of that book are kept deliberately unrhythmical.)

To dispense with Ford's calculated bathos quickly: note in table 6.2 that all our writers approach a 25 percent incidence for cadenced endings, whereas the paragraphs in *The Good Soldier* do not reach an aggregate of even 20 percent. Of our main novelist group, Lawrence is lowest (24.2 percent—here we may recall his trick of undercutting his paragraphs at their conclusions, discussed in chapter three). Even so, Lawrence uses the standard cursus more often than Green and Forster; they, meanwhile, surpass him and the others in using the masculine endings.

This is not to say, however, that I interpret from these counts any

Table 6.2   Rhythmic Closure in Paragraphs

	Number of Paragraphs	Percentage Rhythmic Closure	Standard Cursus		"Henry Green" Cursus	
Back	980	22.7	136	16.7%	59	6.0%
Concluding	1,325	25.9	258	19.4%	86	6.5%
Green aggregate	2,305	24.6	421	18.3%	145	6.3%
The Lost Girl	2,129	25.5	459	21.5%	86	4.0%
Kangaroo	1,711	22.3	307	18.0%	77	4.5%
Lawrence aggregate	3,840	24.2	766	20.0%	163	4.2%
Howards End	868	24.9	156	18.0%	60	6.9%
A Passage to India	624	24.4	116	18.6%	36	5.8%
Forster aggregate	1,492	24.6	272	18.2%	96	6.4%
Tarr	1,396	27.3	296	21.2%	85	6.1%
Self Condemned	1,080	25.0	213	19.7%	57	5.3%
Lewis aggregate	2,476	26.2	509	20.5%	142	5.7%
Dubliners	567	26.1	116	20.5%	32	5.6%
The Good Soldier	547	19.8	90	16.5%	18	3.3%

NOTE: The inclusion of Ford's *The Good Soldier* helps point up a consistency among our writers. He falls below every one of them in both categories. He is weakest in the area of the "Henry Green" cadence, which occurs in only 3 percent of his paragraphs.

The fact that *Back* and *Concluding* both reach 6 percent is significant. *Howards End*, up near 7 percent, seems an anomaly and not much more; I do not regard Green and Forster as being similar. For one thing, Forster writes much longer paragraphs. Green's are shorter and more numerous, so that the opportunity for *hearing* cadence seems greater.

170

similarity between Green and Forster. If the figures reveal anything, it is the marked consistency in Green's case. Only *Back* and *Concluding* (with figures of 6 percent and 6½ percent) show high incidence of masculine closure for a *pair* of novels. Of course this is only to point a direction—the significance of Green's preference for this cadence must be referable to context.

A "gathering" effect is the first thing to mark when a run of unaccented syllables becomes "cinched up" with the final beat. In *Back* this happens more often in medium-length sentences, say of under 40 words, while in *Concluding* many long sentences, running 80 words or more, end this way.

Structurally, the placement of cadenced descriptions early can make them memorable. In *Back,* two paragraphs from the opening graveyard sequence link Charley's infatuation for Rose with the wound he received in France. Green ends these consecutive passages with the same beat. He describes Charley as

> . . . a young man with a wooden leg that did not fit, searching for a tomb. (B 6)

and then considers him thus:

> . . . in his usual state of not knowing, lost as he always was, and had been when the sniper got him in the sights. (B 6)

The whole problem of Charley's past—his state of "not knowing," which Green equates with his fixation for Rose—is fused here in this symbol. The repeated cadence may not be crucial, but it clearly adds to the effect. Early in the novel, moreover, passages have a way of ending with the same sort of resonance on Rose's name.

> And then blamed himself that he did not think oftener of Rose. (B 38)
> . . . the system he had installed . . . had kept him sane throughout the first reflowering of Rose. (B 43)

Later, but still before he realizes Nancy is the one who will save him, Charley muses over the living girl in phrases that take somewhat the same shape. (Green enables himself to balance Nancy against Rose this way, in Charley's psyche.) Though Nancy's name is less alluring than Rose's, Green can do something positive about this (and also about her looks) through his cadencing. This all adds up as a lucky thing for Charley.

> He'd had no idea he could be so excited at the mention of her name. (B 159)

> He laughed in admiration, more particularly of her looks. (B 168)

These short sentences glow with health. In the late rose garden scene, 70-word sentences fulfill the promise, in the descriptions of glowing rose briers and of the kiss Nancy gives Charley. The setting, a blitzed garden at dusk, is more reminiscent of Green's treatment of place in *Concluding:* the sentences are sinuous, occupying whole paragraphs, each ending on this "cursus":

> ... the briers ... were alive, as alive as live filaments in an electric-light bulb, against this night's quick ágōnȳ ōf thē sún. (B 207)

> ... he could see each rose-glowing separate strand [of her hair], then her dark body thrusting heavy at him, and her blood-dark eel fingers that fúmblēd āt hīs néck. (B 208)

Not only does the garden scene parallel the early one, in the graveyard, but the cadences themselves are heard again, those that had given Charley up for lost, "searching for a tomb," and that now reclaim him, "against this night's quick agony of the sun."

In *Concluding,* where places are fraught with a sense of magic, even short passages can resonate as though each locale were charmed.

> ... [it was] as though she were bathing by floodlight in the night steaming lake, beech shadowed, mýstīcāllȳ waŕmed. (C 52)

> ... he had to enter and be lost, as if by magic, in a cube of impénetrāblē sháde. (C 153)

These effects are achieved by placing a long modifier before the final monosyllable. The long vowel sounds of "shade" and "warmed" are made that much more powerful when led up to by the syllable groups that end the qualifiers.* One does not judge these to be facile effects. A good writer might arrive at them, but could hardly prescribe them. Green, one would think, imagining that steaming lake, that shadowed mansion entrance, would find the qualifiers rising up in anticipation—rather than be seeking a formula for a cadence.

Concerning the dance in *Concluding,* which is the most anaesthetizing event in the whole novel, Green has four sentences, among the longest he has written, that end on his masculine cursus. They average 120 words in length. The first two, placed at early and midway stages, are forecasts of how the dance will affect the girls; the second two bring in the headmistresses, who receive comfort and power from it. Buzzers arouse the girls in the first two instances—for breakfast and tea—at which waking point I pick up the sentences:

---

*An ironical charm is even given to a drag on a cigarette taken by Miss Edge, when her unresonant "puff" follows a protracted adjective: "With a languorous gesture, Edge took one more anaésthetīzīng púff" (C 190).

... buzzers called her girls to rise so that two hundred and eighty nine turned over to that sound, stretched and yawned, opened blue eyes on their white sheets to this new day which would stretch on, clinging to its light, until at length, when night should fall at last, would be time for the violĭns aṅd tħe dánce. (C 16–17)

... eyes, opening to reflected light... disclosed great innocence in a scene on which no innocence had ever shone, where life and pursuit was fierce, as these girls came back to consciousness from the truce of a summer after luncheon before the bŭsīnḗss ōf tħe dańce. (C 89)

As the girls turn over "to" a sound, and open their eyes "to" reflected light, so does Miss Edge sense how she and Miss Baker will open festivities "to" waltz music.

Indeed... she was already conscious of a glow within her at the prospect of so much that would inevitably please... when Baker, with herself, in front of all the students dressed in their clear frocks, could sway out in one another's arms at last to open everything to that thúndēr ōf tħe wáltz. (C 113)

Then, lastly, in "spinsterish" command, the two women have their reward, surrounded by "one hundred and fifty pairs in white," while,

... equally oblivious, inside their long black dresses, Miss Baker and Miss Edge lovingly swayed in one another's bony grip, on the room's exact centre, to and fro, Edge's eyes tight closed, both in a culmination of the past twelve months, at spinsterish rest in movement, barely vĭōlābĪe, ālońe. (C 157)

Notice that the fourth of this motif group ends not unlike the first, with the semantics only a little shifted, in the move from "violins" to "violable."

Green has a way of checking this sinister prose. When Edge, at her study window, is anticipating her great moment at the dance, her reverie is interrupted by the approach of Mr. Rock and his͵pig. Green gives this staccato transition: "Bút Eḋge hād caúght sīght ōf tẃo spécks" (C 17). The scansion partly shows what has been true all along—that Rock and his animals represent a potential rebuff to her dreams of conformism. The novel never does conclude with conformity's victory, it only points the way (that is why it is "concluding"). Even after the long sentence above, describing the women as "inviolable," there is a shift to a 20-word paragraph that rescues at least one student—the overnight truant Merode—from the spell of the dance: "Above, locked safe into a sick bay͵ curtains drawn close against the moon, Mérōdḗ's īnfānt bréathīng tóld sħe wás āsléep." Regular iambs here, but again, the scansion is incidental: the short sentence poised against the long is the rescue force. Green insinuates this push-pull, stop-and-go pattern throughout *Back* and *Concluding*. It is a way he has of keeping his writing earthbound. His feeling, clearly, is that ordinary life moves at the behest of this alternating current. It might be described, not as a flow between poles (of attraction and repulsion, say, as in Lawrence), but rather as attraction and cessation, with the arrival of a deadened prosaic "middle," for which Green reserves much value.

Compare two passages from *Back* and *Concluding*, where sixty-word, increasingly lurid sentences are checked by six- and eight-word paragraphs that try to get the characters back to their senses.

> ... He began to take in [Miss Pitter's] forearms, which were smooth and oval, tapering to thin wrists, with a sort of beautiful subdued fat, also her hands, light nimble bones with fingers terribly white, pointed into painted nails like the sheaths of flowers which might any minute, he once found himself feeling late at night, mushroom into tulips, such as when washing up, perhaps.
> He dreaded getting into this condition. (B 48–49)

> ... There was no sign of Marchbanks, which was, perhaps, to be expected after the ridiculous misunderstanding that had been uncovered about not calling the doctor, but Miss Baker was absent, and, most significant of all, Sebastian Birt had not put in an appearance, which was inexcusable after what had occurred, and, for that matter, was still going on, perhaps.
> Because they still had no news of Mary. (C 99)

While the abrupt transitions end a kind of fantasia that has been built up (for different reasons), it should be pointed out that the long sentences have their own check points. Both were readied for a prosaic shift by being ended with "perhaps." In both cases, before that, momentum had been rebuilt by "which" clauses ("which might any minute"; "which was inexcusable"). Earlier, that was how their momentum had begun ("which" clauses occurring at the first pause), only to be checked midway (by "also" and "but"). So, within some of Green's long sentences, there is already some "push-pulling" that can be doubled on by pitting short sentences against the long ones.

It might be better, then, to describe Green's long sentences as "quasi-poetic," in that they reveal methods of checking amplification as well as sustaining it. I have remarked occasions of poetic resonance; it may be well to examine his special kind of syntactic climax, which enables his long sentences to bear his autograph.

In *Back* there are 26 sentences of 60 words or more, in *Concluding*, 48. Averaging the two books, one can expect one long sentence for every five pages of text. This more than doubles the incidence one finds for the other writers being studied (see table 6.3). Green's sentences lack the antithetic parallelism of Forster's; they rarely show the parataxis of Lawrence's long sentences; nor do they feature the absolute constructions and other "pelting" devices observed in Lewis's. Long sentences do need to work on some scheme of repetitiveness; Green's are essentially multileveled, right-branching constructions— they are generated through manifold subordination.

The one pure example of a periodic sentence in either book is this from *Back* about Dot Pitter:

> But when she found an advice note from Braxtons for the joint rings in question, and saw that she had not initialled it, and therefore, that she had never seen the thing, and, consequently, that Mr. Pike, the chief draughtsman, must have kept it back on purpose—when she came into his room again she leaned her head on that beastly green card cabinet, and cried. (B 51)

Here is a movement wholly left-branching, with the "when" clause restated after that opening chain of consequences, bringing Miss Pitter's grievances to a head, after which "she leaned her head . . . and cried." Not only is such staging untypical of Green, but so is the dramatic ordering of the final predicate, which rests the whole sentence on the single word "cried."

A later sentence, less frustrating to Dot (when James Phillips enters her bed), approaches a more typical mode.

Table 6.3   Sentences of Sixty Words or More

	Number of Sentences	Number of Pages	Incidence per Page
Back	26	180	.145 (1/7 pp.)
Concluding	48	200	.240 (1/4 pp.)
Green aggregate	74	380	.195 (1/5 pp.)
The Lost Girl	22	372	.059 (1/17 pp.)
Kangaroo	15	367	.041 (1/25 pp.)
Lawrence aggregate	37	739	.051 (1/20 pp.)
Howards End	12	315	.038 (1/28 pp.)
A Passage to India	24	300	.080 (1/13 pp.)
Forster aggregate	36	615	.059 (1/18 pp.)
Tarr	28	291	.096 (1/10 pp.)
Self Condemned	53	386	.137 (1/7 pp.)
Lewis aggregate	81	677	.120 (1/8 pp.)

NOTE: Where the percentages for Green average out to one sixty-plus sentence in five pages, those for Lewis indicate one long sentence every eight pages; for Forster, one in eighteen; and for Lawrence, one in twenty.

175

Then, after another very enjoyable little party over the road, she went up early to get her beauty sleep, because it was a pity to throw away this good country air which was already doing things to her skin, and she was just dropping off when the door did open a crack, someone came in, into her bed even, the sauce, and, believe it or not, it was that fat James, though everything had been so dark she hadn't known till after. (B 145)

This sentence tends to lose periodicity after its first clause: "she went up early . . . *because*"; the same thing happens again: "and she was just dropping off *when*. . . ." But an important hesitancy occurs when the second clause develops some seriation:

   a. the door did open a crack,

   b. someone came in, into her bed even, the sauce,

   c. and, believe it or not, it was that fat James

These three members are (*a*) neutral; (*b*) right-branching (ending with the free appostive "the sauce"); and (*c*) left-branching (by the interposition of "believe it or not"). Once Green has reinvigorated the passage by that last bit of periodicity, he lets it trail off to the point of bathos. (Sauce indeed, not to reveal who he was "till after"!)

Concluding, which has no purely periodic sentences, presents many declensions similar to this last. In one of its motif statements, describing the settling of starlings, the seriation goes much the same way.

[*a*] They swarmed above the lovely elm, [*b*] they circled a hundred feet above, until the leader, followed by ever greater numbers, in one broad spiral led the way down [*c*] and so, as they descended through falling dusk in a soft roar, they made, as they had at dawn, a huge sea shell that stood proud to a moon which, flat sovereign red gold, was already poised full faced to a dying world. (C 143)

Briefly, the first independent clause remains neutral; the second is right-branching, ending on the "until the leader" clause; the third has three separate embedments that hitch it back toward periodicity: "and so, *as they descended* . . . they made, *as they did at dawn,* a huge sea shell . . . to a moon which, *flat sovereign red gold.* . . ."

With these increments one approaches something close to uniqueness in Henry Green's prose, namely, his tendency to check nonperiodic thought with late semblances of periodicity. Essentially Green is a writer of loose, right-branching sentences that seem to carry the imprint of thought in the making. But as these augment, imperfect parallelism begins to develop. Once this happens, qualifications interjected into the late parallel elements retard the right-branching flow, occasioning a late rhetorical "lift" at the point of syntactic climax. Yet, most typically of all, the last element of a final series will be extended *to the right,* thought and feeling carrying past any regathering "check," as it were, with the vision at the end completed unrhetorically. Despite even the "flat sovereign red gold" holding back the passage about the starlings at the end, the final movement of that sentence is right-branching and downshifting, a relative clause developing out of a relative clause: "a huge sea shell *that* stood proud to a moon *which,* [pause], was already poised. . . ."

Green's long sentences are remarkable for such "downshifting" (often through consecutive relative clauses) while still retaining some architectonic patterning along the way. (And, at last, some final downshift.)

A 62-word sentence from *Back* follows. The pattern is nearly identical to that in *Concluding,* except that the parallels take place in a series of noun clauses.

> Then, with surprising intuition, he supposed [a] that one crisis in this life inevitably brings on another, [b] that she wouldn't have kissed him if Mr. Grant had not been having a relapse (even if they neither of them knew), [c] nor, and here he fell unwittingly on the truth, would she have asked him if it hadn't been for the now doubly serious illness. (B 212–13)

The key to the structure of the middle unit is the parenthesis; it creates an "if" clause following an "if" clause, making a movement that is wholly right-branching. Then, in the third unit, the parenthetical element ("and here he fell unwittingly") is shifted to the left. Again we have retardation before the climax—and are brought to rest, surprisingly enough, on another "if" clause!

A last rendition from *Back* shows how many levels of "downshifting" may occur before Green does something about late parallelism. This sentence of 66 words deals with the hold Charley's dead sweetheart has on him. Coming early in the novel, the syntax well mirrors his confusion. The labeled clauses (*a* to *e*) are of all three types: noun, adjective, and adverb. But some focus comes at the end, with Charley's memories of the girl, which take a parallel form (indicated by my italics):

> He could not even remember her ever saying [a] that she had been in this churchyard, [b] which was now the one place [c] one could pay a call on Rose, [d] whom he could call to mind, [e] though never all over at one time, or at all clearly, *crying,* dear Rose, *laughing,* mad Rose, *holding her baby,* or, oh Rose, *best of all in bed,* her glorious locks abounding. (B 5)

The participles in this series attach to the (*d*)-level of clausation, and their antecedent is "whom." Of the four members of the series, the first two are followed by free appositives ("dear Rose," "mad Rose"), but "holding her baby" breaks that pattern. The pattern is then in-verted: "oh Rose, best of all in bed." Here is Green's brief periodic check, at the climax. But that transposition leaves a gap. As Green fills it, he extends the final element to the right, with the absolute "her glorious locks abounding." In doing so, right at the point of describ-ing Rose in bed, Green focuses on her hair, the allurement beyond all others that Charley cannot fight down as the girl's memory haunts him. The glorious locks, on their syntactic own (as in Wyndham Lewis), have control.

From among *Concluding's* long sentences one can locate several with modulations like these, and the multiple downshifting on the whole is a constant in Green. But some mutant paragraphs in *Conclud-ing* can indicate that book's trend toward more random conclusions. The following one records the suspicions of Edge's deputy, Miss Marchbanks, about the forester Adams, a sinister figure who might have been involved in the schoolgirls' overnight truancy. In the clause structure of this long sentence, the (*b*)-level is serial and so marked. When later levels become phrasal instead of clausal, however, the early parallelism, marked by italics, is vitiated.

> She'd come on [Adams] at such a curious spot, the clearing by the New Plantation, [*a*] where he was seated in a sort of hut, [*b*] *which* she did not recognize, [*b*] *that* seemed to be made entirely of old doors, [*b*] and *which*, [*c*] if behind a dwelling house instead of out in the open, could have been taken [*d*] by anyone [*e*] for the outside privy [*f*] back of an uncultivated garden [*g*] of a few wild, gay, separate flowers. (C 91)

This sentence appears convoluted only at first, because of the shift from "which" to "that," stepping the sentence down another level, at first glance, before the reader corrects himself.[4] It is an ap-propriate confusion for a hut almost obscenely seeming to be made of old doors. After the next "which," amplification about this sinister hut would appear to start. However, the phrasal sequence (*d-e-f-g*) turns out to be extraordinary. These prepositionals do not amplify the "hut"; they successively amplify themselves. It is some supposed "privy" that is back of a garden; the "garden" that grows with gay flowers. The hut has been all but blent out of the picture by all these suppositionals.

The mind—the character's and the reader's—has been led away. Though other examples must help verify this, a thematic difference between *Concluding* and *Back* seems reflected here. The paragraph itself, like the book in which it appears, might be described as "wind-ing down." *Back's* long sentences do not show this symptom. *Back* is a resolved novel—resolved through episodes that have been alluded to:

the death of old Grant, the transference of burden to Ridley, the betrothal of Charley and Nancy. But *Concluding,* as it winds down, leaves its predicaments unresolved when Rock retires at the end of his day. A look at one of its earliest long paragraphs, describing the mist-laden grounds of the Institute, leads to the image of an undressed woman letting her hair down—but the picture has nothing of the effect of the similarly placed one in *Back,* with Rose's "glorious locks abounding."

> At this instant, like a woman letting down her mass of hair from a white towel in which she had bound it, the sun came through for a moment, and lit the azaleas on either side [a] before fog, redescending, blanketed these off again; [b] as it might be white curtains, [c] drawn by someone out of sight, [d] over a palace bedroom window, [e] to shut behind them a blonde princess undressing. (C 6)

Even the way the opening simile leads the eye from woman to hair to towel suggests a principle of replacement instead of serial accumulation. By the end of the passage it is as though the fog has been forgotten in the metaphor of drawn shades—drawn in nonparallel progression "by" someone, "over" something, "to shut behind them" a third thing. (Such was the prepositional pattern of the earlier example.) True enough, the blonde princess undressing is a heartstopping image. But if it fixes the mind's eye it does so to the exclusion of the fog bank that led up to it. I submit this did not happen with the triad "dear Rose . . . mad Rose . . . oh Rose" in *Back.*

The house, equally with the grounds in *Concluding,* comes in for a share of panning-camera description. In one place a 79-word passage suggests a limit to which Green's downshifting clauses may stretch.

> When the owner rebuilt he had replaced a vaulted roof of stone by oak, and put flat oak panelling eight foot up the walls, [a] all of which, including a vast bow window over the Terraces, had been varnished a hot fox red, then, at some later time, treated with lime, [b] until the wood turned to its present colour, the head of a ginger haired woman [c] who was going white [d] as her worries caught up, [e] in the way these will. (C 102)

Again we have a conclusion focusing on a woman's hair, but it would have been enough for the metaphor to have stopped with the color of ginger. Instead, in three subsequent clauses, Green has supposed the woman's hair turning white, the increase of her worries, and the well-known fact that these "will" mount up. At one and the same time, the history of the Institute's paneling has been given and allowed to evanesce, because attention seems to have strayed.

The susceptibility of the people of *Concluding* to sudden and haphazard influence seems the source of sentences spun out like these. In *Back* hammer blows are needed to break in on Charley Summers's preoccupations. Of all Green's characters Charley is the most static, the slowest to react. But in the flux of *Concluding*, distractions and dreads of all sorts—even whetted expectations—galvanize the characters. Assaults on their senses are too strong for their minds. Accumulating loose ends, the long sentences convey the insistence, the pressingness, of things that bid to throw characters out of balance. Such *sentences* are refused balance. An appropriate figure for dread occurs when Merode, the returned truant, is grilled by Marchbanks in the principals' sanctum. The walls of this room have a checkerboard dado that mesmerizes the girl. "And while her horror at this interview increased, so the dado began to swell and then recede, only to grow at once even larger . . ." (C 57). The pulsation itself is a symbol—of sequence without reason, without cause—as Marchbanks tries to cajole the girl:

> Merode could hardly take this in, trapped, [a] as she now was, by one of the more frightening periods of the dado, that immediately [b] before the black square would begin to swell, [c] when the whole stretch was beginning to billow, [d] as if the painted pavement was carried out on canvas [e] which had started to heave under a rhythmically controlled impulse [f] [that was] actuated from behind. (C 57)

If ever a sentence had a migraine buildup, this one has. The sequence (*a-d*) leads through four successively dependent clauses, all adverbial, the last of which enables the tile dado to appear "as if . . . canvas." Now relative clausation begins (*e-f*), as Green supposes a mechanism actuating the whole horrid business from the other side. Understandably, Merode faints.

In all these recently quoted passages, there continues to be a failure of the instinct for final seriation—an instinct which Green possesses, but which he has evidently let be co-opted by *Concluding's* variant and unhealthy theme.

THE ARRIVISTE FACTOR

In the eulogy delivered at St. Paul's, Knightsbridge, after Henry Green's death, V. S. Pritchett indicated he thought Henry "felt *himself* to be mysterious."[5] This remark is instructive as a final way to ponder Henry Green's writing. On the heels of a demonstration of his unusual "half-control"—of his sentences that regenerate their energies in new directions at their close—I would like to make a concluding remark about two habits of his that make for mystery. One is nominal and the other verbal. In either case, the mystery relates to characters' perceptions—usually, sudden discoveries of consequences. Sometimes even aphorisms emerge. "Then, with surprising intuition, [Charley] supposed that one crisis in this life inevitably brings on another..." (B 212-13). The point is that such adventitious moments promote the author's tendency, *along the sentence line,* not to be sure of what he is inking in until it arrives. As author, Green lets his writing take the line of the character's perception quite often. His style becomes affected by what one might call an *"arriviste"* factor: not being able to supply a name for something (the noun habit), or not foreseeing the outcome of something (the verb habit) until there it is.

Noun clauses and infinitives become the style-markers for this way of seeing: specifically, "what" clauses and infinitives of result (they are not infinitives of intention, and lack the sense of "in order to"). A sentence from *Back* illustrates both tactics at once:

> He even asked himself *what he suspected,* only *to find* that he could not think. (B 37)

Here the uncertainty of the clause leads to the surprise arrival of the phrase. The rubric "only to find" is indeed classic in this respect, a standard idiom, but Green does not use it in full form often.

The pattern can be reversed, as a sentence from *Concluding* shows. It records Miss Edge's worst moment, when she faints at the sight of a doll painted in the effigy of Mary. Not immediately identifying it, she only has a premonition at first:

> ... she did turn, then, with a sickening premonition of the worst, *to have the quick comfort to realize* they had found *what was only a short, small object.* (C 113-14)

Thus the infinitive records her unexpected "quick comfort," with her premonition kept in check while the object remains unspecified. (But once she focuses on the thing she faints dead away—that is the point.)

The infinitive phrase of result seems more deviant, linguistically, than the clause; but note that Green could have written "they had found only a short, small object." Adding "what was" involves a lengthening of the process, through the implanting of a moment's further question. It is the profusion of these "what" clauses in Green's style, and not so much their oddity, that calls for commentary—after which I shall conclude on the more unusual infinitives.

While the incidence of such clauses is high for each book (see table 6.4), the number in *Back,* 113, surpasses that in *Concluding,* 86, for probably one reason. This would be Charley Summers's own difficulty at formulation. Mr. Rock, with his deafness and none-too-good

Table 6.4   Incidence of "What"-Clauses

	Number of Clauses	Number of Pages	Incidence per Page
Back	113	180	.628
Concluding	86	200	.430
Green aggregate	199	380	.524
The Lost Girl	77	372	.207
Kangaroo	86	367	.234
Lawrence aggregate	163	739	.221
Howards End	72	315	.229
A Passage to India	87	300	.290
Forster aggregate	159	615	.259
Tarr	93	291	.320
Self Condemend	221	386	.573
Lewis aggregate	314	677	.464

NOTE: Green's average of better than 50 percent—a clause every two pages—doubles the averages of Lawrence and Forster. Lewis's average comes closer to Green's, owing primarily to *Self Condemned*. Its high proportion of "what" clauses seems related to the frequency of its conditional structures. I have in mind this type:

> [He] thrust forward his bristling mouth in *what might be called* the ho-ho-ho position. . . . (SC 6)

> They ordered *what would have seemed* a somewhat elaborate meal to the average Englishman. (SC 31)

Even so, *Back* surpasses *Self Condemned* in these noun clauses, and Green's combined average shows greater homogeneity than the Lewis figures do.

eyesight, also has problems perceiving things; but the specialness of Charley's confusion between living and dead girls goes beyond this. Thus there accrue, in *Back*, no less than 14 noun clauses used like expletives at the heads of sentences. These work in an almost gingerly manner. (Only a half-dozen begin sentences in *Concluding*, and only one shows Rock tentative in the way Charley tends to be.)

> What he meant was, it must be all of five years since Rose was said to have died. . . . (B 59)

> What had come to him, was that this might only be too possible, mother and daughter both suffering . . . from lost memories. (B 60)

> What he thought of himself was, that he was going to lose his reason. (B 105)

> What was before him of the house was in pitch darkness. (B 216)

The last example, coming just before Grant's death upstairs, is virtually a symbol of Charley's mental condition—this time it is a physical cul-de-sac he is in, a pitch-black house. He has to spell out to himself, and so often, just how things are from moment to moment. By not naming, the noun clauses show the dawning process of various inchoate ideas. "He thought he would lose his mind," written so, has nothing of the effect of Green's version: "What he thought of himself was, that he was going to lose his reason."

Green's women, on the other hand, do not usually hesitate in this manner. So when a few sentences, sounding like these, pertain to *Concluding*'s headmistresses, the *verbs* within the noun clauses have direction to them. Italics indicate this in the following samples:

> What [Baker and Edge] had *decided* was, that the police must be casually informed.... (C 17)

> What [Baker] *had in mind* was that, in any case, the staff... could not leave either, at any rate not without scandal. (C 62)

> What [Edge] *could do, and did* without the slightest sense of shock, was to ask herself if he had meant Moira all along. (C 191)

It might be argued there is a playing-for-time quality here (rather than, in Charley's case, a groping for position). In any event, that Green used the clause does reveal something native to him, I think: his way of registering minds confronting the beat of experience. Returning to *Back*, we observe that when women there are calculating in advance, the addition of a conjunction to the noun clause makes for a sureness quite lacking elsewhere. Here is Dot Pitter in one of her moods of petulance toward Charley:

> But *what all this added up to*, she felt at the time, was that those repatriated men came back very queer from those camps. (B 144)

Dot is to be forgiven, yet a fine contrast develops between her irritation and some thoughts that Nancy entertains later on, on the same subject—Charley's reticence:

> But *what she liked about Charley* was how he did not ask for anything, however small, although his need was desperate, a child could tell it. (B 236)

> Really *what intrigued her was*, that she did not know if he didn't, or just couldn't, tell about himself, tell even something of all that went on behind those marvellous brown eyes.... (B 237)

Dot has none of Nancy's tolerance or sapience. Dot can sweep the stage clean with her "what all this added up to." Still, there is force to what both women feel, with the headword the key indicator for this (feminine) variation.*

---

*We noticed Joyce doing something of the sort with his would-be resilient Maria, who was lent false bounce by similar headwords. "But wasn't Maria glad when the women had finished their tea...." (See chapter two.)

The nearly two hundred "what" clauses in *Back* and *Concluding* mostly represent enigmas—which are mainly shunned, though they can often be tantalizing. Green once wrote, in *Caught*, of "the dark cupidity, the need" that surged in so many ordinary people.[6] When it comes to people's appetites being whetted, sometimes the "what" clauses are extended serially. Here is a sample from each novel: one of women in a queue, arrested by Charley's odd antics; the other of Miss Winstanley before the Founder's Day ball, watching her students:

> They turned from *what might be in the shop*, from *what was unseen*, onto *what might be in this young man*, click click they went at him, and Mrs. Frazier noticed. (B 69)
>
> [Winstanley] thought . . . that one and all were in *what she called "the mood*," that . . . the first waltz would send each child whirling forward into her future, into *what, in a few years, she would, with age, become*. (C 145)

Both passages are frightening, the former actively because the women eavesdrop on Charley's despair, the latter possibly more disturbing in Winstanley's complaisance over what is in store for the girls. What "might be in this young man," what each girl "would" become, is sensed but not namable. But it already is in control of them—that is what is fearful, and also alluring. The unnamable quality of that which is in control is best presented at an eerie moment before *Concluding*'s dance, as Rock, his granddaughter and Sebastian approach the mansion in moonlight. "The moon," writes Green,

> . . . coldly flicked the dark to an instantaneous view of *what this held*, it stunned the eye by stone, was all-powerful, and made each of these three related people into something alien, glistening, frozen eyed, alone. (C 152–53)

The hallmark is that the "what" clauses at their most disquieting *cannot* disclose what they are trying to denote. Green cannot say, but can only suggest, "what" the dark holds. The imagery is deadly. The stone mansion is "flicked" into a kind of mausoleum (Sebastian's next words are "I'll leave you now"), but this all has to be read in, with the characters stunned by the unspecified, and the end of the sentence is concerned with the way they are separated, not with what they have seen. No wonder, in these books, that actions are fraught with evasion and dread; as regards the immediate past:

> "I didn't say a word." He was horrified at *what he seemed to have let out*. (B 201)
>
> And this moment he chose to wink, to cajole her not to speak of *what she had just witnessed*. (C 78)

or the immediate future:

> So that, on top of everything else, he began to dread *what was due.* (B 209)
>
> ... Mr Rock, instantly apprehensive, decided ... he would do better to ignore *what was on the way.* ... (C 21–22)

And as regards the present, Green's characters are continually caught short because of what they "take to be" this or that.

> Charley dropped his eyes, but not before he had recognized contempt in *what he took to be his son's.* (B 98)
>
> This small weight woke the girl who, when she first opened eyes, saw *what she dizzily took to be* [Rock's cat] *Alice.* ... (C 125)

These last infinitives, and some of the others that have been cropping up in recent examples, are, incidentally, not the sort with which I was dealing earlier in this section. The "what" constructions are the nebulous items here; the infinitives I would call "bound," in that they flow directly from characters' awareness ("he would do better to ignore," etc.). The other, unexpected type—a "free" infinitive, if you like—works differently in that an action engaged in produces temporal rather than intended consequence. (That is why I used the term *arriviste* earlier.) This infinitive, related thematically to the "what" clauses, is rarely used by other writers (being easily substituted for), and is the best indicator of Henry Green's feeling for immanence. It is a device of style that enables one to perceive "the concrete objects which [were there] all the time if we could have had reason for stopping to see them."[7] That is why "to find" and its variants turn up regularly:

> He could not make out where he was until he tilted himself, *to find* [Nancy] kneeling at his head, which was in her lap. (B 53)
>
> Meantime Miss Baker, going down to this lake another way, for all her fat moved silently *to come upon* the sergeant seated on a log in the traditional attitude, a high helmet on the ground at the side. ... (C 120)

Or, even better, "to show" is sometimes the word:

> Seen from behind her short skirts were lifted, while she stretched, *to show* an inch or so of white flesh above the stockings. (B 128)
>
> ... a great shaft of early sunlight ... bisected the kitchen, *to show* him air on the rise in its dust, like soda-water through transparent milk. (C 18)

One observes that an alternative (a compound predicate) was available in every instance: "until he tilted himself, and found"; "skirts were lifted ... and showed"; "bisected the kitchen, and showed ...." What effect, then, is gained in the originals? Something fairly radical,

I think. Paired verbs must have given the sense of "this: then that"; the infinitive placed next to the verb, conversely, creates a blending point, barely missing simultaneity. What is disclosed has "takeover" force—the force attendant on actions like coming upon a policeman, or being shown a strip of flesh unbeknownst to its owner.

And of course the infinitive has potency, continuance, that a finite verb must lose. Yet the realization of powerful actions can still take place. Consider the hysterical Mrs. Grant, or the amputee Middlewitch, in *Back:*

> ... Mrs. Grant took control by throwing herself back into the sofa *to thrust* her head into one of its soft corners.... (B 22)

> [Middlewitch] put the box up under an armpit, *to dab* with a match at the millimetre of sandpaper that was left exposed. (B 25)

Lightning movements, "to thrust" and "to dab" seem realized by the very irrelevance of infinite form to things so transient. (That would be the argument of Ransom and other critics who might observe deviance in these constructions.) In *Concluding,* ladylike actions may be caught from the side of the eye: here the actions are sympathetic to infinitude ("fanning," "holding"); the syntax alone arrests:

> [Baker] declared she could dance no longer, and sat herself heavily down, *to fan* a cheek with a lace bordered black and white handkerchief. (C 173)

> [Edge] slumped quickly down, in an elegant attitude, *to hold* her cigarette like a wand. (C 191)

And in *Concluding* (which outdoes *Back,* 52 to 30, in these constructions—see table 6.5), Green apprehends a great number of gestures as though through bifocals. They seem half physiological, half motivational, as though the body gives the signal before the mind realizes what it is intending.

> "Sometimes I can't imagine how you put up with me," she said, putting his arm in hers to press it to her side. (C 36)

> Mr Rock straightened his back to wave a hand at the cloud of gnats which rose and fell before his eyes. (C 129)

> He waited for an answer but the old man said no word, just stood to wipe at his face with a handkerchief in a palsied hand. (C 130)

> "Come back, Gapa," she ordered, hanging her whole weight on the arm to pull his old shoulder back to hers.... (C 138)

To consider only the last usage: note if it had been written "hanging her whole weight and pulling his shoulder to hers," the paralleling would have given double weight to Liz's intention. But a touch of

Table 6.5   Infinitives of Consequence

	Number of "Consequential" Infinitives	Number of Pages	Incidence per Page
Back	30	180	.166
Concluding	52	200	.260
Green aggregate	82	380	.216
The Lost Girl	13	372	.035
Kangaroo	15	367	.041
Lawrence aggregate	28	739	.038
Howards End	9	315	.029
A Passage to India	6	300	.020
Forster aggregate	15	615	.024
Tarr	7	291	.024
Self Condemned	8	386	.021
Lewis aggregate	15	677	.022

NOTE: The usages in *Concluding* reach the surprising ratio of more than one such infinitive every four pages; the combined ratio for Green comes to more than one usage every five pages. The other writers offer no ground for comparison with Green, since they use the *"arriviste"* infinitives so sparingly. Still, that they do use them sometimes is of interest: it shows that the idiom is available to a writer when the occasion, ever unpredictable, calls.

affection is left her by Green, since the second action ("to pull") is as much the result of physiology as of desire. It is not "so as to pull"; it is "with the consequence of pulling."

Of course, people become thing-like when their motivations are cut into, when physics begins to control things. And if my dozen examples have stressed the actions of people, it remains true that Green lets many things generate force, to the point of entropy, through this device. Roses and music happen to be the two strongest begetters of compulsion in *Back* and *Concluding*. Significantly, *Back*'s first long description of roses ends in the way the other's first description of music does, on the phrase "to die." This may seem portentous, especially since these are the only occasions when the infinitives become serial (as my italics show):

> For, climbing around and up these trees of mourning, was rose after rose ... those roses gay and bright which, as still as this dark afternoon, stared at whosoever looked, or hung their heads *to droop, to grow stained, to die* when their turn came. (B 3)

> The music was a torrent, *to spread out, to be lost* in the great space of this mansion, *to die* when it reached the staff room to a double beat, the water wheel turned by a rustling rush of leaf thick water. (C 160)

187

Yet *Concluding* and *Back* are not, after all, about dying. They are about the life-throb. On *Concluding*'s last page domestic actions supervene. Mr. Rock, who thought he had lost his goose and pig, finds them home when he gets home. A couple of half-intentional infinitives confirm his near-daydreaming state before he retires. First of all—"And he would never, for the rest of his life, be able to explain why"—on his way past the goose's pen, "he bent down to put a hand inside." He is answered by his goose's hiss; whereupon, passing to Daisy's sty—though mainly still preoccupied with his errant granddaughter—"Mr Rock moved across to shut the gate on his pig." It could have been "bent down *and* put," "moved across *and* shut," but then would not some magic have been lost in this gerundive book with its nonfinite title? As it is, Green can have Rock forever ministering, handling, shutting rather than once and for all having done it.

What of the end of *Back*? In that novel, as the count showed, the "what" clauses tended to take some precedence. And in the one-page finale, the chapter in which Charley breaks down and cries, the novel has the strength of Nancy to bank on. So in its opening paragraph Charley goes to Nancy's room "for the first time in what was to be a happy married life" (B 246). Nancy is lying naked, the light from a pink-shaded lamp spilling over her. And if the return of the Rose-obsession, at "the great, the overwhelming sight of the woman he loved, for the first time without her clothes," breaks Charley down to tears, there is nothing, ultimately, dismantling about that. The final paragraph reassures, through Nancy. "And she knew what she had taken on." Green repeats the assuaging "what" clause. He also repeats "for the first time"—beginning something, giving life beyond the book—as in a different way he managed to do this for *Concluding*. The artistry remains unflagging. So does the language.

NOTES

1

1. G. W. Turner, *Stylistics* (Baltimore: Penguin, 1973), p. 238.
2. Quoted by V. S. Pritchett, "E. M. Forster at 90," *New York Times Book Review,* 29 December 1968, p. 19.
3. And not only the rantings of characters: consider the personal letters in *Howards End,* the newspaper items in *Kangaroo,* the memoir of an eighteenth-century Frenchwoman that takes up the middle of *Back*—all these are models of parodic versatility.
4. Louis T. Milic, *A Quantitative Approach to the Style of Jonathan Swift* (The Hague: Mouton, 1967), p. 17. (My italics.)
5. Ibid., p. 80.
6. Ibid., pp. 78–79.
7. J. Middleton Murry, *The Problem of Style* (London: Oxford University Press, 1922), p. 82. T. E. Hulme once made a statement in keeping with Murry's example, one that would contradict Milic's ideas about priority. "Thought," said Hulme, "is prior to language and consists in the simultaneous presentation to the mind of two different images.... All the connections in language ... only indicate the precise relation ... between the two simultaneously presented images." (*Further Speculations,* ed. Samuel Hynes [Lincoln: University of Nebraska Press, 1962], p. 84.)
8. Richard Ohmann, "Prolegomena to the Analysis of Prose Style," in *Style in Prose Fiction* (English Institute Essays), ed. Harold C. Martin (New York: Columbia University Press, 1959), p. 14.
9. Ibid., pp. 13–14.
10. Richard Ohmann, *Shaw: The Style and the Man* (Middletown, Conn.: Wesleyan University Press, 1962), p. 175.
11. Milic, *Style of Jonathan Swift,* pp. 292–93.
12. Ohmann, *Shaw,* p. 185.
13. While Richard Ohmann has attempted to elucidate some sentences from literary works by means of parsing their deep structure, he has also—in his capacity as editor of *College English*—overseen publication of a searching essay by Eugene R. Kintgen on the unfeasibility of the transformational approach to practical stylistics. See Ohmann, "Literature as Sentences," *College English* 27 (January 1966): 261–67; and Kintgen, "Is Transformational Stylistics Useful?", *College English* 35 (April 1974): 799–824. Kintgen's essay gives an overview of the muddled situation of

transformational grammer per se. A specific inquisition of Ohmann's essay, demonstrating the invalidity of the transformational approach (especially as applied to artistic prose), is David H. Hirsch's "Linguistic Structure and Literary Meaning," *Journal of Literary Semantics* 1 (1972): 80–88. Hirsch demonstrates that the "deep structures" assigned all along by Ohmann to the specimen sentence (from Joyce's "Araby") are in every case violating the actualities residing in the surface components of the original.

14. Stanley Fish, "Literature in the Reader: Affective Stylistics," *New Literary History* 2 (Autumn 1970): 125.

15. Ibid., p. 144. But mark that one of the best linguistic critics, G. W. Turner, who does *not* discount the transformational approach, can say virtually the same thing: "The justification of syntactically difficult [writing] . . . is that we begin to respond before we fully understand; we . . . experience the ordering of thought and mood ourselves as the initially isolated, but already powerfully affective, elements fit into place and we understand the system." (*Stylistics*, p. 99.) All the key words of Fish are present here: "begin to respond," "experience," and, in particular, "affective." We may deduce, as usual, that the critic's platform is not as important as his perspicacity: both accounts give the reading experience its due complexity.

16. Michael Riffaterre, "Criteria for Style Analysis," *Word* 15 (1959): 158. (His italics.)

17. "Defamiliarization" is a favorite term of Russian formalist criticism, utilized by, among others, Victor Shlovsky. See his "Art as Technique" in *Russian Formalist Criticism*, ed. Lee T. Lemon and Marion J. Reis (Lincoln: University of Nebraska Press, 1965), p. 22.

18. Fish, "Affective Stylistics," pp. 157–58.

19. Turner, *Stylistics*, p. 13.

20. Susan Sontag, "On Style," *Partisan Review* 32 (Fall 1965): 557. (The essay appears as chapter two of her *Against Interpretation* [New York: Farrar, Straus and Giroux, 1966], pp. 15–36.)

21. David Lodge, "Towards a Poetics of Fiction: 2) An Approach through Language," *Novel* 1 (Winter 1968): 161.

22. David Lodge, *Language of Fiction* (London: Routledge and Kegan Paul, 1966), p. 36.

23. Alan Plater, "The Artificial Respiration Controversy," in *The Pick of Punch: An Annual Selection*, ed. Nicholas Bentley (New York: E. P. Dutton, 1959), p. 60.

24. Seymour Chatman, "New Ways of Analyzing Narrative Structure, with an Example from Joyce's *Dubliners*," *Language and Style* 2 (Winter 1969): 28–29.

25. Milic, *Style of Jonathan Swift*, p. 147n.

26. The nouns are Susan Sontag's, from "On Style," p. 558.

27. Peter Quennell, *The Sign of the Fish* (New York: Viking, 1960), p. 88. Quennell is actually translating from Joseph Joubert: "Pour bien écrire . . . il faut une facilité naturelle et une difficulté acquise. . . ."

28. Describing what he calls the two uses of tone—persuasion and expression— Richard Ohmann holds that these reflect "ingratiation and personality," which can "become one." ("Prolegomena," pp. 21–22.) His view is similar to the one I advance; I would return to the distinction between "tone" and "voice" to mark these presences, though. But I agree there can be a merger: the actual thing can outrun the terms.

29. Kenneth Burke, *Permanence and Change* (Los Altos, Calif.: Hermes, 1954), p. 50.

30. John Crowe Ransom, "The Understanding of Fiction," *Kenyon Review* 12 (1950): 198. Susan Sontag, along this line, makes a fine distinction about "creative mistreatment," a wilful stylization replacing "secreted" style. This is often the fate of writers who are not discovering their material, but who assume it as "capable of exhaustion," and assume themselves to be in a situation of ownership over it. ("On Style," p. 546.)

31. Ransom, "Understanding of Fiction," p. 201. The notion of dissipation of attention is at the heart of Anton Ehrenzweig's treatise on art, where it is called "creative scanning." (*The Hidden Order of Art* [Berkeley: University of California Press, 1971], p. 5.)

2

1. *Writers at Work: The Paris Review Interviews, Third Series* (New York: Viking, 1967), p. 111.
2. Among Joyce critics, Hugh Kenner, Marvin Magalaner, and the editors of the Critical Edition of *Dubliners*, Robert Scholes and A. Walton Litz, have said some important things about his style, but no one has tackled the problem for the entire book. Among recent linguistics-oriented critics, two of the best, Richard Ohmann and Seymour Chatman, have dealt with "Araby" and "Eveline" respectively. For Ohmann, see note 10 to this chapter; for Chatman, note 24 to chapter 1.
3. Nils Erik Enkvist, "On Defining Style," in *Linguistics and Style,* ed. John Spencer (London: Oxford University Press, 1964), pp. 30–31.
4. Robert Scholes and A. Walton Litz, eds., *Dubliners* (New York: Viking, 1969), p. 225.
5. For comparative purposes I chose collections about the length of *Dubliners* written by perhaps the most well-known story writers just before and after Joyce. In Rudyard Kipling's *Soldier Stories* of 1896 (203 pages), there are 80 semicolons and colons; in W. Somerset Maugham's *The Casuarina Tree* of 1926 (230 pages), there are 241. In Kipling there are only 4 colons; in Maugham, only 14.
6. Scholes and Litz, eds., *Dubliners,* p. 240.
7. Hugh Kenner, *Dublin's Joyce* (Bloomington: Indiana University Press, 1956), p. 13.
8. Joyce's "indulgence"—eliciting the thought processes of Crofton in a story that hews rigorously to the scenic point of view—brings to mind a fine saying of Peter Quennell's: "Whether in personal or in literary conduct, undue asceticism is always blighting; and as important as a capacity to resist temptation is an ability, displayed at the correct juncture, to succumb with grace and gusto; for, in every prose style that gives us genuine delight, an element of restraint and reserve is accompanied by occasional touches of exuberance." (*The Sign of the Fish* [New York: Viking, 1960], p. 95.) In "Ivy Day," the atypical sentence about Crofton certainly qualifies for exuberance.
9. The two exceptions come from the beginning and end of "Grace," when two ingratiations are attempted. In the first Mr. Kernan makes light of his tumble down some lavatory steps: "It was nothing, he said: only a little accident." The second introduces the sermon of the sycophant priest: "But one thing only, he said he would ask of his hearers. And that was: to be straight and manly with God."
10. Richard Ohmann, "Literature as Sentences," *College English* 27 (January 1966): 261–67.
11. In the later stories Joyce does indeed use some noun-derived verbs in finite form. Examples include: "she elbowed her way through the crowds" ("Eveline"); "Higgins and Nosey Flynn bevelled off to the left" ("Two Gallants"); "She buttonholed him as he was limping out" ("A Mother"). These have a racy air to them, not related to the passive participial arrangements elected by the boy. In the rest of *Dubliners,* only three such verbs are used in passive voice, all long naturalized so that they give no special effects: "Their passage had been booked" ("Eveline"); "Their faces were powdered" (A Little Cloud"); "His black clothes were tightly buttoned" ("Ivy Day").
12. Scholes and Litz, eds., *Dubliners,* p. 239.
13. Actually, a sixth sentence, ending the first paragraph, also displays three finite verbs in series, but as opposed to the other five this one seems inconsequential. A seventh sentence, also in the first paragraph, contains three main clauses (the only one of its type), so three predicates are, naturally, found there.
14. Marvin Magalaner and Richard M. Kain, *Joyce: The Man, the Work, the Reputation* (New York: New York University Press, 1956), p. 62.
15. James S. Atherton, "The Joyce of *Dubliners,*" in *James Joyce Today,* ed. Thomas F. Staley (Bloomington: Indiana University Press, 1966), p. 49.
16. Morris Croll, *Style, Rhetoric, and Rhythm,* ed. J. Max Patrick (Princeton, N.J.: Princeton University Press, 1966), p. 353.
17. Ibid., p. 348.

18. Paull F. Baum, *The Other Harmony of Prose* (Durham, N.C.: Duke University Press, 1952), pp. 96–97.
19. Eliseo Vivas, *Creation and Discovery* (New York: Noonday, 1955), p. 125.

3

1. R. P. Draper, *D. H. Lawrence* (New York: Twayne, 1964), p. 88.
2. The Viking Compass editions from which I cite (identical to the Heinemann) each provide 42 lines of type per standard page, with the number of characters per line also commensurate. *The Lost Girl* has 372 pages; *Kangaroo* has 367.
3. Leo Gurko, "*Kangaroo:* D. H. Lawrence in Transit," *Modern Fiction Studies* 10 (Winter 1964–65): 349, 358.
4. Anaïs Nin, *D. H. Lawrence* (Denver: A. Swallow, 1964), p. 121.
5. Ibid., p. 73.
6. John Alexander gives an excellent account of Australian politics at the time of Lawrence's visit in 1922, indicating that there was more actual ferment in Australia than critics of *Kangaroo* had realized. ("D. H. Lawrence's *Kangaroo:* Fantasy, Fact or Fiction?" *Meanjin* 24 [Winter 1965]: 179–97.)
7. Richard Ohmann, "Generative Grammars and the Concept of Literary Style," *Word* 20 (1964): 438.
8. D. H. Lawrence, letter to Edward Garnett of 5 June 1914, in *The Letters of D. H. Lawrence*, ed. Aldous Huxley (London: Heinemann, 1956), p. 198.
9. A related "throwaway" apposition occurs several times in *The Lost Girl:*

She, Mrs. Rollings, had suggested that Madame [use] hot mustard.... (LG 138)

He, Tommy, could quite understand any woman's wanting to marry him.... (LG 319)

She, Mrs. Tuke, had volunteered. (LG 366)

10. Josephine Miles, *Style and Proportion* (Boston: Little, Brown, 1967), p. 17.
11. Richard Hoggart, "The Force of Caricature," *Essays in Criticism* 3 (October 1953): 453. Hoggart is treating an analogous device in Graham Greene's fiction.
12. *Writers at Work: The Paris Review Interviews, Third Series* (New York: Viking, 1967), p. 182.

4

1. George H. Thomson, *The Fiction of E. M. Forster* (Detroit: Wayne State University Press, 1967), p. 95.
2. Northrop Frye, *Anatomy of Criticism* (Princeton, N.J.: Princeton University Press, 1957), p. 308.
3. E. M. Forster, *The Longest Journey* (New York: Vintage, 1962), p. 120.
4. By a "Beerbohmism" I mean a carry-over from dialogue into narrative of a nearly identical locution, as though the narrator has been struck by the aptness of a character's comment. Mr. Wilcox, showing Margaret a room, says, "Here we fellows smoke," after which Forster starts a paragraph: "We fellows smoked in chairs of maroon leather" (HE 153). The device is identified in J. G. Riewald, *Sir Max Beerbohm: Man and Writer* (The Hague: Martinus Nijhoff, 1953), p. 200; Riewald uses the term "Beerbohmism" on p. 182.
5. William K Wimsatt, *The Prose Style of Samuel Johnson* (New Haven, Conn.: Yale University Press, 1941), p. 23.
6. Alexander Pope, *An Essay on Criticism*, ll. 426–27, in *The Poetry of Pope*, ed. M. H. Abrams (New York: Appleton-Century-Crofts, 1954), p. 19.

7. I think it no accident that the name of the Schlegels' loved residence, Wickham Place, sounds a bit like "wych-elm." The residence to which they transfer is thus "Wych-elm Place."
8. Thomson, *Fiction of E. M. Forster,* p. 181.
9. Naturally there are some similarly phrased sentiments. An equivalent to the monk-beast impasse of *Howards End* is the Ronny-Adela relationship: "There was esteem and animal contact at dusk, but the emotion that links them was absent" (PI 150). And Fielding is set at the mean between extremes that makes for proportion: "Neither a missionary nor a student, he was happiest in the give-and-take of a private conversation" (PI 62). Note that, for "missionary" and "student," we could substitute the proscribed "theologian" and "scientist" of *Howards End.* Though my chapter has singled out differences, it is encouraging to be able to find the essential Forster, as one might say, still present—though the books do diverge.
10. Of *Passage's* critics, perhaps Avrom Fleishman best saw the paradox of "positive" negation, when he argued for the contributory role of "nothing": it "becomes a presence when presented," he says; and of Mrs. Moore, "By refraining from intervention, [she] creates a nothingness around Adela which allows her to come out of her muddle." ("Being and Nothing in *A Passage to India,*" *Criticism* 15 [1973]: 109–25.)
11. Quoted in Peter Stansky and William Abrahams, *The Unknown Orwell* (New York: Knopf, 1972), pp. 74–75.

5

1. Robert T. Chapman has summed up this narrative method as a "progression of *tableaux vivants.*" *(Wyndham Lewis: Fictions and Satires* [New York: Barnes and Noble, 1973], p. 81.)
2. Hugh Kenner, *Wyndham Lewis* (Norfolk, Conn.: New Directions, 1954), p. 35.
3. In Bertha's kitchen is a stove, "its gas stars blasting away luridly at sky-blue saucepans with Bertha's breakfast" (T 153). Of this description Kenner has said, "'Blasting' crystallizes the whole observation, somewhere between the auditory and the kinesthetic: Bertha's stove, its essential gesture captured, is present on the page as is no other kitchen appliance in English fiction." (Ibid., p. 36.)
4. William H. Pritchard, *Wyndham Lewis* (New York: Twayne, 1968), p. 153.
5. As to Cartesian dualism, *Self Condemned* is explicit. "René sprang up and stretched . . . as though to shake the concentration out of his body. That he should want to shake it out was evidence of the fact that he lived in two compartments. He shook off what was mental as soon as he was done with it and passed over into the animal playground . . ." (SC 120–21).
6. E. W. F. Tomlin, *Wyndham Lewis,* British Book Council Pamphlet (London: Longmans, Green, 1955), p. 13.
7. Pritchard, *Wyndham Lewis,* p. 37.
8. A peculiar variant in *Self Condemned* finds "such as" becoming the subject of a noun clause! The contexts are the way Canadians display meat and arrange obsequies at a "Mortician's." Both are highly offensive to the Hardings, causing Lewis to use this reductive substitute for a noun:

These show-cases were *such as* are used in Museums for the display of antiquities, and to begin with this method of exhibiting meat is displeasing to English people. (SC 236)

[Hester and René] sat on chairs placed in the corner for *such as* had not reserved seats. (SC 299)

9. Northrop Frye, *Anatomy of Criticism* (Princeton, N.J.: Princeton University Press, 1957), pp. 234–35.
10. Susan Sontag, "On Style," *Partisan Review* 32 (Fall 1965): 546.

6

1. See Edward Stokes, *The Novels of Henry Green* (London: Hogarth, 1959), p. 190; and my *Henry Green* (New Brunswick, N.J.: Rutgers University Press, 1960), pp 48–49.
2. Edward Stokes, "Henry Green: Dispossessed Poet," *Australian Quarterly* 28 (December 1956): 84–91; and "A Poet of Fear," anon. rev. of *Concluding, The Times Literary Supplement,* 25 December 1948, p. 726.
3. All paragraphs are considered, except those ending on unexpanded dialogue guides.
4. Here is a perfect example of the kind of affective stylistics that Stanley Fish proposes in "Literature in the Reader: Affective Stylistics," *New Literary History* 2 (Autumn 1970): 123–62. Perhaps many of Henry Green's sentences would qualify. My final section deals with "arriviste" structures that are precisely suited to Fish's method.
5. V. S. Pritchett, "Henry Yorke, Henry Green," *London Magazine,* N.S. 14 (June–July 1974): 29.
6. Henry Green, *Caught* (New York: Viking, 1950), p. 14.
7. John Crowe Ransom, "The Understanding of Fiction," *Kenyon Review* 12 (1950): 201.

INDEX